Social Alienation as a Consequence of Human Suffering in the Book of Job:
A Study of Job 19: 13-22

Alexander G. K. Salakpi

iUniverse, Inc.
New York   Bloomington

Social Alienation as a Consequence of Human Suffering
in the Book of Job: A Study of Job 19: 13-22

Copyright © 2010 Alexander G. K. Salakpi

iUniverse books may be ordered through booksellers or by contacting:

iUniverse
1663 Liberty Drive
Bloomington, IN 47403
www.iuniverse.com
1-800-Authors (1-800-288-4677)

ISBN: 978-1-4502-4261-5 (pbk)
ISBN: 978-1-4502-4262-2 (ebk)

Printed in the United States of America

iUniverse rev. date: 7/26/2010

Dedication

I dedicate this work to my family: my parents Stephen and Bernadette, most especially Stephen my dear father who died before the completion of this work. He has been my strong support and encouragement, and he is still; my sisters Emelda, Theodora, Charllotte, and their families; and my brothers Stephen, Simeon, Benedictus, Sylvanus, and their families.

Table of Contents

Abbreviations

AB	Anchor Bible
ABD	D. N. Freedman et al. (eds.), *Anchor Bible Dictionary*
ANE	Ancient Near East (or Eastern)
ANET	J. B. Pritchard (ed.), *Ancient Near Eastern Texts*
BAG(D)	W. Bauer, W. F. Arnt, and F. W. Gingrich (2d ed.: and F. W. Danker), *Greek-English Lexicon of the NT*
BDB	F. Brown, S. R. Driver, and C. A. Briggs, *Hebrew and English Lexicon of the Old Testament*
BHS	*Biblia Hebraica Stuttgartensia*
Bib	*Biblica*
BibOr	Biblica et orientalia
BKAT	Biblischer Kommentar, Altes Testament
BTB	*Biblical Theology Bulletin*
CAT	Commentaire de l'Ancien Testament
CBA	Catholic Biblical Association
CBQ	*Catholic Biblical Quarterly*
CBQMS	Catholic Biblical Quarterly Monographs Series
CBSC	Cambridge Bible for Schools and Colleges
Chap(s).	Chapter(s).
GKC	Gesenius' Hebrew Grammar, ed. E. Kautzsch, trans. A. E. Cowley
HALOT	W. Baumgartner et al., *Hebrew and Aramaic Lexicon of the Old Testament*
ICC	International Critical Commentary
Int	*Interpretation*
JAOS	*Journal of the America Oriental Society*
JB	*Jerusalem Bible*
JBC	R. E. Brown et al. (eds.), *The Jerome Biblical Commentary*
JBL	*Journal of Biblical Literature*
JSOT	*Journal for the Study of the Old Testament*
JSOTSup	Journal for the Study of the Old Testament, Supplement Series

KAT	E. Sellin (ed.), Kommentar zum Alten Testament
KHCAT	Kurzer Hand commentar zum Alten Testament
KJV	*King James Version*
NAB	*New American Bible*
NASB	*New American Standard Bible*
NCB	New Century Bible
NEB	*New English Bible*
NIB	*New Interpreter's Bible*
NICOT	New International Commentary on the Old Testament
NIV	*New International Version*
NJB	*New Jerusalem Bible*
NJBC	R. E. Brown et al. (eds.), *New Jerome Biblical Commentary*
NJPSV	New Jewish Publication Society Version, *Tanakh* (1985)
NRSV	*New Revised Standard Version*
OTL	Old Testament Library
OTS	Oudtestamentische studiën
RSV	*Revised Standard Version*
RV	*Revised Version*
TDOT	G. J. Botterweck et al. (eds.), *Theological Dictionary of the Old Testament*
TLOT	Ernst Jenni et al. (eds.), *Theological Lexicon of the Old Testament*
TUAT	O. Kaiser et al. (eds.), *Texte aus der Umwelt des Alten Testaments*
TynOTC	Tyndale Old Testament Commentaries
VE	*Verbum et Ecclesia*
VT	*Vetus Testamentum*
WBC	Word Biblical Commentary
WEB	*World English Bible*
ZAW	*Zeitschrift für die alttestamentliche Wissenschaft*

Foreword

This book is the revised version of the dissertation submitted to the Biblical Department of the School of Theology and Religious Studies of the Catholic University of America, Washington, DC. This revised edition translates, eliminates, or transliterates all foreign languages that are included in the original work. This edition has seven chapters as against six in the original work. It has a detached introduction as chapter one and chapter seven is the expanded form of the original chapter six. Chapter seven also cites other areas of social life that experience social alienation and ends with pastoral suggestions. The original copy is available at ProQuest Information and Learning Center.

It is recommended that readers of this book familiarize themselves with chapters 19, 27, 29, 30, and 31 of the Book of Job. In fact, reading the whole Book of Job is encouraged for a better understanding. Similarly, it is also recommended that Psalms 22, 31, and 88 are read before reading chapter four.

All Biblical references are quoted according to the Hebrew text of the *BHS* and the English equivalents of the Hebrew text, apart from Job 19:13-22 which are taken from the *NRSV*.

Chapter One

Introduction

The Book of Job has attracted the attention of exegetes and theologians for centuries. Several topics have been the focus of scholarly consideration, most importantly the problem of theodicy. Job, the hero of this book, suffers undeservedly and the consequences of his affliction are manifold. Among his sufferings are a progressive alienation from his social network, his friends, and even his closest family. This social disorientation reaches its first climax in chap. 19, particularly in 19:13-22, where Job claims that everyone has abandoned him. His social estrangement exacerbates his alienation from God, but this unexpectedly results in his strongest expression of hope (19:23-25).

Job strongly believed that he had done nothing wrong to deserve his fate; yet, Israel's theodicy held that God rewards the righteous and punishes the wicked. According to this principle, Job is suffering for the wrong he has done. His family, friends, and loved ones reinforce that notion by making judgments on behalf of God. However, while Job's personal suffering is thus made more unbearable by those who loved him, Job's demand for a hearing by God becomes more urgent. Hence, Job repeats and intensifies his affirmation of innocence in chaps. 29–31, where he also contrasts his glorious past with his deplorable present. Particularly in 30:1-31, Job describes the painful rejection by society that his suffering has brought upon him. It is at this point, because Job can forcefully and truthfully maintain his claim of innocence, that the theologically based conviction about divine retribution, proposed as one of the bulwarks of traditional wisdom literature, begins to crumble. Physical and mental suffering is not always, as it now emerges in the Book of Job, a punishment from God, and the social rejection the sufferer goes through is ethically wrong and unjustified.

I. Purpose of This Study

The purpose of this book is to examine how social isolation aggravates the suffering of Job. Taking social estrangement as recounted in Job 19:13-22 as its point of departure, the book studies how the principle of a "deed and consequence" connection relates to

1

the suffering of Job and what theological solution the author of the Book of Job suggests. The book explores this important issue.

II. Methodology

The book uses both an exegetical and a theological approach. It is based on a historical-critical exegesis of Job 19:13-22 and sections of chaps. 27, 29–31. The most important passage in chaps. 29–31 is 31:1-31; it stands out as the climax of Job's assertion of innocence and thus serves as an important textual source for this study. Further literary and contextual analyses of Job 19:13-22 and chaps. 29–31 (mostly lexical and semantic) elucidate the theological problem at stake, that is, the theological problem of theodicy. The book explores the many dimensions of the rejection of the afflicted individual by his family and friends. Since social isolation as a sufferer's fate is not uncommon in the OT, diachronic and intertextual approaches to the relevant materials are used to analyze the problem fully.

Chapter Two includes study of recent findings in sociological research on the social construction of reality and the elements of a sociological theory of religion, with special reference to some notable sociologists. It also studies the human suffering caused by religion and its causes and effects in the context of social isolation, with particular reference to Mesopotamia and Israel.

Chapter Three studies the Book of Job, beginning with a brief study of wisdom literature and with special reference to the "deed and consequence" connection. It also studies the ANE (ancient Near East) stories similar to the story of Job. It treats the authorship, date, purpose, literary style, and theology of the Book of Job. It ends with a current history of research on Job 19 by notable scholars.

Chapter Four presents the exegesis of the text of Job 19:13-22. This chapter brings out factors of social alienation in the text. It begins with a Hebrew transliteration and an English translation of 19:13-22 and a study of chap. 19 as a whole, since this is the immediate context of the passage under consideration (19:13-22), so as to provide a broader understanding of the text. It also studies the structure and poetry of the text and finally provides a verse–by–verse study of the text.

Chapter Five investigates the conceptual attitude of Israelite society toward suffering individuals as attested in the Book of Psalms. Three psalms (22, 31, and 88) are selected for this study.

Chapter Six examines Job's response to his suffering and social isolation. The chapter is divided into three sections. The first section deals with his frustration at the attitude of his family, friends, and neighbors. The second section deals with certain conceptual attitudes of society that alienate people and cause them suffering, with special reference to the case of Job. It also considers Job's displeasure at God's silence. The third section deals with Job's declaration of innocence by way of an oath in 27:2-6, his defense of his integrity (chaps. 29 and 30), his self-examination in 31:1-34, 36-40, and demand for a bill of indictment in 31:35.

Chapter Seven provides a brief summary of each chapter and the principal conclusions reached in each. The chapter also envisions that this study will raise the conscience of members of society about how to avoid social actions that alienate and how to help and support those who suffer social alienation not only in religion but also in other sectors of social life.

III. Contribution and Originality

This book is the first of its kind in the study of the Book of Job. Although the alienation of afflicted individuals from family and friends has been studied with regard to the Book of Psalms, the Book of Job has not yet been considered from this point of view. The exegetical and theological problem at stake has a bearing on suffering in our contemporary world. The book explores this important issue for the interpretation of the Book of Job as it brings to light how some societies in the past have tended to use a misconceived concept of faith to isolate and afflict their members. This phenomenon still occurs in our societies today.

3

Chapter Two

Definition of Social Alienation and Human Suffering

This chapter defines the terms "Social Alienation" and "Human Suffering." The chapter analyzes each term used and studies all the methods that will be applied in the subsequent chapters of this work. My discussion of social alienation considers theories of social life, with a brief treatment on the theories of Emile Durkheim and Max Weber.[1] Particular attention is paid to responsibility for alienation in society. Human suffering is narrowed down to suffering that is caused by social alienation and the possible causes of such suffering. The chapter is divided into two parts: social alienation and human suffering.

I. Social Alienation

Social alienation, the umbrella term used for all forms of alienation that individuals experience in a society, is the separation from society that is experienced by its members. Society is comprised of individual human beings who live and are bonded together by a common goal. Society sometimes distances itself from some of its members and, when this occurs, those members become alienated from the society. This alienation may be done knowingly or unknowingly by society. We shall break down the phrase "Social Alienation" into "Social," "Alienation," and "Social Alienation." To address the issue of social alienation we need first to understand how an individual becomes socialized.

A. Social

The term "social" has to do with human beings living together as a group; since their lives affect one another, their interaction generates social life. Social life is a basic unit embedded in a group of

---

[1] Emile Durkheim (1858-1917) was the French sociologist considered by many to be the father of the discipline and one of the most influential figures in the founding of modern sociology. Max Weber (1864-1920) was a German economist and sociologist and is arguably the foremost social theorist of the twentieth century and principal architect of modern social science.

people called a society. The basic unit of a society is the clan, which is a social aggregate of individual families, each of which has individual members. The family therefore is the smallest unit of a society. For the perpetuation of the society, the society has a code of conduct with which each member of the society is obligated to comply. However, not all actions of an individual in a society can be termed social. To qualify as such, the individual's conduct must be oriented meaningfully towards the behavior of others. For instance, religious behavior is not social if it is oriented towards solitary life. Similarly, economic behavior is not social if it does not concern any other individual in the society.[2] Conduct which is social is such behavior that strongly influences the members of the society.

Among the numerous scholars who have studied the subject of social life, two are outstanding because of their remarkable achievements in the field. These scholars are Emile Durkheim and Max Weber, some of whose concepts will be utilized in this study of Social Alienation in the Book of Job.

1. Emile Durkheim

Emile Durkheim was born in April 15, 1858, in Epinal, France and died in 1917. He was born of Jewish parentage but later became an agnostic. His lifelong interest in religion was academic and not theological. He developed a passion for scientific study that could give moral guidance to people living in society. His main focus was social order.[3] The fundamental issue in Emile Durkheim's theory is objectivity. He advocated the rejection of all preconceived knowledge of any social behavior in order to arrive at a sociological method that would lead to an explanation of social behavior.[4] His method includes a critical study of basic practices of society that have evolved over the

---

[2] Max Weber, *Basic Concepts in Sociology* (trans. with introduction by H. P. Secher; New York: Philosophical Library, 1962) 55-56.

[3] Additional information on Emile Durkheim, his life, his writings, and achievements can be found in George Ritzer's *Sociological Theory* (2nd ed.; New York: Alfred A. Knopf, 1988) 16-18, 72-98.

[4] A detailed treatment of social facts will be given later in this chapter, but for additional information see Steven Luke's introduction in Emile Durkheim, *The Rules of Sociological Method and Selected Texts on Sociology and Its Method* (ed. with an introduction by Steven Lukes; trans. W. D. Halls; New York: The Free Press, 1982) 12.

years. His goal was to arrive at a wholly realistic view of why society behaves the way it does and thereby attain to the real nature of society. He considered religion to be a social fact since no human being is born with religion; and since no human being is born with religion, religion is an element external to all human beings that needs to be scrutinized.[5] His arguments revolve around social facts, social life, and social reality.

Social life is the social context in which human life is lived. A member of a society is born within a world of social facts which need to be scrutinized in order to arrive at objective reality. This does not mean all social facts are negative; some are positive. A society that lives only within the context of social facts alienates its own members.

a. Social Facts

Social fact is the power of an external force that the society exerts on its members. At birth a member of a society discovers ready-made rules, beliefs, and practices of the society. These formulated rules, beliefs, and practices, when taken collectively, constitute what Durkheim refers to as social facts.[6] These practices may be either religious or secular; and, since they predate the individual, he or she inherits them. Durkheim argues that since a person inherits these practices, it means that the set of rules exist outside the person and are foreign to him or her.[7] The practices are taught to the members while they are children. From a very tender age, the child is taught when to sleep and rise, how and when to eat, how to go to school, how to learn; in short, the child is taught "the dos and the don'ts" of society. All of these rules equip the child to live meaningfully in society. As a consequence, the child's ways of acting, feeling, and thinking are foreign properties that exist outside the consciousness of the individual member of the society. No individual develops biologically with a set of rules; rather, he or she becomes informed historically at the dictates of the environment.[8]

---

[5] See Pickering's discussion in his abstract on "Durkheim and Religion" in Emile Durkheim, *Durkheim on Religion* (ed. W. S. F. Pickering; Atlanta: Scholars Press, 1994) 325.

[6] Durkheim, *The Rules of Sociological Method,* 54.

[7] Ibid., 50.

[8] The process of equipping a child with the norms, beliefs, and values of the society is what we refer to as socialization. Socialization involves two processes:

The set of rules and practices of a given society originated with ideas of prominent individuals or groups of individuals. These ideas were embraced by the members of the society and, after a period of time, they became collective ideas and hence accepted as a special authority of the society. It is always the responsibility of a leader of a society to ensure that the society enjoys a minimum level of peace; hence, the need for laws and regulations. However, the leader is not supposed to promote his or her own ideas but to be objective and to preserve the dignity and the good of the society as a whole. When the society deviates, the leader has to find a way to bring the society back to order.

A society's set of rules may sometimes be compulsory because it reacts against and brings back deviants into conformity with the society. In every society there are deviants and these deviants must be brought to conformity. Such an undertaking demands sanctions from the society. The society punishes deviant behavior in different ways: reprimand, banishment, seclusion, deriding, and extermination. Society has the power to take control of its individual member and shape the individual into what the society requires. The operation of such a set of rules and their sanctions shows that the individual depends on the operation of such a society more than he or she depends on himself or herself.

Social facts cannot exist without a defined social organization.[9] It is only when people gather together with a common goal that social facts become obvious. Any group of people needs to be organized. A social organization under the dictates of the society develops social phenomena. In social phenomena, members of society know when to

---

primary socialization and secondary socialization. Primary socialization involves the use of language. Language is an important tool in socialization because it engages the individual with other members of the society (see Peter L. Berger, *The Sacred Canopy: Elements of a Sociological Theory of Religion* [New York: Doubleday, 1969] 18-21). Language is the vehicle of communication and helps bring people together. The child interacts with other members of the society especially with its parents and hereby comes to know the values, norms, and beliefs of the society. The child explores "the dos and don'ts" of the society and lives the life of the society. Secondary socialization involves going to school to learn to specialize in a particular field of life. Socialization is never completed but always an ongoing process.

[9] Durkheim, *The Rules of Sociological Method,* 52.

take certain steps in life, for example, when to begin formal education, the age of marriage, and different religious observances. These social phenomena exert some pressure on the members of the society. On the one hand, the society may be aware of these pressures but still continue to conform to these social phenomena until there is a disaster. On the other hand, the society may be unaware of these pressures and may continue to conform to these social phenomena because the social process has made the members lose their sense and have become unaware of their own selves and as a result act without reasoning. The members of the society may continue to live the life of the society until the bond that holds the society together disintegrates or an individual emerges from the society to point out some of the practices within the society which are not good. It is only then that the individuals of a society will realize how long the society has kept them captive.

The problem with social facts can be that they have been ingrained in the society for a long time and the society has accepted them as a true value of the society. For a change to occur, someone has to explain to the people what is wrong with what they have accepted as true for so long. Human beings are always reluctant to change, but when change does occur and is good, they are happy. All human beings are psychosocial beings. The individual's ability to imbibe all the features of the society may be a psychic response to the biological constitution of the individual; hence, change becomes a psychological problem because such a behavior has been ingrained in the mind. When a society is not able to identify the bad elements in its social facts, the individual members who identify the reality of a social fact may suffer the consequences of alienation because society opposes their view, which in fact is a better way of life.

b. Social Life

For an individual to live in society, he or she has to have the ability to function and develop within the ideas of the society. The individual may or may not be conscious that he or she is acting according to these ideas. Constituent elements of social life are only learned and expressed in a society. If such elements are inherent in the life of the individual, then that individual has no need to learn since the ideas are not distinct from him or her. This concept of learning from the society and acting upon it does not mean that the individual cannot develop his or her own way of life; the point here, is that an individual in society develop his or her own personal features and mannerisms based on the society's way of life. That the ideas of the society are not his or her own ideas, but those of the society, may become known to him or her only later in life.[10]

Living and developing social ideas lead to formation of social sentiments. There are two types of social sentiments.[11] In the first set of sentiments, the individual is linked to other members of the society where he or she experiences daily life. As the individual interacts with others, he or she develops esteem, respect, affection, and fear. All these sentiments experienced by the individuals are what the society requires of its members. These sentiments leave the individual with his or her autonomy, personality, and independence intact. The second set of sentiments links the individual to the social entity where the individual has to behave as a member of a society. With these sentiments, the individual becomes limited in his or her choices with regard to what is to be done. The individual is compelled to accept the decisions of the society; hence, the society imposes on the individual an obligation to follow and to live by. This experience of observing the rules of the society is what is termed the culture of a people.

The members of the society in their day-to-day interactions produce culture. Culture is an essential part of the society.[12] Culture is a human product and is always being produced by human beings. Unfortunately, sometimes individuals can be trampled by their culture when negative elements of that culture are not eliminated. Society sometimes has to question its practices and not just accept existing concepts and compel its members to be influenced by these practices; such a procedure can be dangerous. Just as human beings are responsible for developing the physical products of culture, that is, inventing physical objects for the use of the society in order to enhance the livelihood of its members, such as improved farm implements, clothes to keep the body covered, shelter to give protection and rest, transport for easy mobility, so also human beings are responsible for non-physical products of a culture such as thinking, feelings, and

---

[10] Ibid., 69.
[11] See the review by Jean-Marie Guyau, *L'Irréligion de l'avenir, étude de sociologie,* in Durkheim, *Durkheim on Religion,* 36.
[12] Berger, *The Sacred Canopy,* 10.

emotions which are products of the values, norms, and beliefs of the society. We need then to evaluate what is accepted as culture.

The ongoing existence of the individual in a society depends on his or her involvement in the culture of the society. To be involved means here to share in the objectives of others. The culture of the society must be welcoming and reasonable; if it is not, the individual becomes isolated.[13] Sometimes society becomes a nuisance to its members when it forgets its own principles. When a society fails to meet the demands of individuals and imposes itself on those individuals, imposing excessive punitive measures just to control the members and forgetting its dynamic aspect, it can destroy the individuals of the society and the society as a whole. Respect for the individual is essential in maintaining a well-balanced society.

Society, however, cannot exist without individuals obeying laws and regulations of the society. Norms and regulations are essential for maintaining the society. It is therefore very necessary that individuals obey these rules and regulations. The society fails only when its rules and regulations become more important than the people they are meant to guide and protect. To live in a society is to live in an orderly world; and to have a meaningful life is to obey the laws and regulations of the society. The observance of the laws and regulations of the society is society's process for structuring the individual's consciousness of life. Therefore, when society alienates an individual, very often that person is destroyed because his or her life had already been structured according to the consciousness of the society.

Alienation of individuals from society leaves them vulnerable because their lives were formed by the society that is no longer supportive of them. Alienation is associated with both sociological and psychological problems; the individual perceives himself or herself as a useless human being because life becomes meaningless and senseless without the support of the society. At this point, the reality and the identity of the life of the individual are transformed into what Berger

---

[13] Welcoming and reasonable, in this context, refer to the hope that the society should try to identify itself with the individuals in the society. Consideration and tolerance should be given to individual members of the society. A society should be aware of situations that can lead to isolation of an individual in the society, especially during times of crisis. Special attention and support should be afforded to individuals facing such.

refers to as "meaningless figures of horror."[14] To be a member of a society is to be sane, and it is the responsibility of the society to protect the individual from insanity and help him or her to experience the reality of life.

c. Social Reality

Social reality is the approved societal actions that are beneficial for the life of the individuals in the society. These actions become a societal reality because they represent the actual nature of the society. To ascertain such social reality, social actions must be studied without the preconceptions that exist in the society. This means shaking off all fallacious ideas about a given action in order to arrive at one's own view or conception. This scrutiny may involve questioning societal actions in order to understand why certain actions are approved by the society while others are not. The goal of this scrutiny must not be personal fulfillment but rather the fulfillment of the individuals in a society.

Social life is inseparable from social facts because these facts are its main constituent parts. The scrutiny of social facts leads to social reality, but it is not as if social reality is a new development; it is not. It existed within the society but, unfortunately, was not realized by the members of the society.[15] Durkheim's study on suicide is a good example of the positive and negative consequences of social facts on a society.[16] Unexamined social facts may lead to social destruction.

A protest by an individual in a society which may seem deviant can lead to social reality. Durkheim gives the example of Socrates, who according to Athenian law was condemned as a criminal. His crime was his independence of thought. This crime became useful for the Athenians and the world at large because Socrates' thought gave rise to a new morality.[17]

As with other scholars, Durkheim was criticized for his work on the grounds that he never brought his actual interpretative practices to the level of self-conscious reflection. In his social analysis, he did not take into account the psychological makeup of individuals and society.

---

[14] Berger, *The Sacred Canopy*, 22.
[15] Durkheim, *The Rules of Sociological Method*, 82.
[16] On suicide, see Durkheim, *Durkheim on Religion*, 39-58.
[17] Durkheim, *The Rules of Sociological Method*, 102.

11

He was unable to address the problems of interpretation and to integrate a deductive inquiry into the rules of sociological method.[18] He, however, did lay a solid foundation for the study of social life.

2. Max Weber

Max Weber was born on April 21, 1864, in Erfurt, Thuringia, Germany and died in 1920.[19] He was born into a well-educated family which gave him a sound academic environment and foundation to pursue his studies.

Max Weber won international acclaim for his classic work *The Protestant Ethic and the Spirit of Capitalism.*[20] His interest in the religious influences on modern capitalism and the evolution of Western rationalism led to his empirical study of the world's great historical religions. Weber has been praised for his logical reasoning, systematization, fabulous knowledge, brilliance, lucidity, and intellectual energy.[21] In his famous unfinished work *Wirtschaft und Gesellschaft*, in the chapter titled "Religionssoziologie," he deals with fundamental concepts of sociology, offering an expansive methodological and conceptual analysis that result in a systematic analysis of major areas of human social activities. In particular, he treats social causes, influences, social effects, and the impact of religion upon group life.[22]

---

[18] Steven Luke points out some of Durkheim's limitations in his introduction to Durkheim's book, *The Rules of Sociological Method,* 14-18.

[19] For more information on the life of Max Weber and his education, see H. P. Secher's introduction in Max Weber, *Basic Concepts in Sociology,* 7-23; see also Ritzer, *Sociological Theory,* 99-140.

[20] Controversial as it is, this book is judged as a landmark of recent Western intellectual history. It is also considered as a counterattack against the Marxist assertion of materialism in the historical process. For further information on Weber, see *The Sociology of Religion* (introduction by Talcott Parsons; trans. Ephraim Fischoff; Boston: Beacon Press, 1963) xx.

[21]Ephraim Fischoff makes these remarks about Max Weber as well as about his two friends Ernst Troeltsch and Werner Sombart, who with Weber are recognized as the founders of sociology of religion. For more information about Weber and his two friends, see Fischoff's translator's preface, ibid., x.

[22] This book, although unfinished when Weber died, is considered as one of the most comprehensive and powerful works of social science scholarship. For more information, ibid., xii.

Weber was not a theologian; rather, his main focus was on the relationship between religious ideas and human conduct, especially the economic behavior of the individual in society.[23] He inaugurated a new phase in the study of religion in relation to human life. In his study, he worked with key terms, two of which are differentiation and rationalization.

a. Differentiation

Social process was a major concern of Weber's, just as social facts were for Durkheim. The essential element in the analyses of social process is differentiation. Differentiation helps one to visualize the change that takes place between the "material sphere," which consists of conditions, structures, and utilitarian interests of ordinary living, and the "ideal sphere," which deals with the meanings of various conceptions of the supernatural and other aspects of experience.[24] The study of the two spheres helps us to understand the extent to which different situations are defined in terms of their corresponding actions. Weber places heavy emphasis on differentiation. Talcott Parsons notes that Weber's differentiations are predominantly dichotomous; he always offers a twofold means of solving a problem.[25] According to Parsons, Weber abstracts from the outcome of a social process two principal alternatives for social structuring, after which he proceeds to clarify the differences and the relations between those two alternatives and then presents his grounds for concluding in one direction or the other.[26]

---

[23] Talcott Parsons, an American sociologist, is a structural functionalist. He happened to be at Heidelberg five years after the death of Weber when Weber's influence was still strong. Weber's wife used to hold meetings in her home, some of which Parsons attended. Parsons finally wrote his doctoral dissertation in part on Weber's work. For more comments by Parsons on Weber, see Parsons's introduction, ibid., xx.

[24] Ibid., xxix.

[25] Ibid., xxix; on the "ideal type," see also Secher's introduction in Weber, *Basic Concepts in Sociology,* 14.

[26] The outcome of a social process is what Weber refers to as a breakthrough. Weber makes a primary distinction between a direction that becomes the basis for evolutionary change in the established order and another direction that either strengthens the established order or changes it cautiously. See further Parsons's introduction in Weber, *The Sociology of Religion,* xxix.

b. Rationalization

According to Weber, the social behavior of an individual evokes a social action from others that generates social relation.[27] Individuals in a society base their behavior on the expected behavior of others for their actions to be rationalized. Similarly, religious actions have to be rationalized. Weber defines rationalization as "the master conception through which cultures define their religious situation, and through which the sociology of religion must understand such cultural definitions of situation."[28] To analyze social relation we need to rationalize the ideas that emerge in the society. Examples of social relations are struggle, communalization, aggregation, and corporate groups.[29]

An essential component of the rationalization of behavior is the substitution of a well-ordered meaningful behavior for thoughtless commitment to ancient custom and a deliberately planned adaptation to situations in terms of self-interest of some individuals in society who impose their ideas. In this unjust imposition lie the problems of suffering and evil for those who do not morally deserve to suffer. Therefore, rationalization must take into consideration the intellectual clarification, specification, and systematization of concepts, since every course of behavior has an intended meaning, whether the individual or individuals involved in it understand this or not. This is similar to Durkheim's concept of scrutiny of social facts in order to come to the reality of societal actions. Systematization is necessary because behavior can impinge positively on the conscious realization of ultimate values, or negatively, not only at the expense of custom, but also of emotional values to the detriment of belief in absolute values.

---

[27] See also Secher's introduction in Weber, *Basic Concepts in Sociology*, 15.

[28] See Parsons's introduction in Weber, *The Sociology of Religion*, xxxii.

[29] Weber defines a struggle as the relation in which one individual asserts his will over another. Communalization is a social relation based on subjective feeling, either emotional or traditional, of belonging together. Aggregation is a social relationship based upon a rationally motivated balance or union of interests. A corporate group constitutes a social relation in which authority is vested in a leader and his counselors. These social relations determine the character of a society. The members of the society respond to how the society evolves. See further Secher's introduction in Weber, *Basic Concepts in Sociology*, 15.

Ideas are generated by what Weber called the teleological meanings of human conceptions of oneself and of one's place in the universe. These conceptions legitimize the individual's orientations in the world and give meaning to the person's various goals.[30] Human concepts presuppose metaphysical and theological understanding of cosmic and moral order; therefore, the individual's concepts have to be understood in relation to such wider order. It is good for the individual to understand the usefulness of these concepts which control his or her activities in life.

Rationalization must also take into account normative control or societal sanction.[31] This is necessary because the teleological reference of the concepts in question implies that human actions are goal-oriented. This means human actions should be subjected to the fundamental control of a hierarchy. The need for legitimate leadership to control the affairs of a society corresponds to the normative cultural order of every society. That normative cultural order places teleological demands upon its members. The conduct of each person is regulated by legitimate authority. But even in rationalizing the conduct of individuals, one has to bear in mind that the individual's conception of the nature of this normative order is not constant, because life is dynamic; therefore, there exists a differentiated variety of possible normative orders. All these factors must be taken into consideration when rationalizing because when one examines the conceptions of the normative order of a single society, one realizes that changes have occurred in the course of history. Weber's primary concern is the exploration of these different possible concepts and the direction these concepts have taken. Weber's rationalism is thus intellectual, in that it involves a particular reference to existential ideas that are teleological or normative, rather than empirical, since these concepts place obligations on members of the society with respect to their conduct in life.[32]

Another factor worth noting in rationalization is the concept of motivation towards commitment.[33] This concept not only imposes

---

[30] See Parsons's introduction in Weber, *The Sociology of Religion*, xxxii.
[31] Ibid.
[32] See ibid., xxxii-xxxiii. See also Weber, *Basic Concepts in Sociology*, 71-74.
[33] See Parsons's introduction in Weber, *The Sociology of Religion*, xxxiii.

social and behavioral patterns but also various levels of motivational commitment required for the implementation of these implied patterns of life. Such motivational commitments include beliefs and norms, especially seriousness of commitment to the cognitive validity of the espoused concepts and practical commitment, in the sense of readiness to put one's own self-interest at risk in the service of the concepts. Rationalization in this case concerns the systematization of a pattern or program for one's life as a whole. For instance, the emergence of capitalism, which we shall study soon, gives meaning in terms of an existential conception of the universe in which a given action is performed.[34]

3. Comparing Emile Durkheim and Max Weber

The most significant difference between Durkheim and Weber is that although both thought in evolutionary terms, they operated from different angles without any apparent influence of one on the other. Weber views religion as the source of the dynamics of social change, while Durkheim views religion as the reinforcement of societal stability.[35] Durkheim concentrated on ideas, while Weber focused on a structural analysis of the process of change. Weber advocates sociology of religion, while for Durkheim religion is a product of the society.

Durkheim and Weber were contemporaries. Although I do not agree with a number of their theories on religion, they made useful contributions that are relevant for a holistic understanding of the topic. The theories of social facts, social reality, and social process are of importance to our study, as are also differentiation and rationalization. I believe that the concepts of social facts and social reality help to understand social norms, values, and beliefs better. Critical examination of social facts, differentiation, and rationalization of social ideas will eliminate social concepts that alienate the society's own members. What constitutes alienation will now be considered.

---

[34] Ibid.
[35] Ibid., xxx.

B. Alienation

Alienation means separation of one thing from another. Alienation has a negative connotation because separation can be disastrous. Berger, from a dialectic perspective, looks at alienation as "the process whereby the dialectical relationship between the individual and his world is lost to consciousness. The individual 'forgets' that this world was and continues to be co-produced by him."[36] Berger's definition of alienation mirrors the viewpoint of Karl Marx. Dialectical consciousness is the real consciousness that a person needs to have of the self and of the world, but this is distorted because of the false image of the world that has been generated. The socio-cultural world in which we live is different from the world of nature, because human beings have imposed a different meaning on the sociocultural world and thus suppressed the world of nature, giving rise to alienated consciousness; and as long as alienated consciousness is conceived in this manner, it is false.[37] Alienated consciousness is false because the human consciousness has been transformed into a social world, so that the individual becomes estranged from what he or she does.

C. What Is Social Alienation?

Social alienation is the separation that results after an individual member of a society has been judged as a nonconformist according to the norms of the society. Human society is dynamic and constantly reproducing itself. It is within a society that an individual develops his or her personality and lives out his or her identity as a human being. No human being can exist without a society, and no society can exist without the individuals that constitute the society. It is the society that shapes the individual. For a society to exist, its members must have a certain standard of intellectual and moral probity. This involves mutual respect for others in the society and obedience to the norms, values, and beliefs of the society. For a society to be healthy there must be an interaction among the individuals of the society and such nonhuman factors as animals, machines, and plants because each of these elements contributes to the society as well. A human being is a social being who, when separated from other components of the society, loses his or

---

[36] Berger, *The Sacred Canopy*, 85.
[37] Ibid.

17

her humanity because the life of the individual is embedded in the life of the collectivity that is the human society and in the nonhuman components of the society.

Different factors contribute to social alienation in a society. Some of these factors are religion, politics, economics, health, and prejudice. Religiously, there are different ways that society alienates its members. A person who belongs to a religious society has to conform to the beliefs of the religious group and without such compliance one cannot claim membership; thus one becomes alienated. Religious alienation also occurs when a religious body alienates a person because he or she does not profess its faith.

Political partisanship can also result in alienation. People who do not support a leader of a regime may see themselves estranged from that regime. When leaders become power hungry and corrupt, they listen to no one and terrorize the people they govern with their own laws. Also, political leaders may make economic policies that are egocentric and favor only themselves and thus eliminate others. Economic shackling is a serious problem that alienates. Greed and self-interest constitute the major cause of this alienation.

Prejudice is responsible for racism and sexism in a society. For example, prejudice can sometimes be encouraged by parents. Parents should be careful what they tell their children about others. In some cases, a leader may influence his or her followers to believe certain ideas about others. Their doing this saddles people with a particular kind of thinking that can lead to a particular kind of work or particular manner of behavior, thus stereotyping such a group, and this thinking is transmitted over the years. Racial discrimination is a product of prejudice. It is usually based on skin color or language. People who do not belong to a particular group are weaned away from the other group. Another form of prejudice concerns gender differences. Some societies look down on women and neglect them and this breeds a lot of tension and discontent in the society; when women try to fight back, chaos may result.

Our main focus will be on religion as one of the basic agents of social alienation. Religion occupies a very important role in human society. It has done a lot of good for human society, but when religious concepts are misunderstood they can be very harmful.

D. Religion as an Agent of Social Alienation

1. Religious Bonds

Human beings are religious by nature, in virtue of their own constitution, and independently of all social conditions.[38] The individuals in a religious society are bonded together religiously. This religious bond also attaches each individual to the Supreme Being that he or she looks up to. Religion creates a sacred world in which human beings experience an awesome, mysterious, and superior power that transcends them; this mystical experience makes them believe that this superior power rules the world.[39] Religious beliefs are expressed in religious rites. These rites constitute the external manifestation of the beliefs at the heart of a religious group. Thus, those rites are the expression of the thoughts and actions of the group. Religious rites create, maintain, and reestablish a way of life and a sense of belonging within a society. A religious group may alienate a member of another group because that person does not profess the same creed and thus has no link to the group. Religious bonds are a vital issue in a society. Even a religion that professes one faith but has different denominations alienates others. Religious bonds can cause tremendous instability in societies.

Religion is experienced socially and makes a society a religious one.[40] A religious society cannot exist without the collective beliefs of the society. The stricter the beliefs, the stronger the religious bonds of the society. The religious beliefs that the members profess together become a means of socialization that unite them as one people. The rites of a religious society determine the religious expression and the intensity of the religious concepts of its members. It follows that the greater the number of those religious rites, the more the members of the society are integrated in the expression of their religious belief. The

---

[38] Emile Durkheim, *The Elementary Forms of the Religious Life* (trans. Joseph Ward Swain; New York: Collier Books, 1961) 113.

[39] For more information on the sacred, its origin, its location, or how the sacred is visualized in animate and inanimate objects, and how individual human beings are transformed by this sacred power, see Rudolf Otto, *Das Heilige* (Munich: Beck, 1963).

[40] Durkheim, *The Elementary Forms of the Religious Life*, 22.

common concept of the Supreme Being that the individuals in the society embrace leads them to work towards a common goal. The religious ideas that a people share as a group become the religious representations of that people and these representations become collective realities of the society.[41]

Human beings manifest these collective realities by their allegiance to the society and this is done externally; thereby the individual in a society identifies with the society to which he or she belongs. Thus the members of the society become one in belief and this belief binds them together in a social context in which they think and behave alike. Their togetherness, unity, and peace are realized in the profession of a common creed. Therefore a society tries to maintain a standard of life to ensure that the unity and peace that creed emphasizes is maintained. Any idea against its creed is avoided since that can disrupt social stability, and so any action contrary to its creed by any individual in the society is seen as disobedience to the creed and deviants are punished.

2. Religious Sanctions

The creed of a society goes together with various sanctions, which are imposed by individuals of a society in the name of the sacred.[42] All members of a religious society are obliged to conform to its norms and regulations of the sacred.
Nonconformity to such norms and regulations is scorned and considered deviant behavior and therefore liable to sanctions, which may eventually alienate.[43] It is a fact that for a society to thrive there must be decorum and the members of the society must adhere to the norms of the society. However, when there is deviant behavior, before the person is penalized the crime has to be thoroughly investigated to ascertain the justification for such sanction. The story of Susanna (Daniel 13) is a typical example of an unjustified sentence.

In many religious societies, the laws of the sacred are not tempered with mercy. There is no remedy and the deviant has to face the consequence of his or her actions. In the Gospel of John, the woman caught committing adultery is to be stoned to death (John 8:1-

---

[41] Ibid.
[42] Berger, *The Sacred Canopy,* 94.
[43] Durkheim, *Durkheim on Religion,* 89.

20

12). In Islam, the hand of a thief is cut off because he or she has stolen. Sometimes such harsh sanctions are not actually supported by any legitimate religious laws.[44] They cast a dark shadow on religion when leaders of religious societies impose judgment in the name of the sacred. Even more egregious is the case in which the person conducting the unjust execution knows very well in his conscience that the execution is wrong but says nothing to prevent its occurrence. In reality, the conscience of the executioner objects to the action but, since he or she has to conform to the dictates of the society, he or she keeps quiet and allows the unjust sentence to proceed.

In some societies, certain kinds of suffering, misfortune, or disease are considered signs of punishment for deviant behavior. Such concepts are inherited through socialization and are passed on from generation to generation. These symptoms are viewed by the society as real punishment. In such cases, an individual who happens to fall within the category of these conceptual ideas of society is separated from the general population because the person is deemed to have done wrong and has to be isolated. The society, instead of coming to the aid of the person, abandons him or her to his or her fate.

3. Religious Enthusiasts

Religious concepts reflect the interpretations handed down by earlier generations. The interpretation of concepts gives rise to religious sentiments. In order to study religious sentiments, critical thinking is needed on the interpretation of those concepts. An essential element in such interpretation is to understand one's object of worship because religion arouses sentiments within its adherents, which sometimes become very powerful. One has to be careful about interpretation of religious ideas because when religion is misunderstood, its proponents disseminate the wrong notion of religion. Such false doctrine moulds the life of the individual; the individual becomes excited by strange religious thoughts. The person becomes consumed with passion; his or her vital energies are overstimulated, desire becomes more animated, and his or her sensations become stronger. At this stage of emotion, the individual no longer recognizes himself or herself, because he or she has been transformed.

---

[44] Berger, *The Sacred Canopy*, 94-95.

Religion generates exuberance and that exuberance changes the life of the individual enthusiast. Such new zeal is attributed to a new experience of the object of worship, and consequently the society is transformed in the name of the object of worship. A good example of religious enthusiasts is found among some religious fundamentalist groups. Interestingly, some mainline churches also have them.

Religious enthusiasts do not act the way they do only because they want to but rather because they have experienced something that triggers their zeal. They consider their actions justified because they see religion not only as a system of practices but also as a dogma.[45] They consider it their responsibility to teach others to do what they think is the right thing to do. This self-entrusted responsibility, on their part, may demand the use of force in some cases.

The failure of appropriate socialization may give rise to a false identity within society, and this in turn gives rise to consequent actions. In some cases, the members may not even know that their actions are wrong because those actions have been accepted by the society as proper. This happens when society has false ideas and imparts a false consciousness to its members. Religion, when it is misunderstood, can become a powerful instrument for bad indoctrination,[46] and its consequences can be very disastrous for a society. Zeal for a religion is sometimes due to that religion's doctrine of salvation.

4. Religion and Salvation

Every religion has goals. Religious zeal stems from a concern for salvation. It is essential that a member of a religious society seek for salvation, whatever its form, insofar as this produces certain consequences for practical behavior in the world. Religion is practiced in the context of the world, and so zeal for salvation must lead to a positive orientation to worldly affairs. According to Weber, the quest for salvation in any religious group derives from religious motivation, which is a practical system that orientates the group to certain integral values.[47] These integral values have a goal to attain, and so the

---

[45] According to Durkheim, religion is both a system of practices and a set of religious ideas. I agree, but not with his doubts about the existence of God. See Durkheim, *Durkheim on Religion*, 157.

[46] Berger, *The Sacred Canopy*, 95.

[47] Weber, *Sociology of Religion*, 149.

religious way of life is oriented towards that goal. Such a way of life is oriented to this world because the religious person lives and moves in the world and needs to use elements of the world to promote personal salvation while focusing on the world beyond. In this regard, salvation becomes a quality of devotion that is indispensable, which the individual must acquire and must manifest in his or her pattern of life.[48]

E. Consequences of Social Alienation

When an individual is alienated from the society, he or she becomes vulnerable because he or she has no support from the society any longer. The result is that the alienated person cannot identify with the society. In a situation like this, an alienated person may have recourse to suicide or to violence against other members of the society in an attempt to avenge his or her alienation.

Durkheim made a classic study on suicide. Suicide is a decision to take one's own life because life has become meaningless. These are some of the reasons why people commit suicide: the loss of status in the society, economic depression, lawlessness, loss of a dear one, divorce, deformation due to sickness or accidents, physical separation, and natural disasters. The likelihood of suicide, Durkhiem said, depends on the degree of the individual's integration in the society. This includes confessional influences on the members and their adherence and obedience to the faith. Catholics are more likely to submit their conscience to the control of their faith, while for the Protestant, he or she is the master of his or her own faith. Durkheim concluded that Catholic countries have lower suicide rates than Protestant countries.[49]

As a conclusion, it can be said that social alienation, when not regulated and understood by the person alienated, may lead to the destruction of the person.

---

[48] Ibid., 150.
[49] For more information on Durkheim's studies on suicide, see Durkheim, *Durkheim on Religion*, 39-58.

II. Suffering and Humanity

Suffering began with humanity and has been a problem that all generations have struggled with. Suffering can be caused by oneself or by the society and is experienced within the society. When an individual encounters suffering, the initial reaction is to seek the cause of the suffering. Suffering may or may not be induced. Induced suffering may result from one's own carelessness, greediness of a member of the society, death of a loved one, or oppression or exploitation by a fellow human being. Suffering that is not induced may be the result of natural illness, natural disasters, or in the case of Job, who is relatively unique in that God allows the accuser to afflict him.

A. The Source of Human Suffering: Biblical Perspective

In the Bible, God created everything in a perfect order and found it good (Gen 1:25). The biblical account of the fall of Adam and Eve is an attempt to explain the origin of human suffering in the world. The world is created good. Goodness for Israel is always active; it is something that determines life, something one has to experience daily.[50] Good produces good and evil produces evil. Good and evil create social conditions that can either be productive or destructive for the society. These two factors, good and evil, determine happiness, joy, sorrow, or suffering for humanity.

The good person is called a righteous person and that person enjoys blessings manifested in terms of children, honor, property, wealth, good friends, prosperity, and long life. The righteous person lives happily because he or she knows the path to follow in life. Happiness depends on certain traditional codes of life, and anyone who follows those codes is assured of happiness. Such codes of happiness are something with which Job was familiar (Job 29:2-25). Job enjoyed considerable respect in his society because he led a good life. Respect is the prize of righteousness and is not the privilege of a single person but of all who pursue that course of life. The fruits of blessing for the

---

[50] Gerhard von Rad, *Wisdom in Israel* (trans. James D. Martin; 7th ed.; Harrisburg: Trinity Press, 1993) 77-79.

righteous, as understood by the society, are seen in the individual person.

The doctrine of retribution teaches that every human action has its reciprocal reaction. What a person enjoys or suffers is the direct consequence of his or her previous actions. Thus, the life of the individual is a momentary link with the past, the present, and the future. This means that the individual has no one to blame for his or her misfortunes apart from himself or herself. Similarly, if he or she is prosperous it is because of his or her own efforts.[51] In the religion of Israel, there is only one world of spiritual experience and that is God. It follows that whatever happens in one's life is known to God. This concept of an all-knowing God is the reality that envelops ancient Israel.

According to the biblical doctrine of retribution, suffering is caused by sin. The guilt of sin has to be expiated in order for the sufferer to regain his or her peace. The burden of guilt is seen as the consequence of one's involvement in an evil act, which is disobedience. In the light of the doctrine of retribution, the words of God were understood by Israel to generate either constructive or destructive effects.[52] This thought permeated the life of Israelites and made their lives more comprehensible in that suffering is seen as a consequence of disobedience. The friends of Job occasionally made reference to disobedience as the reason for Job's suffering (Job 4:7-21; 33:8-33), an idea which Job himself rejects several times.

B. The Concept of Suffering in Mesopotamia

It is also worthwhile to look briefly at how some of the neighbors of Israel reacted to suffering. In his study of the Old Babylonian period, William Moran observes that the religious understanding of suffering in society is expressed in confession of sins.[53] The Babylonians believed that people suffer because of the evil

---

[51] Berger, *The Sacred Canopy*, 65.

[52] God's words are constructive when people obey the laws and keep God's commands (Deut 4:40) but destructive if they disobey the law and follow other gods (Deut 6:12-16).

[53] William. L. Moran, "Rib Haddad: Job at Byblos?" in *Biblical and Related Studies Presented to Samuel Iwry* (ed. Ann Kort and Scott Morchauser; Winona Lake, IN: Eisenbrauns, 1985) 173-81, here 176-77.

they have done. What immediately comes to the mind of any sufferer is the need to examine himself or herself in terms of the directives of his or her god. The gods are believed to impose punitive measures for sinful actions. Suffering therefore is believed to be the consequence of sinful action.

Sometimes, after a careful examination of oneself, the sufferer realizes that he or she has done nothing to deserve such punishment. Thus the problem of the reason for the punishment arises. If the gods are truly responsible for punishment, then the gods have other laws that are unknown to the individuals in society, given the sufferer's belief that he or she has done nothing wrong to deserve that punishment. With this realization comes the simultaneous realization that there is something wrong with the theory that people suffer because of their sins. What is sometimes observed in a society is that a righteous prosperous person comes to a wretched end while a wicked person becomes prosperous. It is difficult sometimes for human wisdom to comprehend the suffering of the just person. If the gods are responsible, then the ways of the divine are not known to humans, and what one has to do is to give faith a chance, as in the Book of Job.

In three typical Mesopotamian stories, righteous sufferers describe their suffering, the mystery surrounding the cause of this suffering, and the possible end to the suffering. The three stories are very similar to Job's story in the Bible. They are *The Sumerian Job* (= A man and his god), *Ludlul bēl nēmeqi* ("I will praise the Lord of Wisdom"), and *The Babylonian Theodicy*. We shall come back to them later in the next chapter.

In the traditional ANE creation account, the gods vanquish evil by fighting among themselves.[54] This fight is the expression of the

---

[54] The Babylonian creation story, the Enuma Elish, has the story of the struggle between Apsu and Ea, and the fight between Tiamat and Marduk, the son of Ea. For a full account, see the Creation Epic in *ANET*, 60-72; Richard Clifford, *Creation Accounts in the Ancient Near East and in the Bible* (CBQMS 26; Washington, DC: CBA, 1994) 82-98; and Stephen Dalley, *Myths from Mesopotamia: Creation, the Flood, Gilgamesh and Others* (New York: Oxford University Press, 1989) 228-30. Ugaritic literature also tells a similar story. Baal (lord of the sky, also known as the storm god) tries to establish his kingship and has to fight with the god Yamm (the god of the sea), his enemy. Baal later fought with the god Mot (death divinized, the god of the underworld) and the god Athtar (an astral god who is

struggle between good and evil. The struggle is a sign that there is no perfect society. In the Book of Job, God makes both human beings and monsters. Those monsters are considered by humans as evil because they are a threat to humanity, but God created all of them and he admires them as his creatures (cf. Gen 1:25). What human beings consider evil is not evil in the sight of God (Job 40:15).

C. Evil as a Source of Human Suffering

To ascribe suffering solely to the devil would be denying human involvement in suffering, because suffering sometimes originates with human beings. If the devil is responsible for human suffering, then human beings cooperate with evil to cause their suffering. The demon responsible for an evil act does not operate on its own but needs an agent to effect its action, and human beings become the agents of such evil acts. An individual has to allow himself or herself to be used by the demon. The demon sometimes finds expression in the social segregation experienced in a society. Good is in opposition to evil, so when goodness ceases to exist, evil takes its place. When human beings become selfish, they cooperate with evil consciously and inflict pain on others and, sometimes unknowingly and unintentionally, on themselves. In other cases, the evildoer may not be conscious that he or she is inflicting evil upon others. To resolve this problem, one has to judge one's action conscientiously from the point of view of the other. To say "the devil made me do it" is a fallacious way of excusing one's action; every individual has to pursue righteousness.

Righteous life is promoted and greatly rewarded in any society. The unrighteous person according to the "deed and consequence" concept is considered to end miserably (Job 5:3-7; 8:11-13). A righteous life benefits not only the righteous person but also the generations that follow. Conversely, the wicked perishes with his or her generation (Prov 11:21; Job 15:34-35; 18:5-21; 27:13-23; Sir 44:9).

---

perhaps a natural irrigator of the land). Baal has to fight these other gods because he wants to establish his kingdom, as he does eventually. These four warrior gods rule different parts of the cosmos. For more details, see Simon Parker, ed., *Ugaritic Narrative Poetry* (tans. Mark S. Smith; Atlanta, GA: Scholars, 1997) 81-180; Clifford, *Creation Account*, 118-26.

The reality of good and evil determines a person's way of life and becomes an important social fact that is promoted by all societies. For example, the society of ancient Israel pursued righteousness and considered anything unrighteous as evil. What Job encounters is what we can term evil. What makes Job's affliction morally evil is that his accuser does not deny the piety of Job but rather questions the motive for Job's piety (1:9-11; 2:4-5).

Israel considers God all-knowing, and Job in his piety knows that his suffering is known to God and so he presents his plight to him. He appears to be resigned to the belief that "the Lord gave, and the Lord has taken away" (Job 1:21b), later declaring "Shall we receive the good at the hand of God, and not receive the bad?" (Job 2:10b). These are words of complete faith and trust. These expressions of faith and trust (Job 1:21b; 2:10b) made Job accept his suffering although uncertain of what the real problem is; but despite the acceptance of this mysterious affliction, he has another problem to confront. Job is now forced to deal with the taunts of his family and friends. He has to convince his family and friends that he has done nothing evil because the sort of affliction perpetuated by the accuser on Job was thought to happen only to evil people. These taunts from his family and friends and Job's task to convince them of his innocence compounded his problem.

God does not promise a life without suffering in the Bible. However, the story of creation shows that suffering was not the intention of God. God created other things only after he created human beings so that human beings would lack nothing, and all God created was good (Gen 1:25). Suffering became part of the created order only after the fall of Adam and Eve. In the Book of Job, God's permission to the accuser to test Job implies that God did not promise a life without suffering (Job 1:12; 2:6). All who trust in God must prepare for trials and tribulations.

D. Disregard for Normative Order as a Consequence of Human Suffering

The reason for suffering sometimes lies with the human quest for what an individual values in life. Most of the value systems in a society are institutionalized in normative orders and become rules for the life society lives. The one who fails to conform to the normative order has to suffer the consequence of his or her actions. Suffering sometimes emerges from selfish desires that people hold as essential, because in the selfish desires, which are considered essential for them, lies their interest and satisfaction. On one hand, those who do not share in this interest suffer if the person imposing his or her interest happens to be the leader of the society. On the other hand, individuals who hold onto their personal interest face consequences from society if society does not deem their selfish interest essential. Hence, conformity or nonconformity with an established normative order has its consequences. Some norms, however, need more rationalization because they are complex. Weber notes the more rationalized an order, the more the tension and the higher the frustration in the meaningless things that happen in the society.[55] The more incomprehensible a norm, the more tension it generates and, if the tension is not properly handled, it results in suffering for innocent people as well.

Conclusion

Social actions, when not consciously thought out, can be alienating. Norms, values, beliefs, and other social practices are essential for an orderly society. However, some of these norms, values, beliefs, and practices sometimes may have outlived their usefulness or do not contribute positively to the mutual growth of the society, and that is why it is necessary that these practices be reviewed periodically. The failure of positive social attention to these practices may cause suffering to individual members of the society.

Suffering in human society is a mystery and inevitable. The sufferings that no human reason can comprehend are supposed to be endured with the support of the society, but those that human beings might impose on their fellow human beings should be avoided. Sin is not always the cause of suffering. A sinner can inflict suffering on a sinless person without the sinner, himself or herself, sharing in that suffering. Society can make headway only if every individual in society pursues "the objective good" of the society, becoming more conscious of others in society. Those who suffer need support of others

---

[55] Parsons's introduction in Weber, *The Sociology of Religion*, xlvii.

in society to endure their unfortunate situation. The next chapter studies the Book of Job—where a misinterpreted religious concept intensifies Job's suffering.

Chapter Three

The Book of Job

The Book of Job is one of the greatest literary works of all time; it has universal significance.[1] The book is a drama cast in poetry, itself set in a prose framework that presents the biography of a man who suffered the disintegration of his life and was later restored to life again. It teaches about undeserved suffering, the nature of God, and God's relationship with human beings in his created world.[2] The book is characterized by tensions and resolutions. Some of the themes that run through the book include the transcendence of God, the problem of good and evil, human suffering, retribution, and rejection by family, friends, and loved ones. It is a didactic book and the longest ancient Hebrew poem that has survived.[3]

The Book of Job belongs to a category of books in the Hebrew Bible called wisdom literature. The book is unique among the wisdom literature books because of what it addresses, namely, the problem of the suffering of "the righteous." The suffering of "the righteous" and the prosperity of "the unrighteous" is a common theme in the wisdom literature books. The theme of "the righteous" and "the unrighteous" dominates the Books of Psalms, Ecclesiastes, and Ben Sira but the radical protest of Job is not to be found in any of the other wisdom books.

The Book of Job does not offer wisdom instructions and proverbs like the other books mentioned above; rather, it features a critical inquiry into the central tenet of Judaism that has been accepted worldwide as true wisdom: the law of retribution.[4] Accordingly, the "deed and consequence" connection states that the righteous are rewarded and the unrighteous suffer in this life.

---

[1] Norman Habel, *The Book of Job* (OTL; Philadelphia: Westminster, 1985) 21, 60; Gustavo Gutiérrez, *On Job: God-Talk and the Suffering of the Innocent* (New York: Orbis, 1987) xvii, 1.

[2] Richard J. Clifford, *Wisdom Literature* (Nashville: Abingdon Press, 1998) 20.

[3] R. A. F. MacKenzie "Job," *JBC*, 511.

[4] Henceforth, the law of retribution will be referred to as the "deed and consequence" connection.

This chapter studies the Book of Job as a wisdom book with keen interest in the "deed and consequence" connection, since it is a major theme the author seeks to address. To help bring out human isolation as the cause of Job's suffering, a brief study is also made of similar stories of suffering individuals in some ANE texts; this is followed by a brief survey of the Book of Job. Finally, there follows a history of research on the text, 19:13-22, since that is the focus of the dissertation.

I. Wisdom Literature

The adjective *ḥākām* taken literally as "wise," as in English, is not confined exclusively to professional wise men. The adjective denotes a type of skill and competence.[5] The phrase "wisdom literature" means a writing that intends to impart skills and competence, but the definition of what constitutes wisdom literature is disputed.

Wisdom literature in the Hebrew Bible refers to the books of Proverbs, Job, and Ecclesiastes. Ben Sira and the Wisdom of Solomon belong to the Protestant Apocrypha but are recognized as canonical books in the Catholic and the Orthodox Bibles. In addition to these writings, there are psalms and prophetic passages that are regarded as wisdom writings (Psalms 1, 37, 43, 73, 104, 112, 119, 127, plus parts of Amos and Isaiah).[6] Among the canonical wisdom books, the core work is the Book of Proverbs. Some elements of the Book of Proverbs date back to the origin of Israel; it appears to be a teaching instruction manual for Israelite society.[7]

The search for wisdom includes the pursuit of ethical and theological truth. Wisdom teaching became accepted as part of the

---

[5] Some examples in the Bible are Exod 31:3; 35:35; 36:8; 1 Kgs 7:14; Jer 10:9; Ezek 27:8.

[6] Ronald E. Clements, *Wisdom in Theology* (Carlisle: Paternoster, 1992) 16. See also Donn F. Morgan, *Wisdom in the Old Testament Traditions* (Atlanta: John Knox, 1981).

[7] Hartmut Gese identified nine major divisions in the Book of Proverbs: 1:1–9:18; 10:1–22:16; 22:17–24:22; 24:23-34; 25:1–29:27; 30:1-14; 30:15-33; 31:1-9; 31:10-31. See H. Gese, "Wisdom Literature in the Persian Period," *The Cambridge History of Judaism* (4 vols.; ed. W. D. Davies and L. Finkelstein; Cambridge: Cambridge University Press, 1984) 1. 189-218; see also David J. A. Clines, *Job 1-20* (WBC 17; Nashville: Thomas Nelson, 1989) lxi.

revealed will of God. The Torah became identified with wisdom in the Book of Ben Sira (Sir 24:22). Torah determines the moral life of the people.[8] However, it is inappropriate to present wisdom as if it were solely a religious phenomenon of postexilic Israel.[9] Some of Israel's wisdom literature was common to the ANE and not specific to the religion of Yhwh.

No one can talk about the wisdom literature of Israel without mentioning Israel's neighbors. It is imperative that we consider those neighbors because the teaching of wisdom in Israel was greatly influenced by that country's neighbors. After the Israelites settled in Canaan they were dominated by the Assyrians, and the Assyrian influence lasted through the eighth to the seventh centuries B.C. The seventh to the sixth centuries B.C. saw the rule of the Babylonians. The Persian domination lasted quite a long period from the sixth to the fourth centuries, B.C., ending with Alexander's conquest, beginning in 334 B.C. These nations, as they ruled, transmitted familiarity with their own literatures to their subjects and this accounts in part for their influence on the Israelites. Israel's wisdom literature shows features similar to its neighbors.[10] Although Israel was not similarly dominated by Egypt over a long period, its literature also shows strong Egyptian influence.

Literature recently discovered or long preserved shows that as early as the third millennium B.C. down to the late period, wisdom books existed in Egypt.[11] The content of the wisdom book of Amenemope shows similarities with that of the biblical Book of Proverbs, Prov 22:17–23:11 in particular. In Egypt, the close counterpart to *ḥōkmāh* was *ma'at;* a concept linked to the political life of Egypt.[12] *Ma'at* determined the economic and moral life of the people.[13] Similarly, the wisdom of Israel is associated with the ruling

---

[8] Clements, *Wisdom in Theology*, 19.

[9] von Rad, *Wisdom in Israel*, 9.

[10] I shall discuss in detail examples from the ANE under the heading "Literary Style of the Book of Job" on p. 61. For further literature on the influence of the ANE wisdom literature on the wisdom writings of Israel, see Clifford, *Wisdom Literature*, 23-42.

[11] von Rad, *Wisdom in Israel*, 9.

[12] *Ma'at* has a wide variety of meanings: truth, right, justice, basic order, and world order. See von Rad, *Wisdom in Israel*, 72.

[13] Clements, *Wisdom in Theology*, 22.

class and addressed the moral life of the people. Most of the wisdom writings in the OT are attributed to Solomon by literary convention. However, Israel's earliest wisdom developed in the clans and was later nurtured in the royal court.[14]

Wisdom writings teach the art of living a good life and assume human freedom, but this freedom is achieved only within the social milieu of the individual. The individual interacts with family and friends within the society; if the society is religious, then the interaction takes place in the context of religion. The Book of Job, like the other books of wisdom, advances the idea of acquiring wisdom in order to live a good life. The Book of Job teaches trust in God, perseverance, and consistency with oneself. Job was accused of disobedience by the friends, and his suffering attributed to his evil deed(s).

One of the fundamental teachings of wisdom literature is the difference between good and evil, between righteous and unrighteous persons. The Book of Job presents Job as a righteous man. Good and evil represent two worlds that are antagonistic to each other. Wisdom literature theologizes human action in terms of cause and effect; the relationship of cause and effect was encapsulated in the extremely ancient traditional concept of "deed and consequence." [15] Good actions produce good results and evil actions produce evil results.

II. "Deed and Consequence"

Good and evil deeds are performed in all societies. von Rad cautions that the idea that good acts occasion good and evil acts occasion evil is not strictly a wisdom teaching.[16] The idea had been in existence for quite some time and was later adopted as part of wisdom teaching. It became very deeply rooted in Israel and forms a significant element of the teaching of the prophets and the sages (Deut 30:15-20; Jer 6:19; 14:16; Prov 11:21; 12:7; 15:6; 16:4-7; Job 18:5-21; 20:4-29; 27:13-23).

---

[14] Ibid., 23.

[15] von Rad, *Wisdom in Israel,* 124-37, 195-226; K. Koch, "Is There a Doctrine of Retribution in the Old Testament?" *Theodicy in the Old Testament* (ed. J. L. Crenshaw; Issues in Religion and Theology 4; London: SPCK, 1983) 57-87.

[16] von Rad, *Wisdom in Israel,* 128.

The society drilled this concept of "deed and consequence" into its members during their primary socialization. It was the responsibility of the parents to teach their children the culture of the society (Exod 10:2; Deut 6:7, 20-25). In Proverbs, parents give moral formation to their children (Prov 1:8; 6:20; 31:1). The concept of "deed and consequence" might be a motivation to live a good life; however, its formulation was sometime exaggerated to the point of invalidating itself. Good and evil actions occur in every society. We see evil people prospering and righteous people suffering in every society, so it is wrong to assert that only good people prosper and only evil people suffer.

Threats to life are an experience of every age. A reaction to a threat could emerge in different ways. The way the society considers certain matters depends on that society's experience over the years. Wisdom writings multiplied after the exile; the Israelite sages taught the people how to live a good life. Different aspects of human life were touched on by their teachings (Prov 1:20-33; 8:2-36; Sir 6:34; 9:16). Wealth is a reward for a practiced virtue and poverty is punishment for evil (Pss 1:3; 112:1-3; Prov 10:15-16; 15:1-33). Deuteronomy 4:40 and 30:15-20 promise a good life for obedience of Yhwh's laws. In the history of Israel, God is considered as all-knowing and all-powerful; therefore, anything that happens is accepted as coming from the hand of God. For instance, when God reveals the sin of Eli to Samuel, and Samuel is afraid to tell Eli, Eli realizes this and asks Samuel to tell him. After Samuel does tell him, Eli says, "It is the LORD; let him do what seems good to him" (1 Sam 3:18b).

von Rad observes that the "deed and consequence" concept became rooted in the people in such a way that personal illness or major disorders, such as national disasters, were looked upon as the result of divine wrath. To appease God's wrath, the whole nation has to observe a public fast and confess their sin. The cultic performance is intended to ward off the effects of sin; von Rad thinks that such cultic performances created more tension in the people and filled them with fear because they believed that they were being punished by God for their misdeeds. [17]

---

[17] Ibid., 196.

The practice of turning to God in times of calamity and searching for peace is a common practice in the Bible. After the defeat of Israel at Ai, Joshua turned to God and discovered the sin committed by Achan. Once the sin was expiated, Israel won the battle (Josh 7:6-8:29). Saul also sought an oracle from God but God remained silent. God's silence was due to Jonathan's violation of Saul's oath (1 Sam 14:38-46). A three-year famine in Israel led David to inquire into the cause of the problem. He learned that it was because of the blood guilt of the house of Saul. David arranged for this to be expiated (2 Sam 21:1-14). The story of Jonah is another example. Jonah sinned and the only way to expiate his guilt was to throw him into the sea (Jonah 1:4-17). The idea of sin and guilt was already in existence.[18] The "deed and consequence" concept inherited that idea and expanded upon it. From the above examples, we learn why it was not difficult for the friends of Job to believe that Job had indeed sinned.

The concept of "deed and consequence" became so intense after the exile because the exile had made Israel more conscious of sin and guilt. The concept "deed and consequence" is not a divine law, but unfortunately it could be assumed to be the teaching of the Torah (Psalm 1). This assumption was easy and clear because it was elaborated upon by wise people who, having experienced exile, came to the conclusion that teaching strict observance of the law was necessary to avoid a future disaster. The experience of the exile of 587 B.C. gave a new impetus to Israel's wisdom literature. Wisdom teaching became a way of educating the people and giving them spiritual guidance. There was the need for Israel to know why they went into exile. Typical of Israel's negligence were the absence of true worship of Yhwh and the observance of the law, as the prophets had complained. "Deed and consequence" became a motivating factor for observing the law.

Generally, ideas develop in a society over a long period of time. These ideas of the society are what Durkheim refers to as collective representations.[19] Collective representations are the collective personal

---

[18] The law and the prophets teach that justice will prevail in the life of every person. For more on the operation of the "deed and consequence" principle in the law and the prophets, see Robert Gordis, *The Book of God and Man: A Study of Job* (Chicago: University of Chicago Press, 1965) 135-56.

[19] Durkheim, *The Elementary Forms of the Religious Life*, 22.

experiences of the individual members of the society, and the exile gave a new impetus for the returnees to live a just and a good life. The effect of "deed and consequence" on the society was due to the collective representations of the society, such collective representations being more efficacious in their implementation by society and more stable than individual ideas. An individual can easily change his or her mind because the individual is conscious of the slight changes that take place in his or her environment, while in the case of a collective representation only regularly occurring events can succeed in affecting the mindset of a society. As a consequence, "deed and consequence" lingers on in the society and becomes the collective wisdom that surpasses the wisdom of the individual and thus becomes a concrete representation of the society and hence enforced by the society. One understands why the friends of Job collectively agreed that Job had sinned and his lone voice was not heeded since they were the representatives of the view of the society. The friends serve as the epitome of the understanding of the society and its environment.

von Rad observes that most "deed and consequence" teachings in the Bible are presented as if these were a rule, as in Prov 11:21; 12:7; 14:22; 15:6; 26:27.[20] These are wisdom observations; they do not mete out blessings or curses. In texts in which the blessing of God is invoked on a righteous person (e.g., Prov 19:17), such blessing is not necessarily a matter of retribution. The problem one faces with "deed and consequence" is precisely where to draw the line that determines how the righteous and the unrighteous are requited. von Rad condemns the theory of "deed and consequence" as "alien to life," a concept that could only end in theological catastrophe.[21]

A. Similar Concepts of "Deed and Consequence" in Other Societies

Similar examples of the idea that generated the concept of "deed and consequence" exist in other societies and religions as well. Such concepts emerge depending on the understanding and interpretation that those societies place on a particular value of the culture. A society develops a specific pattern of life for its members.

---

[20] von Rad, *Wisdom in Israel,* 129.
[21] Ibid., 195.

Weber, for example, made a detailed study of the emergence of capitalism in the West as well as the social life of the Chinese and the Indians.

Human beings have the tendency to acquire and make money. Economic acquisition becomes the ultimate purpose of the capitalist. The quest for economic success is reflected in Prov 22:29, which says, "Do you see those who are skillful in their work? They will serve kings; they will not serve common people." Calvinists took this idea strictly as an obligation and translated it into their earthly work; success in business became a calling and a means to enter heaven.[22] The comparison between capitalism and the "deed and consequence" concept illustrates how religion was able to influence human beings to enhance their own social relationships within a given environment. The individuals in the society try to excel in economic life, believing that this will earn them their eternity.

Weber first visited the United States in 1904 when he attended a scientific World Congress held in St. Louis.[23] While in the United States, he observed in the working force of the society the need for bureaucratic structures to govern them. That same year, he published his book *The Protestant Ethic and the Spirit of Capitalism,* in which Weber raised serious issues in the field of human social action in terms of the Protestant ethic.

Similarly, Weber studied the Chinese and the Indian societies. The Chinese had a system based on the educated class, rather than the wealthy.[24] They had a closed society and avoided any outside influence and this was the objective pattern of life that the Chinese government wanted for its people. Similarly, the Indians operated with a caste system and adhered to the restrictions imposed by custom on the individuals despite their enterprising culture, which might have given them the opportunity to develop a capitalist society.[25]

---

[22] For more details on emergence of capitalism in the West, see Max Weber, *Max Weber on Capitalism, Bureaucracy and Religion* (ed. Stanislav Andreski; London: George Allen & Unwin, 1983) 115, 136.

[23] See Secher's introduction in Weber, *Basic Concepts in Sociology,* 11.

[24] For the development of the Chinese bureaucratic system, see Weber, *Max Weber on Capitalism, Bureaucracy and Religion,* 67-84.

[25] For a full history of the emergence of Indian culture, see ibid., 83-90.

B. Conclusion on "Deed and Consequence"

In every society what has been traditionally handed down acquires a valid authority.[26] Hence "deed and consequence" was not an invariable rule guaranteed by God. Rather, it was an interpretation and an understanding that acquired greater significance in wisdom teaching after the exile. It was not God who promoted capitalism; Calvinists based their interpretation of the biblical text (Prov 22:29) and developed the doctrine from which capitalism evolved. Like the Chinese, the Indians also protected their society from any external influence in accordance with the pattern they wanted for their society. Every society has it own objectives and priorities and seeks to perpetuate its values toward that goal.

Laws are formulated in order to deal with and regulate the needs and the behavior of people living together in a society. As with the rules that promoted capitalism, the Chinese and the Indian cultures favored their desired goals. The norms and regulations of societies change over time. Laws have never provided true universally valid solutions to problems because sometimes they do not promote the ultimate good, a fact which accounts for the repeal, abrogation, and amendment of laws. When it comes to human decisions concerning what is desirable and undesirable, laws sometimes give a good solution or a partial solution; at other times they may be a misleading guide for a society.

III. A Brief Survey of the Book of Job

The Book of Job bears the name of its main character, Job. The name Job is not used of any other individual in the OT. Job is a symbol of wisdom and righteousness (Job 1:1). Job is from the land of Uz in the region of North Arabia or Edom.[27]

In the prologue, Job is portrayed as one of the legendary figures of antiquity. He was a pious man who, together with the wife and children, is blessed with wealth. At a divine assembly, God calls Job's

---

[26] Weber, *Basic Concepts in Sociology*, 68.
[27] David J. A. Clines, *Job 1-20*, lvii.

exemplary life to the attention of the accuser.[28] The accuser doubts the disinterestedness of the piety of Job and challenges God to allow him to put Job to the test; God agrees, but with a condition (1:6-12). In the first test, the accuser strips Job of all his possessions and family (1:13-19). Job accepts his misfortune (1:20-21). The accuser is not satisfied and requests another chance from God. He is allowed that chance, on the condition that he not touch Job's life (2:1-8). He inflicts a second series of attacks on Job and on this occasion directly strikes his physical life with horrible diseases. Job is disfigured and can no longer live among human beings. His abode is the dung hill where he scrapes himself with a potsherd (2:8). The story of Job is a complex one that still poses a problem for theologians. Job represents the vitality of the human spirit that refuses to be humiliated, even by God and especially not by theologians.[29] However, the suffering of Job, the wise and the righteous person, calls to mind the wisdom axiom articulated in the law of "deed and consequence."

A. Author

The author is not named, but in all likelihood he was an Israelite, possibly in the Diaspora. He may have known the stories of the ANE because his style of writing appears similar to some stories of the ANE. He is a firm believer in the religion of Yhwh and tries to reveal the true nature of the God of Israel. He used Job and the friends to correct the misinterpreted concept of "deed and consequence" that only evildoers suffer. He is a good poet whose manner of writing shows the depth of his theology and knowledge.

B. Date of the Book of Job

The date is uncertain; there is no evidence in the book to help us determine the date. The book makes no reference to the past history of

---

[28] The "accuser" or the "Satan" is the English translation/transliteration of the Hebrew *haśśāṭān*, "adversary," or "Satan." In the Hebrew Bible, the word occurs in Job chaps. 1–2 and Zech 3:1-2 with an article, which indicates that the position was an office of one who performs a functionary role. And so, Satan is shown as a member of God's court whose responsibility is to accuse human beings before God. In 1 Chr 21:1, "Satan" is personalized and so has no article, being presented as one who gives bad advice and misleads.

[29] Clines, *Job 1-20*, xii.

Israel and its language is very different from that of other biblical writings. However, it is possible that the story of Job had been in circulation before it finally appeared in the present form. As early as the sixth century, the prophet Ezekiel mentions Job, Noah, and Daniel who will be saved by their righteous deeds (Ezek 14:14, 20). Job was a righteous man; he speaks of his righteousness (Job 12:4) and vows not to let it go (Job 27:6). Job's righteousness ranks with that of Noah (Gen 6:9).[30] The Daniel of Ezekiel is possibly the Dan'el, a Canaanite king about whom tablets were found in the ruins of the second-millennium B.C. city of Ugarit.

The author of Job is cognizant of other books of the Bible. The suffering of the innocent is a theme found in both Second Isaiah and the Book of Jeremiah from the sixth century. There is similarity between Jer 20:14-18 and Job 3:2-19. Likewise, the story of the accuser in Job 1:6–2:7 resembles the Satan stories in Zech 3:1-2 and 1 Chr 21:1-8. The author may also have been influenced by Psalms 49, 73, and 139. Although there is a tendency to regard the book as postexilic, its date is unknown.[31]

C. Purpose of the Book

It is difficult to pinpoint a particular purpose of the book.[32] However, it is clear that after the fall of the monarchy particular moral and spiritual problems emerged.[33] The problem was in grasping the true nature of God in order to know his will and his intention for humanity, in order to live a life worthy of him. The sages took it upon themselves to reveal the true faith of God in their writings and teachings. The Book of Job is a work of these sages; it represents a clear, prolix, and fearless critical inquiry into the truth of the "deed and consequence" concept.

---

[30] Édouard Dhorme, *A Commentary on the Book of Job* (trans. H. Knight; London: Nelson, 1967) xvi.

[31] R. A. F. MacKenzie and Roland E. Murphy, "Job," *NJBC*, 466-67.

[32] Clines says that whenever scholars think that they have mastered it, new ideas emerge from the book to create a different meaning in the mind of readers (*Job 1-20*, xiv).

[33] Some of the prophets within this era also denounce the moral and spiritual degradation of the Israelite society in their writings (see Jeremiah 12; Ezekiel 18; and Malachi 3).

According to the concept of "deed and consequence," if you live a righteous life you will find favor with God (Psalm 1). This would mean that only righteous people are prosperous and happy, and all evil people suffer because they are denied God's favor. But this is not reality. In real-life situations, both the righteous and the unrighteous suffer. There are unrighteous people who are rich, happy, and prosperous; they lack God's favor, yet they are prosperous and happy. Similarly, there are unrighteous people who are poor and suffering. Among the righteous, some are rich and prosperous while others are poor and unhappy as well. The misleading element in the concept of "deed and consequence" was equating the favor of God with wealth and happiness. Success in business is presumed to indicate closeness to God. This misleading factor needs to be exposed.

The author tried to point out possible reasons for suffering in the world. Suffering can be a result of one's faults or that of society or of the divine will. The author, based on his own experience with God, shows that fidelity to God must not depend on the fear of punishments for one's sins or the hope for reception of good things from God, but rather on one's love for God. Suffering is not only for unrighteous people. We may not understand why we suffer because the human mind is limited in its ability to comprehend. Human beings cannot understand the divine. To illustrate his point, the author used a story of ancient tradition, familiar to the people, of the man Job of Uz.

The book may have been directed to a specific group of people.[34] It is possible the book was written to address the rift between the poor and the rich. The author's society may have had a problem with the "deed and consequence" concept, knowing very well that evil people become rich and live long and have healthy lives while good people suffer and die prematurely. The righteous who were poor may have been grieved that God is partial in showering blessings on evil people because the righteous poor were aware that these evil people cheat and abuse them. Likewise, the rich, who were righteous but suffering, realized that suffering is not always a punishment for evil deeds. In response, the author refutes the argument that suffering is solely a consequence of bad behavior.

---

[34] Clines, *Job 1-20*, lxi.

The book also attempts to resolve the alienation that can occur in a society when inaccurate interpretation and understanding is given to a doctrine, in this case that of "deed and consequence." The book gives hope to the suffering in the society who might conclude that God is punishing them, gives them hope and consolation, and prevents them from feeling that they are condemned and are suffering because of their evil deeds. Societies often have no respect for those who suffer and sometimes offer them no support. Job was a prominent figure in his society and did a lot of good things for the people (29:12-17; 30:24-26; 31:16-22), yet he was not shown any support or respect during his ordeal. After Job's fortunes were restored, all those who previously abandoned him came back to rejoice with him (42:11).

The book teaches that to judge God in terms of human justice with human wisdom and understanding is useless (chap. 28). Nor are we to analyze God and interpret him in the context of traditional wisdom, as was done by the three friends of Job. The friends did not speak the truth about God (42:7-8). The divine purpose is inscrutable; human beings cannot assume that they have authority over the world. God did not promise a world without evil or suffering, as Job 1:12 and 2:6 clearly indicate.

D. Literary Style of the Book of Job

The book belongs to the category of wisdom literature. Scholars are divided on the literary unity of the book.[35] The prologue and the epilogue are different from the main body of the book because they are written in prose while the latter is written in poetry.[36] The characters in the prose and the poetry sections include God, the accuser, the "sons of God" (i.e., the heavenly court), Job, Job's wife, Eliphaz, Bildad, Zophar, and Elihu.

---

[35] Linguistic and stylistic differences contribute to different suggestions regarding the author(s) of the book. There are five suggestions made by scholars: (a) there are multiple authors; (b) the book has a single author; (c) a single author used different sources; (d) a primary work has undergone redaction; (e) a single author worked over an extended period of time.

[36] The "patient Job" appears in the prose section of the book, "the impatient Job" in the poetic section. See Clifford, *Wisdom Literature,* 74.

The book includes mythological imagery that is similar to that of the ANE, and the story of Job is similar to some of the ANE stories that we shall study. Three such stories are dated before the composition of the Book of Job. The Book of Job in this study will be treated as a literary unity, the admirable work of one author.

1. The Composition of the Book of Job

The book, as we have it now, has raised a number of questions, including the following: the difference between the prologue and the epilogue and the rest of the book; the reason for the lack of the third speech of Zophar; the wisdom poem of chap. 28; the Elihu speeches; and the integrity of the speeches of Yhwh. The book also has evidences of disappearing characters. For example, the accuser disappears after chaps. 1 and 2; the wife of Job (Job 2:10) never appears again, apart from being mentioned in 19:17. Elihu likewise disappears after delivering his speech; nothing is heard of him before or after. Each scholar has answers to these questions and the answers are countless. There is no need to go into such arguments here, since they lie outside the scope of this study; however I shall touch upon them in the following pages.

The prose section at the beginning of the book features the conversation between God and the accuser and serves as the introduction of the book (1:1–2:13). The other prose section in the book chronicles the restoration of Job and serves as its conclusion (42:7-17). The main section of the book is poetic.[37]

The poetic section starts with Job's lament and continues with the speeches of the three friends, Eliphaz, Bildad, and Zophar, and Job's responses to them. Job's bitterness increases as the argument with his friends progresses. The poetry features meter and parallelism.[38] The combination of prose and poetry in a book is not unusual. In ancient times, as von Rad notes, poetry was part of the daily life of the people and this fact holds true today. The movement from prose to poetry, he states, was easily understood at that time,

---

[37] Some claim that the book was originally prose but that the main part of the book was lost and was replaced by the poetic section we have today. See Bernhard Duhm, *Das Buch Hiob erklärt* (KHCAT; Tübingen: Mohr, 1897) vi.

[38] P. W. Skehan, "Strophic Patterns in the Book of Job," *CBQ* 23 (1961) 125- 42.

because it was a common phenomenon. So it is not unusual to find a book employing such a pattern. He reasons that the form of writing is a poetic manifestation of the human intellect, as is true also of those books written in poetic prose.[39] An Egyptian work of second millennium B.C. has prose in its prologue and epilogue with its center section in poetry.[40]

In the third cycle, Zophar makes no speech and that of Bildad's seems very short (25:1–26:5-14). It is not a must that Zophar deliver a third speech just because the friends have, but that has been the pattern beginning with chap. 4. Various reasons have been given to explain the absence of Zophar's third speech, but a probable reason could be that during the book's transmission a scribe left it out or mixed it up with Job's speech. For example, 27:13-22 is identified as Zophar's third speech because the argument found is the kind used by Job's friends, and 26:1-4 and 27:1-12 are attributed to Job.[41] Clines assigns 27:7-10 to Zophar's speech.[42] The argument in vv. 7-10 is against an enemy and Job already considers his friends as enemies (6:14-30; 19:29), while vv. 11-12 suggest that he is addressing his friends. The friends cite the fate of the wicked in their argument, but they never attack Job directly as an enemy—as happens in vv. 7-10.

The wisdom poem of chap. 28 is often thought to be an intrusion because it does not conform to the flow from chap. 26 when Job becomes the sole speaker until chap. 31. The poem is, however, relevant to the book because it expresses the inscrutability of God's ways and the limited nature of the human mind. Wisdom has to be pursued with eagerness. The poem serves as a good transition to Job's last speeches once he and his friends have failed to use their wisdom appropriately.

Job's friends annoyed him and contributed to the emotional imbalance that escalated into his agitation. Elihu's four speeches

---

[39] For more information on the possible reason for the use of both prose and poetry in the Book of Job, see von Rad, *Wisdom in Israel*, 49; Francis I. Andersen, *Job: An Introduction and Commentary* (TynOTC 3; Downers Grove, IL: InterVarsity, 1976) 41-55, esp. 45; John Job, *Job Speaks to Us Today* (Atlanta: John Knox, 1977) 8.

[40] See John A. Wilson, trans., "The Protest of an Eloquent Peasant," *ANET*, 407-10.

[41] Job, *Job Speaks to Us Today*, 8.

[42] Clines, *Job 1-20*, 645.

(chaps. 32–37) are all monologues, and Job does not respond to these speeches as he did to the speeches of his three friends. Elihu's speeches are directed to the three friends who proffered false images of God and to Job (cf. 33:1). He refers to the dialogue between Job and his friends (e.g., 32:12). Elihu's speeches are considered secondary because of their linguistic and stylistic peculiarities. They are judged by many commentators to be secondary, a later attempt to respond to Job's arguments because the friends failed to make good arguments.[43] On the one hand, those who hold that Elihu's speeches are secondary support their argument with the fact that Elihu is mentioned neither in the prologue nor in the epilogue (2:11; 42:7; 42:9). On the other hand, those who advocate the speeches' originality within the book support their argument with the fact that Elihu is a youth who claims to be wiser than his elders (32:6-9); because he is an inexperienced youth he would not need to be mentioned as a major character.[44] A youth in Israel was not accorded much importance in biblical times.[45] The Elihu speeches really do belong to the book, however, in the sense that they add meaning to it. Any attempt to remove these speeches will create a vacuum in the book. The speeches are part of the plan of the author because they dwell on the argument between Job and his friends and prepare the ground for Yhwh's speeches.

Yhwh's speeches are not intended to make up for his silence until his final verdict. God's silence is frequent in the psalms. Even today, God's silence is still experienced by his faithful ones. The Yhwh's speeches do not only address Job, they also expatiate on how God operates in the world. The author of the book is quite skillful. It is intriguing to note the similarity between the double meeting of God and the accuser in the beginning and the pair of discourses between

---

[43] For more information on the matter, see Clifford, *Wisdom Literature*, 87; see also Clines, *Job 1-20*, lviii-lix; Andersen, *Job: An Introduction and Commentary*, 50. Wolfers thinks Elihu speeches are part of the original. See David Wolfers, *Deep Things out of Darkness: The Book of Job Essays and a New English Translation* (Grand Rapids: Eerdmans, 1995) 66.

[44] See Clifford, *Wisdom Literature*, 87. It was culturally wrong for a youth to sit and talk among the elders. The young were less esteemed in Israelite society, so it is not strange that Elihu was not included.

[45] Philippe Ariès, *Centuries of Childhood: A Social History of Family Life* (trans. R. Baldick; New York: Vintage Books, 1962) 58.

God and Job at the end. The speeches are an integral part of the book; they are appropriate and fit very well where they stand.

The book recounts a favorable final restoration of Job after his incomprehensible suffering. The composition of the book also reveals much use of the Book of Psalms (Job 7:17-19; 8; 9:5-12; 12:13-25), Proverbs (Job 5:10, 17; 8:11; 12:11), and of similar features of the ANE literature.

2. The Influence of the Ancient Near Eastern Texts

A distinctive feature in the Book of Job is its similarity with some other ANE texts. The book contains mythological ANE allusions, prominent among which is the cosmic struggle between Yhwh and the sea represented by the dragon, Rahab or Leviathan (3:8; 7:12; 26:12; 38:8-11; 41:1-34). Some scholars suggest that the descriptions of Behemoth and Leviathan in chaps. 40–41 mirror Egyptian imagery drawn from the myths of Horus and Seth. The description of creation and cosmic chaos in chaps. 26 and 38 also alludes to the mythology of the ANE cultures.[46]

The problem of suffering is very much evident in the poetic literature of Mesopotamia and Egypt. No fewer than seven works on suffering have been found in Egypt, Babylonia, and Sumeria.[47] Three works of Mesopotamian literature feature social alienation of the sufferer on account of a mysterious misfortune. The tablets on which the stories were written are broken at places and some of the writings are not very legible; nevertheless, the stories are comprehensible. They are *The Sumerian Job, Ludlul bēl nēmeqi,* and *The Babylonian Theodicy.*

a. *The Sumerian Job*

The Sumerian Job was once a wise and a rich man who became a victim of cruel and undeserved misfortune; humbly, he persisted in

---

[46] Clifford, *Wisdom Literature,* 92-93; Habel, *The Book of Job,* 45, 57-60; Marvin H. Pope, *Job* (AB 15; Garden City, New York: Doubleday, 1979) xxii, xxiv, xxix, xxxii-xxxiv; and Richard Gordis, *The Book of Job, Commentary, New Translation, and Special Studies* (New York: Jewish Theological Seminary, 1978) xxix.

[47] Job, *Job Speaks to Us Today,* 7.

prayer before his god and was finally vindicated.[48] The poem is a prayer of lamentation to his personal god.[49] He recounts a series of complaints such as slander, disgrace, and marginalization by friends and enemies. He made a request to his mother, sister, and wife to plead his cause. Finally, his god was so pleased with his confession that he was moved to compassion, accepted his prayer, saved him from his misfortunes, and turned his suffering into joy.

b. *Ludlul bēl nēmeqi*

This is a hymn of profound piety. The hymn celebrates the god Marduk, who rescued the individual who prayed to him.[50] The hymn portrays the dependence of the individual on a god, in this case Marduk. It is only the gods who can save.

The story is dated around the third dynasty of Ur (2250-1925 B.C.) and is about a king who was plagued with all kinds of diseases. The story is told on four tablets consisting of about 400-500 lines. Only the first three tablets are well preserved. The story demonstrates social alienation of the sufferer (a king) by the society because of his ill health. He complains that he does not know the crime for which he is being punished. He had seven experienced courtiers who took advantage of his situation and plotted against him with slander, lies, and every kind of mischief. Their slander and lies brought shame for him and he walks shamefaced, unnoticed as he passes by. He became a social outcast, hated by his friends, who avoided his company, abused in public by his slaves, disowned by his family; he became a recluse that society frowned on. He called on his god, but received no help; he prayed to his goddess, but she did not raise her head; his spirits and angels did not help either.

Supernatural agencies were thought to be responsible for his disease and suffering. In the speaker's mind, the gods repay evil for good; his suffering is unjustified, he complains that he has met the fate

---

[48] *ANET*, 589-91; *Texte aus der Umwelt des Alten Testaments* [*TUAT*] (Gütersloh: Mohn, 1990) 3, 102-9.

[49] A personal god intercedes for human beings before the assembly of gods; see *ANET*, 589.

[50] For the full text, see William G. Lambert, *Babylonian Wisdom Literature* (henceforth, *BWL*) (Oxford: Clarendon, 1960) 21-62; William L. Moran, "Notes on the Hymn to Marduk in *Ludlul bēl nēmeqi*," *JAOS* 103 (1983) 255-60.

of a wrongdoer. He recounts his faithfulness to his gods and finally is saved by Marduk.

c. *The Babylonian Theodicy*

This text is a dialogue of twenty-seven stanzas, some of which are illegible. The dialogue occurs between an unnamed man, the sufferer, and his friend, a sage. The sufferer went to the sage for wisdom and consolation.[51] The sufferer protests against his misery and describes the injustice of the world and the unfriendly attitude of the gods. His friend defends the divine rationale behind the world and the fairness of the gods and urges the sufferer to ask for clemency from the gods.

The sufferer calls the sage's attention to human atrocities, which the sufferer believes have the gods' support. Human beings hail a strong man who killed and humiliated a powerless person who had done no wrong. They endorse the crime of the wicked, fill the storehouse of the oppressor with gold, and despoil the beggar of his provisions. The sage reflects on these statements and reexamines the sufferer's earlier statements and his experience; the sage acknowledges that the gods created both good and evil and have done evil and perverse things to humanity. The sufferer proclaims the sage a kind friend and avers that his attitude was not one of pride or arrogance but rather an appeal against injustice, which is the cause of his suffering. He is humble, wise, and suppliant but has never received help. The sufferer prayed to his god, who has neglected him, to come to his aid, to show him mercy and assistance.

In general, the three stories have similarities to the story of Job in the Bible. A significant difference between them and the Book of Job is that Job's misfortune is permitted by God and initiated by the accuser. The God of the author of the Book of Job is all-knowing and all-powerful and is responsible for all that happens in the world, that is, good and evil; but such was not the case in Mesopotamia. Given this concept of the God of Israel as the all-good, all-powerful, and all-knowing, it was very difficult for an Israelite to understand the problem

---

[51] The work is dated by Lambert around 1000 B.C. and was widely read. For the full text, see William G. Lambert (ed.), *BWL*, 63-91; see also Benjamin R. Forster, *Before the Muses: An Anthology of Akkadian Literature* (2 vols.; 2nd ed.; Bethesda, MD: CDL, 1996) 2. 790-98.

of evil and suffering, unlike someone in Mesopotamia, who knows that the gods fight among themselves and are responsible for good and evil.[52]

However, the stories share the same idea about the problem of evil. *The Sumerian Job* acknowledges human weakness and shows that human beings are prone to sin. *The Babylonian Theodicy* tells of uncertainty regarding the gods because one cannot understand why things are the way they are. *Ludlul bēl nēmeqi* acknowledges human deficiency in understanding the gods. Since human beings are unable to understand the gods, they can only trust and depend on the gods for assistance. All three stories are dated before the composition of the Book of Job. Suffering is a problem for all cultures and so it is not surprising that the stories are similar.

E. The Structure of the Book of Job
The Book is divided into five sections.

1. First Section: Prologue (1:1–2:13)
This section consists of the prose section and is a didactic piece that inculcates selfless piety. The characters are God and the accuser. Their conversation is quite unusual for the Bible, but that the accuser is permitted to act within certain limitations shows that God is in control of the situation. The accuser is an adversary of God and not of Job, because the accuser's challenge concerns how God governs and relates to his creatures.

Job is from the land of Uz. He is a just and God-fearing man and this causes God to be pleased with him. God blessed him with children and wealth. His fear of God is further expressed by his care in sacrificing for the potential sin of his children.

The plot presents Job as being unaware of the conversation between God and the accuser. That conversation leads to the destruction of his property in the accuser's first attack on Job.

The first attack did not yield the result the accuser foretold, so God allowed a second test, a direct attack on Job's person. Behind the scenes, Job has to persevere with all his integrity in order for God to be vindicated. The prologue gives the real reason for Job's sufferings and

---

[52] Clifford, *Wisdom Literature*, 73.

is the key to understanding the book; otherwise, the meaning of the book would elude the reader.

2. Second Section: Job and His Three Friends (3:1–31:40)

This section is the core of the book and is subdivided into three divisions (3:1–11:20; 12:1–20:29; 21:1–31:40). The first division begins with Job's lamentation (3:3-26), followed by Job's responses to the arguments of his three friends: Eliphaz of Teman, Bildad of Shur, and Zophar of Naamath. The three friends defend the traditional understanding of retribution, which they are convinced is true (Psalm 37).

The arguments in this section focus on the "deed and consequence" concept with a seeming repetition of themes and ideas (5:2 and 6:2-3), using legal terminology such as guilt, innocence, appearance in court, hearing in court, fair trial, and judgment. Midway through the second division, the speeches become shorter while the tension between Job and his friends mounts and Job's responses become more incisive.

The third division addresses the incompatibility of suffering and divine justice. It contains the longest of Job's uninterrupted speeches (chaps. 29–31). The division is interrupted by a hymn on the inaccessibility of wisdom (28:1-28). In fact, the isolation of Job becomes very obvious; he makes an oath in 27:5, challenges God, and seeks a hearing (31:35-37); all this prepares the reader for God's response. The text is also very corrupt in this division.

3. Third Section: The Speeches of Elihu (32:1–37:24)

Elihu is not mentioned as one of Job's friends and was not introduced at the beginning of the book, unlike the three friends. He appears only when the three friends have finished speaking. Unlike Job's three friends whose country we know, Elihu is introduced with his genealogy, country, and family: "Elihu son of Barachel the Buzite, of the family of Ram" (32:2). His speeches are four in number and are all monologues, unlike those of Job and his three friends. The speeches are directed more against the friends who gave false views of God. His

51

speeches serve as a link to God's speech, which is centered on earthly wisdom and divine justice, which is Elihu's theme as well.[53]

Elihu claims to be a wise person, and he demonstrates the differences between the sage and the fool. In his speech, Elihu shows that God speaks to people in a variety of ways, which include dreams (33:15-18), suffering (33:19-22), and healing (33:23-28). Elihu defends God's character and shows how justified God is and calls Job to repent for his offensive words about God (34:16-30).

4. Fourth Section: The Speeches of Yhwh and Job (38:1–42:6)

God's speech is a response to Job's demand for answers to his suffering. Job's request climaxes in chaps. 27 and 29–31 where he hauls God into court. Job is a mortal who summons his God. God addresses Job as one who arraigns his God before a court (40:1). God has been the center of discussion in the entire book. God's response is chronicled in two stages: chaps. 38–39 and 40–41. The first stage of the response (chaps. 38–39) features cosmology and meteorology. It describes animate and inanimate objects, the relationship of the creator to his creatures, and divine governance of the world. It ends with a short speech by Job (40:1-5). The second stage of the response (chaps. 40–41) discusses divine justice and also ends with a speech by Job (42:1-6). This speech of God addresses Job's anger concerning his birth (3:3-10) and his ultimate refusal to accept his condition as one of the creatures on earth. The speech contains words that are threatening, intimidating, and humiliating. It condemns the human wisdom of Job and places Job in the circle of human beings, because he has denied the divine wisdom and accused God of inability to care for his creatures.

To God, all his creatures have a purpose in this world; even the ostrich with all its peculiarities has a purpose (39:13-18). Human wisdom must seek to understand the divine purpose on earth. The speech reveals that God does not control evil for the sake of human beings. The world does not belong only to human beings, but also to other living beings, as well as to inanimate objects. Beasts live alongside human beings; although beasts may threaten human life, God protects human beings. Contrary to Job's accusation that God hunts

---

[53] Clifford, *Wisdom Literature*, 87.

him like a lion (10:16), God does not do this; God rather hunts prey for the lion (38:39-40). God is ever protective of his creation. God's protection is already revealed to the reader in the prologue when Yhwh told the accuser not to take Job's life (1:12; 2:6).

5. Fifth Section: Epilogue (42:7-17)

Job's persistent fidelity vindicated God in the sight of "the heavenly beings" (1:6; 2:1) who presented themselves before "the LORD." God spoke approvingly of Job in the prologue (1:8 and 2:3) and now blesses him above his three friends. The universe belongs to God, who controls it. Yhwh is still the God of Job. Job has to intercede for the friends who misrepresented God. It is always good to say the right thing about God in difficult times, especially when one is not in control of things.[54]

F. The Theology of the Book

Theologically, the book addresses the issue of human beings and their trust in God (1:9). Trust in God is the driving force that enables a sufferer to adhere to his or her righteous life. If Job had not persevered in his integrity, the accuser would have been vindicated. The book refutes the idea that suffering and prosperity is the result of the "deed and consequence" nexus. Job's life involved a struggle against a teaching concerning God and Job has to live, think, and struggle against that teaching. The book teaches that one should not believe in God out of fear or to win God's favor.
Rather, God is to be worshiped because God is loving and trustworthy; the worshiper worships because he or she is convinced of who God is. In times of suffering, God appears to be hidden from the sufferer; in such times, the sufferer needs to put forth renewed energy because the feeling of God's absence can cause terror and panic.

Job trusted God and that trust helped him to persevere until the end. Job knew God as one who cares, saves, protects, and answers those who call on him. He could not understand why God did not intervene earlier in his plight. God's silence made him seek a trial with God to prove his innocence (9:2-35; 13:13-28; 16:18-22; 19:23-27;

---

[54] von Rad, *Wisdom of Israel*, 208; see also Georg Fohrer, *Das Buch Hiob* (KAT 16; Gütersloh: Gütersloher Verlagshaus, 1963) 35.

23:1-7; 31:35-37). Finally, God's response proves both Job and his friends wrong. The response has a severe tone tempered with ironic humor and seems to address the right of human beings to question God. It also expatiates on the limits of the human mind and explains how God operates in nature. Our limited ideas of the world contribute in part to suffering because we fail to pursue the objective good to which all humankind is called.

IV. History of Research on Job 19:13-22

Although Job 19:13-22 is the main focus of my study, I shall consider the whole of chap. 19 in order to have a better understanding of the segment's context. Job's response in this chapter is the shortest of all his responses to his friends. This chapter portrays Job's friends exaggerating Job's sin and blowing it out of proportion. It also demonstrates the physiological and psychological agony of Job. Job is alienated from family and friends. Even his servants no longer respect him as the master of the household. When he is out in public, children make fun of him. Job has lost all respect and dignity. In the midst of all the rejection and desolation the chapter has a distinctive character in that it draws on themes that renew his hope for restoration.

Many scholars identify this chapter as unique in the whole book because it is the epitome of what Job is suffering. This section intends to review some of the scholarly works that have engaged in critical discussion of the chapter and consequently advanced the interpretation of the term "social alienation" in the Book of Job. These books will be treated in chronological order.

Francis I. Andersen (1976)

Andersen considers this chapter to be very important because in it Job's faith is rejuvenated in spite of Job's suffering and social neglect.[55] Job's audacious faith reaches its climax in v. 25, when it leaps to a new height from the state of despair caused by the reproaches of his friends (vv. 2-6), his devastation by God (vv. 7-12), and his sense

---

[55] Andersen, *Job*, 190-95.

of utter forsakenness (vv. 13-22). His certainty of vindication (vv. 23-29) shines forth against this dark background.

According to Andersen, Job's description in chap. 19 is not unlike what has been going on earlier in the book. He sees chap. 19 as a reproduction of chap. 16, but only to the extent it is an answer to Bildad's speech. Job admits that his condition is similar to that of anyone suffering retribution. Job knows God was the cause of his suffering and accuses him openly (v. 6). With his knowledge about God, Job cannot understand why God is acting in such an uncharacteristic manner. To make matters worse, although God, the judge, has not condemned Job openly, Job is shocked at the friends' conclusion that he had sinned. The friends ally themselves with God in their assault on Job, just as their forces are combined to make war on him in chap. 16. The friends are totally detached from the truth of his suffering. Bildad did not see how horrible it is for a God to impose such suffering on a just person.

Andersen makes a relevant observation on Job's pain of isolation. The chapter, he affirms, reveals the real state of Job's mind. Job's ardent desire for God does not make him insensitive to human relationships. Any normal human being knows that the two are inseparable. Job needs his human relationships. Job's list of social neglect in vv. 13-19 reveals his capacity for enjoyment of good things, and equally his agony when deprived of the solace of company, the respect of his employees, and intimacy of family. It is sacrilegious to show disrespect to a helpless old man, but the urchins did just that to Job. The bonds of moral obligation and affection were cut off (v. 19). Job is treated like an outcast.

Job is the center of a surprising scene that calls for pity. Job describes his condition of emaciation and horror. Job has lost his dignity and self-respect. He lies broken under the blows of God and the words of his friends. To the friends he appeals for pity, to God for justice. Both God and human beings pursue him. Andersen opines that Job's bitter complaint is about the silence of God. That there is no justice does not mean that there is injustice. The verdict has not yet been pronounced on him.

Robert Gordis (1978)

Gordis regards the chapter as the briefest of the speeches of Job.[56] Job, he believes, touches here on both the depths of despair and the heights of faith. The depth of his despair began with Job's bitter arraignment of the friends who have scorned him and ignored his misery. Job reminds them that it is God's enmity that has led to his estrangement. Job's hopelessness continues with abandonment by his kinsfolk and the contempt of slaves. Gordis refers to the children who mocked Job as young upstarts. In his desperation, Job made a final plea to his friends for their compassion (vv. 21-22). Job's innocence led him to wish that his words were engraved, so that he can be vindicated. Despite his unjust persecution, Job still believes that there must be justice in the world. He sees a vindicator, the God of righteousness, coming to his defense. Gordis identifies the vindicator as God.

Gordis views vv. 23-27 as an ecstatic moment in which Job experiences mystical exaltation. Job feels his reconciliation with God in his very flesh. According to Gordis, Job's ecstatic moments disappear only when he returns to his state of pain to warn his friends about their cruelty and consequent punishment. Gordis has a problem with the warning Job gives to his friends because he notices a contradiction between Job's belief that the friends will face God's judgment for their unworthy defense of God's cause and Job's constant denial of the existence of justice (13:15). Since Job denied the existence of justice, his friends cannot be brought to justice. Gordis considers this a logical difficulty. Psychologically, however, Job is incapable of abandoning his conviction that justice must triumph in the world. He voices his affirmation of faith in his ultimate vindication (19:25; cf. 16:19) and thus believes that justice exists.

Marvin Pope (1979)

In analyzing the chapter, Pope divides it into four units (vv. 1-5, vv. 6-12, vv. 13-22, and vv. 23-27)[57] and takes careful note of the individual words and interprets them.[58] Pope described the comforters

---

[56] Gordis, *The Book of Job*, 195-208.
[57] Pope considers vv. 28-29 "jumbled and probably misplaced;" see Pope, *Job*, xix.
[58] Pope, *Job*, 138-48.

(friends) of Job as annoying. They have a devastating effect on their friend, and this is expressed in the use of the verb "crush" in v. 2. Pope notes that the use of the verb "pull down," or "break down" in v. 10 shows that Job's house has been demolished. The verb, he says, is always used in reference to the destruction of houses or walls. It shows how Job has been destroyed, socially and psychologically.

Pope traces the alienation of Job's wife, family, and friends to his physical condition. He identifies the disease as halitosis, with other symptoms such as eruption and itching of the skin (2:7-8), the change in appearance (2:12), skin lesions and putrefaction of the flesh (7:5), nightmares (7:14), weeping and loss of vision (16:16), emaciation (19:20), osteitis (30:17), discoloration and peeling of the skin (30:30). All these ailments form part of his suffering and explain why Job is isolated.

Pope expresses surprise at Job's loss of social status. The slave, the least of all humans, who should always be concerned about his master (see Ps 123:2), ignores Job's call, and Job in his abjection entreats his slave. Whether the entreaty is effective or not, the humiliation is already complete when a slave is supplicated rather than commanded. Comparing the attitude of this slave to the manner in which Job treats his slaves in 31:13-15 is a cause for pity. Children also make fun of him.

Norman C. Habel (1985)

Habel's commentary offers great scholarly insight into understanding the author of Job.[59] He calls chap. 19 a celebrated speech in three units.[60] The three units (Job 19:6-12, 13-20, 21-29, with 2-5 as introduction) deal with Job's alienation and betrayal by the community within which he lives. His friends and family have no empathy with his anguish. The first unit is a complaint against God as the enemy responsible for his suffering. Job is a solitary mortal under siege, surrounded by the troops of God subverting his ways and preventing his progress. The integrated character of the unit, Habel notes, is evident from the framework of the argument and the repetition

---

[59] Norman C. Habel, *The Book of Job* (OTL; Philadelphia: Westminster, 1985).

[60] Ibid., 289-309, here 294.

of terms of mourning; this, he believes, is a technique the author intended to highlight the emotional pitch of Job's hope at the end.

The speech, Habel notes, comprises a catalogue of social intimates who have rejected, deserted, or disowned Job. The list moves from loved ones in his household to loved ones outside his home. The chapter reveals how Job's social world has been completely turned upside down, such that he is forced to entreat his servant rather than command him. His friends have become scavengers, intending to consume his flesh (v. 22). The appeal Job made in vv. 21-22 to his friends, Habel thinks, is a mockery of the friends because Job already knows that they will not change their minds. Job warned them against the impending judgment because at that time he will be vindicated. According to Habel, the issue is simple: if Job had committed a sin it is a matter between Job and his God rather than the prying eyes of the friends. Job has lost his family and friends in this context of suffering. He now longs for a friend who will be his advocate before the heavenly court (16:19-20). Job believes his redeemer will testify to his innocence. The redeemer stands in direct opposition to the friends. The redeemer is an ultimate friend, a defender, and an advocate. The chapter, Habel concludes, gives a portrait of utter personal alienation and social isolation.

John E. Hartley (1988)

Hartley points out that the nature of the speech of Bildad (chap. 18) vividly portrayed for Job the terrible fate of the wicked and thus made Job feel even more miserable.[61] In this speech, Hartley notes, Job laments the grief and the shame that his friends are causing him and also his brutal treatment by God. The reality of his suffering is objectified as alienation from all his relatives and friends. Job is depressed by the loneliness of his isolation but, exercising genuine faith, boldly confesses that he has a "kinsman" who will stand up to testify on his behalf. Hartley sees this redeemer in the person of God and notes that although Job is unsure when God will act as his redeemer, he is convinced that it will be during a public occasion at which Job himself is present. He is also convinced that his experience

---

[61] John E. Hartley, *The Book of Job* (NICOT; Grand Rapids, MI: Eerdmans, 1988) 281-99.

of God as an enemy is not illusory. However, Job is more certain that God, acting as his next of kin, will secure his redemption and a full acquittal with honor.

It is clear that Job has charted a specific course to win his acquittal. While continuing to lament his agony, he seeks to move God to fulfill his legal responsibilities to him, specifically to verify his confession of innocence. The redeemer has to be kin, a member of the family, but the family has abandoned him. God is his redeemer. This assurance energizes Job's spiritual search and buttresses him against succumbing to depression, to his pain, and giving in to his friends. According to Hartley, as his body weakens, his faith is lifted up in order to keep him from wallowing in self-pity or seeking an easy avenue of escape from suffering, such as repenting in order to receive blessing; to do that would mean yielding to the taunts of the friends. His faith, however, will not be authenticated until God breaks through and reciprocates Job's trust in him. The speech is heavily influenced by language of personal lament.

David J. A. Clines (1989)

David J. A. Clines did a very thorough study on the Book of Job. His commentaries rate among the best ever written on Job.[62] He observes that the structure of Job's speech in chap. 19 is unusual. Job addresses his friends at the beginning (vv. 2-6), midway (vv. 21-22), and at the end (vv. 28-29), a pattern Clines says never occurs anywhere else in the book.[63] He also observes that this is the only chapter, other than chap. 3, in which Job does not address God, and that there is no place in the book where Job more vehemently expresses his isolation than in this passage. This makes the chapter unique.

Clines claims that the language of Job's speech is a lament in the form of a disputation. It has a legal tone, which is unusual for wisdom literature. He notes that the rhetorical question "how long?" (v. 2) is an indication that his friends should stop their persecution, and the verb "know" in v. 6 is an appeal to his friends to be reasonable in their arguments. He considers the speech in vv. 13-19 to be very concrete and breathtaking. Each line is charged with the pain of the

---

[62] David J. A. Clines, *Job 1-20* (WBC 17; Nashville: Thomas Nelson, 1989); *Job 21-37* (WBC 18A; Nashville: Thomas Nelson, 2006).

[63] Ibid., 428-70, here 435.

disintegration of Job's relationship with family and loved ones. According to Clines, the passage is a cry of an isolated human being, a cry that is wholly credible as literal truth. He compares vv. 13-19 with vv. 7-12 and notes that while we hear of physical violence in vv. 7-12, in vv. 13-19 no one raises a hand, a weapon, or a voice against Job because of the expression of his intense pain. He concludes that vv. 13-19 is the climactic expression of Job's suffering from the beginning of the book. The suffering becomes more intense with his bad breath (v. 17a) and his repulsive appearance that lead to his loss of dignity and respect (v. 18). What reads like a plea in vv. 21-22 is not only a demand for the friends to remain quiet but also a kind of irony on the part of Job that shows the kind of friends his interlocutors truly are.

Clines concludes that the chapter makes clear that withholding affection, concern, and love amounts to mental violence. Job wants to show the extent to which God's violence has affected him, leading to alienation from his family and friends. For Job, everything is an act of divine violence against him.

Carol Newsom (1996)

Newsom detects no irony in 19:13-20.[64] For her, the passage is descriptive, and the very first verse reveals God as the agent of Job's isolation (v. 13). According to her, Job employs a traditional lament motif, that is, alienation from family and friends.[65] She identifies twelve different terms for social and kinship categories in vv. 13-19 (e.g., "brothers," "friends," "kinsfolk," "guests"). Unfortunately, as she points out, the precise meaning of many of these terms is unknown or disputed, but the context of the passage is so clear that the reader readily grasps the message that Job is trying to convey to his family and friends, that is, his exclusion from his social world.

Job's lament begins with vv. 13-14 and ends with vv. 18-19, thus placing domestic factors in the center of his lament (vv. 15-17). Newsom observes that the verbs used in this passage differ from those

---

[64] Carol Newsom, "The Book of Job," *NIB* 4 (Nashville: Abingdon Press, 1996) 319-637, here 476.

[65] Newsom gives similar examples from the psalms where the psalmists are alienated by loved ones: Pss 31:12-14; 38:12; 41:10; 55:13-15; 69:9, 19. Job's lament is more detailed than those in the psalms, however.

in the rest of the book. Those verbs characterize and express alienation; for instance, words such as distancing, estrangement, and forgetting (vv. 13-14); moreover, there is a change of attitude by members of his household, family, and friends and their resultant failure to perform the customary obligations to a member of the society.

James Wharton (1999)

Wharton looks at the chapter as a direct response to vindictive hostility that dominates Bildad's latest attack (chap. 18).[66] Job is tormented, shattered, reproached, and shamelessly wronged by the friends who have betrayed the fundamental value of friendship (19:1-3; see 6:14-29; 16:2-5; 17:5). According to Wharton, 19:4 seems to suggest that even if Job were guilty of some error worthy of retribution, it would be wrong, in the spirit of true friendship, for the friends to take sides in an issue that God and Job have to resolve. But the friends use the opportunity of Job's suffering to argue against him and vaunt their moral and spiritual superiority over him (19:5).

For Wharton, the issues facing Job are numerous: first, Job's plight makes it appear to him and to all who know him that he is a victim singled out as the special object of God's wrath. Second, the issue of misunderstanding between Job and his friends results from the ungodly test contrived by God and the accuser. Third, the question in heaven is whether Job will be able to "persist in his integrity" in the "groundless assault of suffering and loss" (2:3). So for those who have behind-the-scenes access, the plot contrived by God and the accuser is understandable; but for those without such access the question is why God has attacked Job without cause. The friends, like us, will not believe that a just God will allow such an evil thing to happen to any of his faithful ones. In this regard, the friends of Job are correct in saying that it is a blasphemy against God's justice for Job to persist in maintaining his innocence. What is left for Job is his integrity. But his integrity demands that he tell the truth.

Job voices the truth of his situation; God has placed him in a dreadful place of loneliness (v. 5). More than elsewhere, Job in vv. 13-

---

[66] James A. Wharton, *Job* (Westminster Bible Companion; Louisville: Westminster, 1999) 85-91.

19 laments his unbearable social isolation, in which family, acquaintances, relatives, close friends, houseguests, wife and children, intimates, loved ones, all the people whose presence can make even the intolerable somehow bearable, have been taken away by estrangement. The sense of estrangement is most agonizing for Job, who in v. 19 states: "All my intimate friends abhor me, and those whom I loved have turned against me."[67]

Wharton notes that the litany of isolation in 19:13-19 is rendered even more poignant by Job's direct appeal to his friends (19:21-22), whom he expected to understand and to recognize that he has been speaking about them, especially in 19:14-15. The friends are expected to show compassion to the innocent sufferer (v. 21); but, to the contrary and to Job's surprise, the friends follow God's lead, pursuing him like prey and tearing at his flesh like insatiable predators (v. 22). The power of this renewed accusation, Wharton thinks, lies in its capacity to bring the crisis between God and Job closer and closer to what Wharton calls a "critical mass," that is, the point at which the crisis must simply explode into an encounter with God in which Job will be either annihilated or vindicated. At the same time, Wharton concludes that 19:2-22 render the gulf that separates Job from his friends even wider, if not altogether unbridgeable.

Samuel Terrien (2005)

Samuel Terrien has produced one of the most comprehensive commentaries on Job.[68] According to him, Job's response in chap. 19 is provoked by the unkind words of Bildad (see 18:21).[69] Job retorts with a violence that has not been heard since the beginning of the book. This speech is Job's second response to Bildad. Terrien notes that Job began his speech with "how long" (v. 2), which is the same way that Bildad began his two speeches (8:2; 18:2). Terrien regards the phrase "how long" as a mockery of his interlocutors. Job could not understand why they would try to humiliate him before God so many times. He expected the friends to be ashamed of their intruding on his affairs; he

---

[67] See also Job 6:14-21. The same theme occurs several times in the Psalms (38:11; 55:12-14; 69:8).

[68] Samuel L. Terrien, *Job* (CAT 13; 2nd ed.; Geneva: Labor et Fides, 2005).

[69] Ibid., 191-203.

says, "Mon erreur ne concernerait personne d'autre que moi" (my error should not be anybody's concern but mine).[70]

Terrien observes that Job's feeling of isolation intensifies with the failure of his friends to understand him. Job pitied the friends because their theological passion demonstrates their spiritual insecurity ("Leur rage théologique est le signe de leur insécurité spirituelle").[71] God has already driven Job to a dead end because God has become unethical. Just like the merchants who use fake scales to cheat people, God has distorted justice and robbed Job of honor. Terrien notes that God's silence should not be interpreted as his disregard for Job because God has actively engaged himself against Job. Terrien maintains that the words "glory" and "crown" (v. 9) should be taken literally because God has robbed Job of his princely quality (vv. 7-12). Terrien affirms that the hostility of God is the basis of Job's pain, which resulted in his "excommunication" by his associates and left him in absolute loneliness. Job expresses his abject loneliness by addressing each category of associates (vv. 13-18), ending painfully in v. 19 with the words "and those whom I loved." For Terrien, that is the climax of Job's suffering of ostracism: "Le motif de l'ostracisme atteint son maximum d'intensité avec la mention des amis intimes et celui que j'aime" (the motif of ostracism attains its maximum intensity with the mention of the intimate friends and those whom I loved, vv. 13-22).[72]

According to Terrien, Job's misery leaves him in doubt about what future generations will think of his character (vv. 23-24). His wish that his words be written down (vv. 23-24) arises, Terrien says, because Job has reached the climax of his isolation. His hopelessness leads Job to dream again of the heavenly witness (cf. 16:19), and he rises higher than before in a feeling of certainty of seeing God (vv. 25-26).

Conclusion

All scholars identify social alienation in the Book of Job, but this alienation, they also agree, is caused by God. None of the scholars

---

[70] Ibid., 192.
[71] Ibid.
[72] Ibid., 194.

cited above recognize Job's alienation as a product of his society. Job's argument shows that even if he has disobeyed God, this was between him and his God and not the concern of anyone else. In his cry, Job argues further that family, friends, and loved ones should continue to treat him as they had been accustomed to (vv. 2-6, 21-22, and 28-29).

The story of Job shows that Job, his family, and his friends, were all under the influence of their society. The conviction of that society made Job believe that he was being punished by God. God allowed the accuser to afflict Job, but God never asked the family and friends to isolate Job and persecute him. Job deserved sympathy and love from his wife, family, and friends, but what we see is rejection and disrespect on the part of his servants, children, friends, family, and wife.

We have seen that the Book of Job reflects a misunderstanding of a religious concept that was diffused within the society and implemented by the people. A society that is religious has a strong cohesion and holds dearly to its culture, that is, its norms, values, and belief systems. In such a society, when an incorrect idea is held by the society, it affects the society and each individual of the society. The Book of Job shows how God has been misunderstood by his society. The misconception of God in the society of Job and the consequent social actions meted out against Job by his family, friends, and neighbors, is a case study of social alienation. We shall now study exegetically the text of Job 19:13-22 in order to bring out this aspect.

Chapter Four

Exegesis of Job 19:13-22

This chapter gives the exegesis of Job 19:13-22. In Job 19:13-22 we see that it is not only God and his council who are against Job (19:6, 8-12) but also his family, friends, and loved ones (19:13-19). Job, for his part, has a right to the defense of a kinsman (cf. Lev 25:25-34, 47-55; Jer 32:6-15), but no one came to his rescue because his kin and loved ones have become estranged from him (19:13-19). God's action against him led to alienation from his kin and loved ones, and their abandonment intensified his suffering. He calls on his friends to stop persecuting him and instead to show him mercy (19:21-22). The following exegesis of 19:13-22 is divided into five main parts:

a) The text and its translation
b) Immediate context
c) Literary analysis
d) Structural analysis
e) Verse–by–verse analysis.

In this chapter we see a total breakdown of Job's social network and his struggle for reintegration into society. This fails, and the result is the continuation of his rejection and alienation. Nowhere else in the Book of Job does Job give expression to his social alienation as strongly as in 19:13-22.

The structure of chap. 19 is as follows:

Verses 2-6: direct address to his friends against their reproaches
Verses 7-20: complaint about his psychological and sociological trauma:
   vv. 7-12: complaint about his devastation by God
   vv. 13-20: complaint about his isolation from family, friends, and loved ones
Verses 21-22: direct address appealing to his friends for compassion
Verses 23-27: expression of his desire for vindication

65

Verses 28-29: direct address to his friends about his certainty of vindication.

Chapter 19 is a complaint that Job addresses to his friends. In three instances, Job addresses them directly (vv. 2-6, 21-22, and 28-29). The "indirect" address includes vv. 7-20 and vv. 23-27. The first "direct" address (vv. 2-6) registers his advice to his friends to back off and leave matters to him. He cautions that it is God who is responsible for his suffering. The first "indirect" address (vv. 7-20) embraces the greater part of the text under discussion (19:13-22) and is subdivided into vv. 7-12 and vv. 13-20. Verses 7-12 register Job's complaints about God's attack on him and have nothing to do with family, friends, and loved ones. Verses 13-20 register Job's complaints about isolation from his family, friends, and loved ones. The second "direct" address (vv. 21-22) to his friends comes immediately after Job has registered his bitterness about the breakdown of his social network. Job needs comfort, which is not forthcoming from God; God is already responsible for his social alienation, and so he calls on his friends to come to his aid and not to join forces with God. This plea in vv. 21-22 is appended to vv. 13-20 because vv. 21-22 serve as a continuation to vv. 13-20. The second "indirect" address (vv. 23-27) registers Job's wishes, desires, and rejuvenated faith and has nothing to do with relations to family, friends, and loved ones, while the third "direct" address (vv. 28-29) is a warning against his friends' false solidarity and righteous attitude. This delimitation leaves us with vv. 13-20 and vv. 21-22 as a discrete unit for our study of social alienation in the Book of Job.

I. The Text (Job 19:13-22) and Translation[1]

ʾaḥay mēʿālay hirḥîq   13

He has alienated my brothers from me;

---

[1] The English translation of these verses is my own.

wəyōḏ‘ay ʾak̠-zārû mimmennî

and my friends are also estranged from me.

ḥāḏlû qərôḇāy 14

My kinsmen have forsaken me;

ûməyuddā‘ay šək̠ēḥûnî

my friends have forgotten me.

gārê ḇêṯî wə’amhōṯay ləzār taḥšəḇūnî 15

The guests of my house and my maidservants treat me as a stranger;

nok̠rî hāyîṯî ḇə‘ênêhem

I have become an alien in their eyes.

lə‘aḇdî qārā’ṯî wəlō’ ya‘āneh 16

I summon my own servant, but he does not answer;

bəmô-p̄î ’eṯḥannen-lô

with my mouth, I entreat him.

rûḥî zārāh lə’ištî 17

My breath is repulsive to my wife;

wəḥannōṯî liḇnê ḇiṭnî

I am loathsome to my own children.

gam-ʿăwîlîm māʾăsû bî   18

Even children scorn me;

ʾāqûmāh wayədabbərû-bî

when I arise, they speak against me.

tîʿăbûnî kol-mətê sôdî   19

All my intimate friends abhor me;

wəzeh-ʾāhabtî nehpəkû-bî

those I have loved have turned against me.

bəʿôrî ûbibśārî dābqāh ʿaṣmî   20

My skin and my flesh cleave to my bone;

wāʾetmallətāh bəʿôr šinnāy

I have escaped by the skin of my teeth.

honnūnî honnūnî ʾattem rēʿāy   21

Have mercy on me, have mercy on me, you my friends;

kî yad-ʾĕlôᵃh nāḡʿāh bî

for the hand of God has struck me.

lāmmāh tirdəpūnî kəmô-ʾēl   22

Why do you pursue me like God?

ûmibbəśārî lō^ɔ ṭiśbāʿû

Have you not had enough of my flesh?

II. Immediate Context (Job 19:1-29)

My discussion of the immediate context takes into consideration chap. 19 as a whole because it frames the text under discussion. It is the fifth speech of Job and a response to the speech of Bildad (chap. 18). The chapter is one of the more famous passages in the Bible.[2] In this poem Job laments the absence of his family and friends. He addresses his friends directly in vv. 2-6, 21-22, and 28-29. Verses 7-20 and 23-27 register his complaints. The complaints in vv. 7-20 can be subdivided into vv. 7-12 and vv. 13- 20. Verses 7-12 are direct attacks on God and vv. 13-20 are complaints about isolation from his loved ones. The complaints in vv. 23-27 express desires based on Job's rejuvenated faith. Job knows he is innocent and believes this strongly.

The impetus behind chap. 19 comes from the words of Bildad in chap. 18. He strongly accuses Job and lays bare the terrible fate of the wicked.[3] Bildad senses the suffering Job is experiencing and his terror of his misfortunes but for him this is *de minimis* compared to what is yet to come; a more horrible fate awaits Job because he is treading the path of the wicked. One is perplexed regarding the intention of Bildad in this chapter. Was it an attempt to stir strong emotions of revulsion in Job so that he might forsake his claims to innocence and humbly repent and be saved, or was it a speech of condemnation foretelling the fate of the wicked? Bildad's words appear to be conclusive; seemingly, he believes that Job's fate is irreversible. Therefore, he considers it his job to instruct Job about the certain, miserable destiny of all who do not know God.

I will now treat individually the different divisions of chap. 19 as listed above. This treatment helps to understand more clearly Job's

---

[2] Clifford, *Wisdom Literature,* 82; see also Clines, *Job 1-20,* 435.
[3] Hartley, *The Book of Job,* 281-99.

woeful anguish and the evil effect in his abandonment of family,
friends, and loved ones in vv. 13-22.

A. Verses 2-6: Job Addresses His Friends

V. 2

Job starts with a rhetorical question *ʿad-ʾānāh* ("How long?"),
as does Bildad in 8:2 and 18:2. The phrase signifies Job's unhappy
state and is a direct blow at the friends. It reflects the heat of the
argument and underlines the misunderstanding between him and his
friends.[4] The plural form of the verbs shows that Job is addressing all
three friends. The verb *tôḡyûn* ("torment") expresses the allegedly
unjust suffering the friends are imposing on Job. Habel observes that
the verb *tôḡyûn* ("torment") in the hiphil is used to express God's
anger toward his people (Lam 1:5, 12) and so, like God, the friends are
afflicting more pain on Job (19:22). The verb *dāḵāʾ* ("crush") calls to
mind Job's earlier wish for God to crush him to death and relieve him
of his misery (6:9).[5]

V. 3

Job's anger of v. 2 continues in v. 3, with Job accusing his
friends of shameless abuse and verbal assault. According to Clines,
"How long?" in v. 2 corresponds to *ʿeśer pəʿāmîm* ("ten times") in v.
3; "ten" is a symbol of full measure (Num 14:22; cf. Gen 31:7, 41; Lev
26:26).[6] So Job is telling the friends that they have reached the limit.
Their intention is to force Job to admit that he is guilty and to repent.
They "humiliate" him and "shame" him with their "words" (v. 2) and
actions.

V. 4

Job continues to maintain his innocence. According to Job,
even if he has erred (*šāḡîtî*) he expects that his friends will support him
by easing his suffering rather than causing him more pain (16:3; 19:20-

---

[4] Clines, *Job 1-20*, 438; Dhorme, *The Book of Job,* 270; Terrien, *Job*, 191.
[5] Habel, *The Book of Job*, 299.
[6] Clines, *Job 1-20*, 439.

22). Job gives his friends a serious rebuke and his words are sarcastic.[7] His message for them is to back off, mind their own business, and avert their prying eyes from him.[8]

V. 5

Job warns his friends that even if they maintain that his suffering is due to his sins (17:4), they should know that his misfortune is not due to his negligence (v. 6). The idiom "if indeed you magnify yourselves against me" is present elsewhere in the OT (cf. Jer 48:26, 42; Ezek 35:13; Zeph 2:10; Ps 35:26); in most cases it is used in the context of a quarrel. The expression *ʾim-ʾomnām* ("if indeed") indicates that there is tension and Job expresses his dissatisfaction with his friends' self-righteous attitude.

V. 6

The reason for Job's attack on his friends in vv. 2-6 is made clear here. The phrase *dəʿû-ʾēpô* ("know then") is an unfriendly judgmental remark by Job (cf. 2 Kgs 10:10), very forceful and unapologetic, and has a link with vv. 25 and 29.[9] The full statement, "know then that God has put me in the wrong, and closed his net around me," is a strong accusation against God. Job maintains that God has perverted justice. Dhorme notes that the verb *ʿiwwətānî* ("to warp justice") is used deliberately by Job in response to Bildad, who used it in reference to God (8:3). Now Job is using the same word to show how God perverts justice because God is responsible for his suffering.[10] Job could have escaped if he had the chance, but he is trapped; just as Marduk cast his net over Tiamat in the Babylonian Creation epic,[11] so God spreads his net over Job.

---

[7] Habel, *The Book of Job*, 299.

[8] Dhorme, *The Book of Job,* 271; Andersen, *Job*, 191; Habel, *The Book of Job*, 299.

[9] See Clines, *Job 1-20*, 442. The phrase with its judgmental tone has a link with Job's hope for a vindicator in v. 25 ("For I know that my Redeemer lives") and his words of judgment in v. 29 ("So that you may know there is a judgment"); and the link is the verb *yādaʿ* ("know") that occurs in the three verses (vv. 6, 25, and 29).

[10] Dhorme, *The Book of Job,* 272.

[11] *ANET*, p. 67, line 95.

B. Verses 7-20: Job Complains about His Suffering

These verses demonstrate how intense Job's suffering has become. God has laid siege to Job, and that siege is evident in his physical deformity (vv. 7-12). His physical appearance has made it impossible for anyone to acknowledge his innocence. God's affliction results in the alienation of his closest relations, namely, his wife, his family, friends, and neighbors (vv. 13-19). These people are responsible for his intense pain. For Job, God has perverted justice for God's own purpose. Verses 7-20 can be subdivided into vv. 7-12 and vv. 13-20.

1. Verses 7-12: Job's Alienation from God

These verses explain the pain and the frustration God has caused Job. They are marked by poetic words that describe the physical violence that Job has experienced. The metaphor used in this context is one of military action.[12] This section is similar to Lam 3:7-9. God's attack on Job is harsh and life-threatening, and Job's choice of words depicts its severity. For instance, the author used the preposition *ʿal* ("against") and *sābîḇ* ("all round") quite frequently to depict Job's being hemmed in on all sides (vv. 8, 10, 11, 12).

V. 7

The verb *ṣāʿaq* ("cry") describes the anguish that Job experienced while lamenting the *ḥāmās* ("violence") that God has afflicted upon him. Despite his cry, there was no one to *ʿānāh* ("answer") and vindicate him. The verb *ṣāʿaq* occurred earlier in 16:18, and in both occurrences it connotes a plea for vindication rather than a cry for deliverance.[13] He calls for vindication, since there is "no justice," "there is no one to answer" him and to help him pursue his justification.

---

[12] Gordis, *The Book of Job,* 201.

[13] Clines, *Job 1-20,* 443. The verb *ṣāʿaq* occurs later on in the book in both verbal and noun forms, but in those occurrences it signify a cry for help (27:9; 34:28; 35:12).

V. 8

This verse demonstrates Job's frustration. He is almost at his wit's end; there is no alternative for him in this life. The verb *gādar* ("wall up") recalls 3:23 where Job compares himself to a man whose path is hidden. If a path is hidden, one cannot get to his or her destination. In Hos 2:8, God builds a wall across the path of his unfaithful wife to prevent her from pursuing her lovers, but in Job's case God built a wall around him so that he cannot escape his suffering. The "path" is understood to be his way to life, and blocking his path means God has thwarted Job's progress and prosperity in life.[14] What lies ahead for him is death, which is symbolized by the metaphor of darkness.

V. 9

Job is stripped (cf. 22:6) of the glory that he had enjoyed with family, friends, and neighbors (see also 29:14).[15] Job has come to the end of his glory; all his good deeds have come to nothing. Job has become an evil person, ridiculed by friends and neighbors.

V. 10

Job has come to his end; he is dislodged. He is destroyed like a building; his hope of redeeming himself is shattered. The verb "perish" means to pass away or to die.[16] Job is snatched away; he has no chance of redemption or survival. Like a tree, his power of defense is uprooted and destroyed. Job is done away with. Job is destroyed from every side; his integrity has been marred.[17] He cannot withstand God and for this reason he says, "I am gone"; he has given up.

---

[14] See Clines, *Job 1-20*, 443. Habel, *The Book of Job*, 295 explains that Job's way is subverted, walled up, and enveloped with darkness, to prevent any movement or progress.

[15] "Honor" and "shame" are often considered as garments that may be put on or stripped off (Job 8:22; 29:14; Isa 61:3; Ezek 16:39; 23:26) and as a crown (Job 31:36; Jer 13:18; Lam 5:16).

[16] *BDB*, s.v.; see also Gordis, *The Book of Job*, 201; Dhorme, *The Book of Job*, 274.

[17] Habel, *The Book of Job*, 300.

V. 11

Job believes that God has made him an enemy but is uncertain as to why he has become God's enemy. His suffering is due to a deliberate act on the part of God and demonstrates that God is angry with him. Job is embroiled in a battle that he is unprepared to wage.

V. 12

The verse's poetic diction is military. The army of God encircles Job. Job is attacked and destroyed like a besieged city. It is no longer God alone who is at war with Job (see 16:10-11) but also the host of heaven. The numerous metaphors are meant to portray the disparity between God and Job (7:12, 17-20; 10:16-17; 13:25; 16:8, 14; 30:12). Ironically, this massive siege work is against a lonely unprotected person who dwells in a tent.[18] Fohrer understands the "army" to mean the forces that brought the disaster on Job.[19] For Clines, the army metaphor is used to express God's role as a warrior and assailant.[20]

2. Verses 13-20: Alienation of Job from Family, Friends, and Neighbors

Verses 7-12 set the tone for vv. 13-20. Verses 7-12 show the suffering inflicted on Job by God, while vv. 13-20 document the result of this affliction, which has resulted in his isolation and rejection by family, friends, and neighbors. He has lost the respect he had in society as a consequence (vv. 18-19). The effects of Job's affliction and subsequent alienation are evident in his flesh, skin, and bones (v. 20). He believes that the oppressed person in society has a right to support from his or her societal members. Job has already called several times for help without response (9:16; 12:4; 13:22; 14:15). In this section, Job gave a detailed account of alienation from his loved ones.

C. Verses 21-22: A Call to Friends for Help

Job calls on his friends for help. This is linked to his address to them in vv. 2-6 because he has already explained to them that his fate is

---

[18] Habel, *The Book of Job*, 295, 301; see also Clines, *Job 1-20*, 444.

[19] Fohrer, *Hiob,* 314; see also Gordis, *The Book of Job,* 201.

[20] Clines, *Job 1-20*, 445.

the result not of a sin he has committed but rather of God's unfairness.[21]

D. Verses 23-27: Complaint Expressing Belief and Hope

A number of lament psalms end with a statement of future hope. In these verses (23-27) we have a wish, a conviction, and a desire.[22] Job's wish is that his good deeds be recorded for posterity so as to justify his existence (vv. 23-24); his conviction is that his friends will come to know the truth of his affliction (vv. 25-26), and his desire is for his vindication (v. 27).[23]

V. 23

After Job has made an appeal to his friends (vv. 21-22), he wants to make an appeal to posterity. This verse is one of the many hopeful wishes expressed by Job (6:8-13; 13:3-6, 13-18, 23-24; 14:13; 16:21-22; 19:25-27; 23:3-7; 29:2-17; 31:35-37).
It is a wish that demands justice without bias. Job hopes to have a full legal documentation of his anguish and sorrow written on durable material. His desire for redemption is very strong, but since human beings are mortal, it is wise for him to write his verdict down before he dies so that future generations can have it as a witness to his case. Job's anger is not only against God but also against his friends who have "the words" (see v. 2) to argue with him, "humiliate" (v. 3) and "shame" him (see also 1 Sam 20:34). Documenting his case will ensure that everybody will come to see the truth of his plight. The strength of Job's desire is seen in the emphasis of the words "write" and "inscribe" (or "cut in," or "decree"; see Isa 30:8; Ezek 23:14). Job has a cause to plead and that cause is the regaining of his integrity.

---

[21] Ibid., 436.

[22] Ibid., 437.

[23] Job's desire for vindication is based on his belief in God, and he seeks to commit his cause to God, knowing that God does great things and will surely justify him (6:8-9). At the same time, Job knows that it is impossible to undertake a lawsuit against God because God's might is greater than his and God holds an advantage. Accordingly, Job asserts that a moral order does not exist; he recounts his unhappiness to God to entice God to intervene in his cause (chaps. 9–10). He wishes to dispute with God because Job believes he is righteous (13:3, 13-15, 18, 22); his hope is that his redeemer will plead his case in heaven (16:19-21; 17:3).

V. 24

    The statement "with an iron pen and with lead" is an indication that Job wants his record to be permanent. The niphal of *ḥāśab* ("hew out," "engrave in") highlights its indelible character; it cannot easily be erased. The word *ʿēṭ* for a metal pen appears in figurative language in Jer 17:1:

> The sin of Judah is written with an iron pen; with a diamond point it is engraved on the tablet of their hearts, and on the horns of their altars.

In some other places in the Bible, *ʿēṭ* designates a brush or a reed pen (Jer 8:8; Ps 45:2). Job's wish in vv. 23-24 was not fulfilled because his words were not written. The rhetorical language is meant to convey the extent to which Job longs for his vindication.

V. 25

    The opening verb *yāḏaʿtî* ("I know") is an indication of Job's conviction about what will happen at the end.[24] The verb occurs in other parts of the book, but in those instances it indicates Job's understanding and knowledge of God's capabilities (9:2, 28; 10:13; 13:18; 30:23; 42:2). The term *gōʾălî* ("my redeemer") is translated by Pope as "my vindicator."[25] The *gōʾēl* who "redeems a kinsman" is a person's closest relative, who acts as the next of kin. In the OT, the *gōʾēl* has many responsibilities: he recovers family property for the family (Lev 25:25-34; Jer 32:6-15), redeems a slave (Lev 25:47-54); conceives an heir for a dead brother (Deut 25:5-10; Ruth 3:12; 4:1-6), and avenges the death of a relative (Num 35:12, 19-27; Deut 19:6-12; Josh 20:2-5, 9; 2 Sam 14:11).[26] The term is used poetically to refer to Job's kinsman having to act on his behalf against God because the redeemer is supposed to defend the needy and the oppressed and Job finds himself in the category of the oppressed (Prov 23:10-11; Jer

---

    [24] Habel, *The Book of Job*, 304. In forensic contexts *yāḏaʿ* means "I firmly believe or I have a strong conviction." See also Clines, *Job 1-20*, 458.

    [25] Pope, *Job*, 146.

    [26] Helmer Ringgren, "גאל," *TDOT*, 2. 350-55.

50:34; Lam 3:58; Ps 119:154). The term is also used for Yhwh as the one who delivered Israel from bondage (Exod 6:6; 15:13) and exile (Isa 43:14; 44:22-24; 49:7, 26; Ps 78:35). Yhwh is also well known for delivering people from death (Ps 103:4; Lam 3:58), so in this regard God could act as a "redeemer" for Job.

Unfortunately for Job, all his family members have abandoned him. It is very uncertain who Job's redeemer will be. Job has no one to depend on but himself (17:3). In 16:20-21, there was no human being involved in his pleading before God. The *gōʾēl* is the witness, advocate, or spokesman (16:19), who is Job's proof of his innocence. It is correct to say that his words of lament claiming his innocence are personified as his vindicator.[27] Just as his redeemer pleads in the heavens, so accordingly in this verse Job will be vindicated on earth. Now that his plea is heard in heaven, he has to be exonerated on earth because it is on earth that he was humiliated, and God is the only one who can declare him innocent.

Scholars are divided on this issue of God as Job's redeemer. Some scholars argue that Job is referring here to God.[28] Habel, by contrast, rejects this notion that God is Job's *gōʾēl*. For Habel, God cannot be the *gōʾēl* because Job has already accused God of causing his suffering, and it is impossible to view the plaintiff as also the redeemer:

> Earlier Job had appealed to the earth not to cover his blood since the violence he has experienced at God's hands was tantamount to murder and he wanted his outcry to be heard in heaven (16:18).... From the outset, it is clear that God is the "enemy" (16:9) who has attacked Job viciously and reduced him to a mangled mess (16:9-14). It is also apparent that Job considers God as his accuser and adversary at law (9:14-20; 13:19-23; 31:35). Job, however, is unable to present his case before an impartial court because of the intimidating tactics of

---

[27] Clines, *Job 1-20*, 459; see also 465.

[28] Bernhard Duhm, *Das Buch Hiob erklärt* (KHCAT; Tübingen: Mohr, 1897) 102; Samuel R. Driver and George B. Gray, *A Critical and Exegetical Commentary on the Book of Job* (ICC; Edinburgh: T & T Clark, 1958) 171; Dhorme, *The Book of Job*, 283; H. H. Rowley, *Job* (NCB; London: Oliphants, 1978) 172-73; Gordis, *The Book of Job, 205*; Terrien, *Job*, 198.

his adversary (9:16-17, 34-35; 13:20-21; 23:15-16). Moreover, God has placed Job under siege to prevent his "hope" of vindication from being realized (19:6-12). Thus the odds are completely against him. His God is his accuser, adversary, enemy, spy, destroyer, hunter, and siege commander. Against this opponent Job needs a *gōʾēl*, one who will take up his case and bring it before the court of heaven for public resolution. That this *gōʾēl* would be one and the same person as his cruel opponent seems quite illogical, inconsistent, and, from Job's perspective, intolerable.... If, as we said, a "satan" figure can arise within the council of heavenly beings (*bᵉnē hāʾᵉlōhīm*, "sons of God," 1:6-7) and act as the prosecuting attorney inciting God to perform his *opus alienum,* there is no valid theological reason why Job, who considers God his enemy and adversary at law, should not conceive of a corresponding figure who rises in the council and moves God to perform his *opus proprium* of vindicating Job.[29]

Although the accuser stood before God to ask permission (1:6-12; 2:1-7), it does not necessarily follow that another heavenly being can do this as well. Job did not know that there was an accuser in his case such that he would think that a heavenly being would intercede for him. That Job accuses God does not mean God cannot also be his redeemer. Job accuses God of injustice. Job knows he is innocent of his friends' charges. God never accuses Job. If Job is accused of committing evil and thus offended God and God punished him as a result, then God is the only one who can prove him innocent. Therefore, if God is not doing what he is supposed to do, Job has the right to seek the face of God. Some scholars, such as Habel, think the redeemer is a heavenly being in the court of God, who could be an angel or some other heavenly being but clearly not a human being (1:6 and 2:1).[30] These scholars find some support from the speech of Elihu about an angel in 33:23-25. But angels, according to Eliphaz, are not righteous before God (5:1) and so they cannot act as redeemers on

---

[29] Habel, *The Book of Job,* 304-6.
[30] Pope, *Job,* 146; Habel, *The Book of Job,* 306; Terrien, *Job,* 198; W. A. Irwin "Job's Redeemer," *JBL* 81 (1962) 217-29, here 217-19.

behalf of Job. Earlier in the book, Job himself made clear that there is no "arbiter" to mediate between God and him (9:33), so this citation in 9:33 is an indication that God is the redeemer that he means. Considering the uncompromising monotheism of the book, there is no reason to assume that there is a third party who will wage a contest with God on Job's behalf.[31]

V. 26

This verse is not very clear. The first half of the verse "and after my skin has been thus destroyed" gives the impression to the reader that Job's desire will be fulfilled after his death, which contradicts the second half of the verse; it states that "then in my flesh I shall see God," which presumes that Job hopes to see God while still alive. The verb *nāqap̄* ("go around") is intransitive, and its piel form means "have struck off"; here it means "after his skin has been struck off" (or "destroyed entirely"). The verb occurs in Isa 10:34, where it is used in the sense of "trimming," an allusion to destruction as in Job. The noun form of *nāqap̄* used in Isa 17:6; 24:13 means to shake fruits from a tree. In the light of these texts, we can read the verse to mean "and after my skin has been shaken off" (or "trimmed off"). The process of trimming the skin might refer to Job's disease that is consuming his skin (see 2:7; 7:5; 30:30).

The word *ûmibbəśārî* ("in my flesh"), literally "and from my flesh," is interpreted by many scholars as referring to Job's desire to see God while alive and see his name cleared.[32] The same desire is expressed in 23:3-7, 10. His desire becomes stronger and stronger, even though there is no indication that it will be fulfilled; he simply believes that he will be vindicated. Job's hope of seeing God himself is confirmed in v. 27. What makes this verse perplexing is the mention of the destruction of his skin. How can his skin be destroyed while he is yet alive? How can he survive in the physical flesh without his skin? Job's hopeful expression stems from the conviction of innocence that he has reiterated numerous times in the book.

---

[31] Gordis, *The Book of Job,* 206.
[32] Clines, *Job 1-20,* 458 and 461; Dhorme, *The Book of Job,* 285.

V. 27

Several times Job has expressed the desire to see God (9:32-33; 13:3, 15, 20, 24; 19:26; 23:3). Job went against traditional wisdom and insisted on having an audience with God, despite the danger involved in seeing God (see Exod 33:20 and Judg 13:22). Job believed in his righteousness, and since traditionally the righteous shall see God he has the courage to seek the face of God (Pss 11:7; 17:15; 63:2-3). According to Clines, Job's ongoing desire to see God overrides his desire for a redeemer.[33] These are not necessarily two different things, because God is the redeemer who will vindicate Job, here as well as above. Therefore, to see God is to see the redeemer. The last part of v. 27 reveals Job's passionate longing for the moment of his final justification.[34]

Verses 23-27 are very complicated. Clines, sums up their thought as follows:

> (i) that there is a contrast between what Job *believes* will happen (his death before vindication, but vindication thereafter) and what he *wishes* would happen (a face to face encounter with God this side of death); and (ii) that what pleads for Job in the heavenly realm is nothing but his own protestation of innocence.[35]

It is true, Job is not sure of seeing God while he is alive. What he desires vehemently is his justification. This verse (v. 27) foreshadows the theophany later in the book, where we see his wish fulfilled. Job was vindicated on earth and had an audience with God (chaps. 38–42).

E. Verses 28-29: A Warning to His Friends

Job warns his friends against their unjust persecution. Their false judgment and condemnation are punishable. According to his friends, Job deserved his suffering because of his evil life. Job assures them that he will be vindicated and warns them against the consequences of their action. He threatens them with the sword (v. 29).

---

[33] Clines, *Job 1-20*, 462.

[34] Gordis, *The Book of God and Man: A Study of Job*, 207. See also J. Gerald Janzen, *Job* (*Int*; Atlanta: John Knox Press, 1985) 144-45.

[35] Clines, *Job 1-20*, 465.

The sword of God is his vengeance (see Deut 32:40-43; Zech 8:6-8). Job threatens the friends with an aggressive attitude.[36] Job's final warning and the reference to impending judgment in these verses make the reader aware that the argument in this chapter has reached an impasse.

Job's anger in v. 2, his reproach of his friends in vv. 3-5, his appeal to his friends in vv. 21-22, his confidence in v. 25, and his threat to his friends in vv. 28-29 do not indicate someone in need of help but rather bespeak a person of conviction. Job is a model of firmness and consistency.

III. Literary Analysis of Job 19:13-22

My literary analysis relates the text to a similar story in the ANE and highlights the poetic nature of the text. The analysis describes the total breakdown of Job's social system.

A. A Brief Background History of the Ancient Near Eastern Social System

Job is presented as a devout person. The family structure is that of the ancestral or patriarchal household known as *bêt-ʾāb* ("house of the father") and the father is the head of the family.[37] The family includes a father, a mother, children, the wives of the children, servants, the resident aliens, widows, and orphans who live within the household.[38]

The family can be very large, depending on the number of generations it includes and also the type of people accepted into the family. No one is left alone in the family; the members interact together and care for and about one another. The family serves as the

---

[36] Ibid., 439.

[37] Philip J. King and Lawrence E. Stager, *Life in Biblical Israel* (Louisville: Westminster John Knox, 2001) 36.

[38] Roland de Vaux, *Ancient Israel. Its Life and Institutions* (Grand Rapids: Eerdmans, 1997) 20. For more on the ANE and its households, see King and Stager, *Life in Biblical Israel*, 9-19 and 36-60; Joachim Wach, *Sociology of Religion* (Chicago: University of Chicago Press, 1962) 77.

religious, economic, social, and political center of society.[39] The family forms the household; and a household deriving from one ancestor constitutes the clan. Traditionally, the clan is bonded by blood ties.[40] The clan members called themselves "brothers" (1 Sam 20:29). The family serves as the basic unit of the society and is the domain in which the consequences of good and evil emerge. Since the family is a protective kinship group, any form of unrighteousness is avoided by the members of the family. It is in this regard that the misfortune of Job affected his family and the society.

Social alienation results when members of a society neglect their role of solidarity. The neglected members feel insecure and vulnerable and they may consider doing violence either to others or to themselves. Family members, if they are religious, may share common values, and those values bind them together as one people. Job's suffering was caused by God (13:6-12) and was intensified by the alienation of his family and friends.

Job 19:13-22 forms a unit of its own. It is an epitome of social alienation. A similar episode occurs in the Babylonian *Ludlul Bēl Nēmeqi*. There the sufferer, like Job, has been isolated and longs for true companions, as can be seen from the following passage:

[84]My friend has become foe,
[85]My companion has become a wretch and a devil.
[86]In his savagery my comrade denounces me,
[87]Constantly my associates furbish their weapons.
[88]My intimate friend has brought my life into danger;
[89]My slave has publicly cursed me in the assembly.
[90]My house…, the mob has defamed me.
[91]When my acquaintance sees me, he passes by on the other side.
[92]My family treats me as an alien.
[98]I have no one to go at my side, nor have I found a helper.[41]

---

[39] King and Stager, *Life in Biblical Israel*, 21.
[40] de Vaux, *Ancient Israel*, 21.
[41] Lambert, "The Poem of the Righteous Sufferer *Ludlul Bēl Nēmeqi*," in *BWL*, 35; I, lines 84-92 and 98.

There is a close resemblance to the story of Job: Job was abandoned by his wife; his friends pretend not to know him; he is chastised as a sinner by his friends; his slave disobeys him; and children make fun of him.

B. Poetical Analysis of Job 19:13-22

The passage is poetic and a lament in form. It has poetic features such as strophic structure, parallelism, and figures of speech. The strophic structure is not uniform, but a 3+3 meter dominates the poem. There are 20 lines in toto:

1. 13a and 13b = 3+3
2. 14a and 14b = 2+2
3. 15a and 15b = 4+3
4. 16a and 16b = 3+3
5. 17a and 17b = 3+3
6. 18a and 18b = 3+3
7. 19a and 19b = 3+3
8. 20a and 20b = 4+3
9. 21a and 21b = 3+3
10. 22a and 22b = 3+2

Some scholars emend lines two and three to give them respectively a 2+3 and a 3+3 meter.[42] Clines notes that the words of v. 20a also appear in Ps 102:6 without "skin" and suggests that probably line 8 (i.e., v. 20a) should be emended to 3 words instead of 4, eliminating "skin" to give the verse a meter of 3+3 like line 9,[43] but I do not accept such an emendation just to make the line 3+3 and thus retain "skin."

The passage uses figurative language to express Job's feelings towards his family and loved ones. Job describes the nature of his familial and societal alienation in an artistic manner. All the verses in the text arouse a feeling of sympathy towards Job. These are some examples, his servant refuses to answer his call even after Job pleaded with him to come to his aid: "I summon my own servant, but he does not answer; with my mouth, I entreat him" (v. 16); Job became

---

[42] Clines, *Job 1-20*, 428.
[43] Ibid., 452.

repulsive to his family: "My breath is repulsive to my wife; I am loathsome to my own children" (v. 17); Job pleads for comfort from his friends: "Have mercy on me, have mercy on me, you my friends; for the hand of God has struck me" (v. 21); Job rejected by his bosom friends: "Why do you pursue me like God? Have you not had enough of my flesh?" (v. 22).

In his social relationships, Job mentions groups of people that we can categorize in two ways: particular and general. For example, particular groups include: "my brothers," v. 13, "the guests of my house," v. 15, "my maidservants," v. 15, "my servant," v. 16, "my wife," v. 17, "sons of my womb," v. 17, "children," v. 18, "all my intimate friends," v. 19; general designations are: "my known ones," v. 13, "my near ones," v. 14, "my known ones," v. 14, "those I have loved," v. 19, and "my friends," v. 21. Those in particular categories can also be included in the general ones. For example: wife, servants, friends, and guests are people who are "known" to Job. Similarly, "my brothers" and "sons of my womb" refer to Job's family; "my friends" (yōdᶜay, ûməyuddāᶜay, and rēᶜāy) and "all my intimate friends" pertain to the category of his friends; "my kinsmen" (v. 14) and "those I have loved" (v. 19) embrace both family and friends. All these words may mean more than we realize today.[44]

The author of the Book of Job vividly expresses Job's social alienation by using the following verbs and phrases: "he made far" ("he has alienated," v. 13), "they are estranged" v. 13, "they have forsaken me" v. 14, "they have forgotten me" v. 14, "The guests in my house and maidservants treat me as a stranger; I have become alien in their sight" v. 15, "repulsive" v. 17, " I have become loathsome" v. 17, "they scorn" v. 18, "they speak against me" v. 18, "they abhor me" v. 19, "they turned against me" v. 19, "I have escaped" v. 20, "you pursue me" v. 22. The use of these words helps us identify the theme of the text and concretize the poet's thought. Each verse has something to suggest about Job's social alienation.

---

[44] Clines, *Job 1-20*, 446.

IV. Structural Analysis of Job 19:13-22

A. Verses 13-14: Alienation from Kinsfolk and Friends

These verses deal with family and friends. The brothers and kinsfolk referred to may include brothers, cousins, nephews, and uncles.[45] The friends may be close friends with whom Job interacts on a daily basis.

B. Verses 15-16: Alienation from the Dependents of Job's House

This category of people includes those that he welcomed into his house because of his goodwill and hospitality. The guests may be either people who work for him or strangers who seek a place to stay.

C. Verse 17: Alienation from the Immediate Family

The immediate family includes his wife and children (1:18-19).

D. Verses 18-19: Alienation from Intimate Friends and Neighbors

These verses mention children of the neighborhood who consistently mock Job. Their mockery highlights the abject condition that he has been reduced to, such that even children make fun of him. The phrase "all my intimate friends" v. 19 might include Job's elite friends, confrères, and intimates with whom he sits under the oak tree making decisions for the society or executing judgment (29:7-12).

E. Verse 20: Summarizing Description of Job's Suffering and Pain

This verse appears distinctive in that it mentions nothing about family or friends as the preceding verses do but rather articulates what appears to be an expression of both internal and external pain. It is a summary of all the pains that Job has endured from God, his family, friends, and loved ones. The verse is placed here because it helps elucidate Job's cry that follows in vv. 21-22.

---

[45] de Vaux, *Ancient Israel,* 20. For further information on the household in ancient Israel, see King and Stager, *Life in Biblical Israel,* 9-19 and 36-60.

F. Verses 21-22: Cry against Alienation from Friends

In times of difficulty, the first people one turns to are family, friends, and loved ones. If God is responsible for Job's suffering, at least fellow human beings should be able to show sympathy and help him in his struggle.

V. Verse–by–Verse Analysis of Job 19:13-22

This section provides a through analysis of the words of the text 19:13-22 in order to bring out its meaning and interpretation.

A. Verses 13-14: Alienation from Kinsfolk and Friends

ʾaḥay mēʿālay hirḥîq

He has alienated my brothers from me;

wəyōdˁay ʾak̲-zārû mimmennî

and my friends are also estranged from me.

ḥād̲lû qərôb̲āy

My kinsmen have forsaken me;

ûməyuddāˁay šək̲ēḥûnî

my friends have forgotten me.

V. 13

God is responsible for the loss of Job's property and human relationships. The creator surpasses all creatures, and in Job's experience of his affliction God treats the righteous and the wicked alike, laughing at the despair of innocent persons (9:22-24). God has become a sadist and unfair. Job's physical condition and his sudden loss of property led to neglect by his family. The first group to isolate

Job is his brothers "my brothers." Job's first complaint about their withdrawal from him was in 6:14-30. The term "brothers" in this verse may refer to his siblings with whom he grew up or family members because clan members also called themselves "brothers" (1 Sam 20:29).

The word "far away" features prominently in psalms of lament. This term expresses the state of alienation and separation from loved ones, as well as the sufferer's longing for an answer to his or her plea for deliverance. The sense of "far away" here appears in other wisdom books and psalms (see Prov 15:29; 27:10; Pss 38:12; 69:9; 88:9, 19).

Job's "friends," those who know him very well and with whom he interacted on a daily basis, perceive him as a stranger. His alienation is not only due to his physical appearance but also because he has been judged a sinner. The once wise, revered, and welcoming man is no longer approachable.

V. 14

The word "my near ones," refers to "kinsmen" and may include "my brothers," in v. 13, family members, closest relatives (Lev 21:2-3; cf. Lev 25:25; Num 27:11), or have a precise meaning to which we no longer have access.[46] Despite the obscurity of the phrase, the context shows that with it Job must be referring to his family and clan members. The responsibilities of the clan include helping needy clan members, paying debts of its members whenever possible, and when the need arises, waging war against its enemies to protect and secure its member(s). The clan avenges the blood of its members. Job's identification with his clan made him yearn for the avenging of his blood and name (16:18-21). It is the duty and responsibility of the members of the clan to share joys and sorrows together; yet, Job's clan abandoned him in his time of need.

The participle "my known ones," that is, presumably friends, is also parallel to the "my friends" mentioned in v. 13 (cf. 2 Kgs 10:11). The "known ones" or the "near ones" also appear in many of the lament psalms where they stand far off from the sufferer (see Pss 31:12; 38:12;

---

[46] Clines, *Job 1-20*, 446.

87

55:14; 88:9). Psalm 31:12 communicates a message more like this passage than any of the other examples noted above:

> I am the scorn of all my adversaries,
> > a horror to my neighbors,
> an object of dread to my acquaintances;
> > those who see me in the street flee from me.

Job's friends "forsake" him and "fade away" like the evening sun (see 7:16; 10:20).

B. Verses 15-16: Alienation from the Dependents in Job's House

gārê beṭî wə'amhōtay ləzār taḥšəbūnî

The guests of my house and my maidservants treat me as a stranger;

nokrî hāyîtî bə'ênêhem

I have become an alien in their eyes.

lə'abdî qārā'tî wəlō' ya'āneh

I summon my own servant, but he does not answer;

bəmô-pî 'etḥannen-lô

with my mouth, I entreat him.

This text suggests that Job has lost his power of control. A person of Job's standing (29:1-12) must be very grieved at such loss of control, even to the point that his maids and servant pay him no respect.

V. 15

Job is a hospitable person (29:11-25) who expects the "guests of my house" will show him compassion because he received them into his home. The term, "guest of my house," could be interpreted as "resident aliens," or "wage earners." These are persons not related by blood who need someone prominent to accommodate them, as Job did.[47]

1. Resident Alien

A resident alien is called "a sojourner," and occupies a middle position between a native and a foreigner.[48] A sojourner is usually someone who has left his or her homeland as a result of famine, politics, economic, or other circumstances and seeks protection in another society. He lives among people who are not his blood relatives and thus lacks the protection and privileges which come from blood relationship and a common place of birth. His status and privileges are dependent on the hospitality of the society in which he sojourns.[49] The LXX translated "sojourner" as "proselyte" through assimilation of faith and race.[50]

2. Wage Earner

The wage earner is called *śākîr*, "hired laborer" (Exod 12:45). The wage earner works for payment. Social stratification involves some people working for others. Traditionally, the poor work for the rich and Job had people working for him whom he paid well (Job 31:39).

3. Job's Household

Job laments that even his "maidservants" look upon him as a stranger. Traditionally, maidservants are at the mercy of their master or mistress, but in Job's case they are looking down on their master. In 31:13, Job tells us how fairly he treated his male and female servants. The slave is expected to obey the master. Although Prov 29:19, 21 and Sir 33:25-33 advise masters to treat their slaves sternly, Job treated his slaves humanely and with justice. Job never neglected his slaves, because he considered them as what they truly are, God's creatures

---

[47] Clines, *Job 1-20*, 446.

[48] R. Martin-Achard, "גור," *TLOT*, 1. 307-10, here 308.

[49] Diether Kellermann, "גור," *TDOT*, 2. 439- 49 here 443.

[50] Ibid., 448.

(Job 31:13-15). However, Job in his affliction did not receive a like treatment from his maidservants.

The term "stranger" as used by Job for himself is very pathetic. The guest and the maidservants came as strangers and were accepted into Job's household. The one who welcomed them into his house they now look upon as a stranger. The text's poetical artistry shows the depth to which Job has been lowered and his consequent pain. Job is treated as an "alien," a native of a different country (Deut 17:15; Judg 19:12; 1 Kgs 11:1). "Alien" is comparable to "stranger" and highlights Job's abject state in the verse.

V. 16

The reversal of the normal order of Job's life continues in this verse. The term *ᶜebed* denotes a "slave" or a "servant." Servants and maidservants are to be at the beck and call of their master or mistress. Servants act on the signal from the master or mistress (cf. Ps 123:2), but this servant of Job was very arrogant and even though Job pleaded with him, something Job should not have to do, the servant did not attend to him.[51] According to Clines, the humiliation of pleading with his servant is not the worst of all that befalls Job because he had an egalitarian attitude towards his servants. Job ensures respect and dignity for his servants, who should not treat Job in the manner they do (31:13-15).[52]

Every society has a social order; King and Stager note that the rural-urban contrast was not pronounced in ancient Israel. There were inequalities, for example, superior and inferior, before and at the early stages of the monarchy, but there was no social stratification along class lines.[53] The term *ᶜebed* covers a range of persons from slave to an

---

[51] The servant degraded Job (see Habel, *The Book of Job*, 301). The singular noun *ᶜebed* used for Job's servant suggests that this servant has a special status in his house. For instance, in Gen 15:2-3, Abraham has Eliezer of Damascus. Abraham had a servant who was in charge of his property (24:2); and likewise Joseph became the overseer of the house of Potiphar (39:4).

[52] Clines, *Job 1-20*, 447.

[53] King and Stager, *Life in Biblical Israel*, 5.

official in the court of the king (1 Sam 19:1; 21:8; 2 Sam 11:13). [54] The term has to be understood in light of the social context in which it is used. Class systems developed later with the monarchy and appear to have been in existence during the time of the composition of the Book of Job. Job's agony will be better understood when we become conversant with the status of slaves in ancient Israel.

4. Slaves

A distinction should be made among free people, adopted children, wage earners, resident aliens, and slaves. De Vaux notes,

> By "slave" in the strict sense we mean a man who is deprived of his or her freedom, at least for a time, who is bought and sold, who is the property of a master, who makes use of him as he likes; in this sense there were slaves in Israel, and some were Israelites. [55]

The daily life of a slave depended on the master. It is outrageous for Job's slave to behave as he does, ignoring Job even after he had pleaded with him.

C. Verse 17: Alienation from the Immediate Family

rûḥî zārāh ləʾištî

My breath is repulsive to my wife;

wəḥannōṯî liḇnê biṭnî

I am loathsome to my own children.

This verse is Job's most pitiable statement in the chapter. To be abandoned by spouse and family is the worst that can happen to any

---

[54] As illustrated by seals nos. 6-11 in Nahman Avigad and Benjamin Sass, *Corpus of West Semitic Stamp Seals* (Jerusalem: Israel Exploration Society, 1997), reproduced in King and Stager, *Life in Biblical Israel*, 5.

[55] de Vaux, *Ancient Israel*, 80.

human being. Some commentators believe that his wife and family abandoned Job because of his bad breath due to his disease.[56] Clines observes that the verse does not show that Job was alienated on account of his bad breath; rather, it was the totality of Job's sufferings which is the reason for his isolation.[57] The appearance of Job's body and his suffering may have been responsible for his repulsiveness.

The word *rûaḥ* ("breath," "wind," "spirit") is sometimes translated as "life." The form in this verse *rûḥî* could mean "my spirit," "my life," or "my breath." The context suggests "my life" rather than "my breath," although "my breath" is favored in many English versions.[58] Breath gives vitality to the body, hence life. The word *rûḥî* appears in 6:4 where it has the sense of "vitality" and similarly in 10:12 and 17:1.
This evidence from elsewhere in the Book of Job supports the translational choice of "life" over "breath."

The verb *zārāh* ("stink") also means "be strange." Some scholars prefer "strange" because *zārû* in v. 13 comes from the verb *zûr* "be strange." Snijders, one of those scholars who favor the translation "strange," maintains that no verb meaning "stink" or "be repulsive" exists in Hebrew; rather, the sense is "be strange," as vv. 14 and 27 suggest.[59] However, the classic study of Wernberg-Møller refers to an Arabic poem that uses the cognate verb in the sense of "repulsive" in the context of a husband becoming stinking or noisome to his wife.[60] Further, repulsiveness is parallel with loathsome in the second line of the above verse. Given all this evidence, the verb should

---

[56] Gordis, *The Book of Job*, 202; Pope, *Job*, 142; Driver and Gray, *Job*, 167.

[57] Clines, *Job 1-20*, 448; see also Habel, *The Book of Job*, 302.

[58] *NRSV* "My breath is repulsive to my wife"; *NEB* "My breath is noisome to my wife"; *KJV* "My breath is strange to my wife"; *NAB* "My breath is abhorred by my wife"; *NAS, NIB,* and *NIV* "My breath is offensive to my wife"; *NJB* "My breath is unbearable to my wife"; *WEB* "My breath is strange to my wife"; *RSV* "I am repulsive to my wife."

[59] L. A. Snijders, "The Meaning of זָר in the Old Testament," *OTS* 10 (1954) 1-154, here 14-16; see also Clines, *Job 1-20*, 429.

[60] For more information on *zûr*, see P. Wernberg-Møller, "A Note on זור 'to stink,'" *VT* 4 (1954) 322-25; see also Dhorme, *The Book of Job*, 277. He adopts the meaning "repulsive," with the understanding of "hate" or "detest" rather than "stinking."

be translated "be repulsive" or "stink." The life of Job has become repulsive to his wife. The life of Job that has become repulsive is not only his physical appearance and the possible odor of his breath but the entire misfortune that has befallen him.

Clines claims that the verb *ḥānan* (II; "be loathsome") is parallel to *zūr* "stinks" and thus supports the rendering "repulsive" or "stink" in the first colon.[61] *ḥānan* in this meaning ("be loathsome") is attested only here in Hebrew.[62] The normal rendering of *ḥānan* is "show favor," "be gracious," or "supplicate" (Pss 25:16; 102:14; Prov 26:25; Isa 26:10; Sir 40:17, 22).

The phrase "to the sons of my womb" is figurative speech. The word *beṭen* ("belly") basically means "interior," which is equivalent to *koilia* and *gastēr* in Greek, as is evident in the LXX.[63] The association of womb and males does not occur frequently in the Bible. However, a few examples in the Bible show that a man can speak of children as coming from his womb, idiomatically as "the fruit of my womb." In these cases, *beṭen* means "body," which implies that the children come from his body and not from his belly (see Mic 6:7, also Ps 132:11). The word *beṭen* is also used for a man in Judges (when Ehud killed Eglon—Judg 3:21, 22). The word appears elsewhere in Job, that is, Job 38:29 and 40:16, but in these two appearances the word *beṭen* refers to the upper cosmos and the belly of an animal, Behemoth, respectively. Driver and Gray think "my womb" may refer to the womb of the mother, as already in 3:10.[64] This interpretation is difficult to accept since the context has no connection with Job's mother. Therefore, some scholars, among them Dhorme, Pope, Gordis, and Habel, believe that Job is talking about his own children.[65] Although the prose prologue reports the death of his children, it is reasonable to assume or surmise that Job means his own sons, if we argue that the poetry is independent of the prologue.

---

[61] See also Clines, *Job 1-20*, 429.

[62] "Be loathsome" is an alternative meaning of "show favor," "be gracious," or "supplicate" of *ḥānan*.

[63] David N. Freedman and J. Lundbom, "בֶּטֶן," *TDOT*, 2. 94-99, here 94.

[64] Driver and Gray, *The Book of Job*, 168; Clines, *Job 1-20*, 449.

[65] Dhorme, *The Book of Job*, 277-78; Pope, *Job*, 142; Gordis, *The Book of Job*, 202; Habel, *The Book of Job*, 302.

D. Verses 18-19: Alienation from Intimate Friends and Neighbors

gam-ʿăwîlîm māʾăsû bî

Even children scorn me;

ʾāqûmāh wayədabbərû-bî

when I arise, they speak against me.

tīʿăḇûnî kol-mətê sôḏî

All my intimate friends abhor me;

wəzeh-ʾāhaḇtî nehpəḵû-bî

those I have loved have turned against me.

V. 18

Job has become a laughing stock for people of all walks of life (12:4), a victim of his society. The once powerful Job has become an object of mockery, leveled to the dust (12:5). Job has reached the nadir of dehumanization, such that even "children" make fun of him. What actually provoked these children to laugh at Job may be the depth of his abject condition because the children have no knowledge of the traditional concept of "deed and consequence" that would cause them to accuse Job of any sin. Habel remarks that children are often free of social opinions.[66] If this is indeed so, then they may be making fun of him because of his physical appearance. Children will point at a mad or insane person who is not well dressed or well behaved.

Job the wise, rich, and righteous person has become a worthless creature. Job, who lived like a king among his equals (29:25), is now "scorned," "humiliated," "despised," and "rejected." The verb *māʾas*,

---

[66] See Habel, *The Book of Job*, 302.

when followed by "*b*" before an individual's name, shows the person in question to be the object of scorn. The word *māʾas* ("scorn") occurs several times in the book (7:16; 8:20; 9:21; 10:3); in all these instances, it expresses Job's abject state. The term conveys the same idea in other parts of the Bible as well (see Jer 4:30).

The verb *qûm* ("arise") needs elaboration; it cannot be literally rendered as "arise" here but has to be understood in the light of the context. The verb occurs only a few times in the book. In 1:20, it expresses "getting up"; when Job heard of his lost property he "got up." In 7:4, the verb refers to getting up from sleep; and in 30:28 it is used in the sense of "getting up" to speak. It seems unlikely that the children ridiculed Job when he went to address an assembly. The likely meaning of the verb here is that the children made fun of him whenever he appeared in public. We therefore render *qûm* as "appeared" instead of "arise" in this context, where this rendering fits the following verb "they speak about me," or "they ridicule me," or "they talk against me." The verb *dābar* with "*b*" before a personal complement means "mock at," "scoff at," "speak against" (see also Ps 78:19), which applies perfectly to Job's situation.

V. 19

Job's intimate friends are men of the council, who discuss confidential matters.[67] The word *sôd* ("council" or "counsel") is used in the context of an exchange of counsels in the following texts: Jer 6:11; 15:17; Pss 55:14-15; 89:8. It is possible that the phrase "all my intimate friends" refers to a group that sits regularly at the city gate to adjudicate issues of the community. The silence and the withdrawal that Job is experiencing in his present state are in stark contrast to the reverence and the attention he received from the youngsters and the elders when he went to the city gate (29:7).

The "loved ones" may be the persons already cited in vv. 13-19a. The cruelest thing that can happen to a sufferer is for his or her loved ones to become enemies and to persecute and abandon the sufferer. Desertion of loved ones should not happen, but as Habel says,

---

[67] Driver and Gray, *The Book of Job*, 168.

"a lifetime of love and concern (cf. ch. 29) is dismissed when an individual bears the marks of God's curse."[68]

E. Verse 20: Summarizing Description of Job's Suffering and Pain

bəᶜôrî ûbibśārî dābqāh ᶜaṣmî

My skin and my flesh cleave to my bone;

wāʾeṭmalləṭāh bəᶜôr šinnāy

I have escaped by the skin of my teeth.

Verse 20 poses a real challenge to scholars. Clines calls it a "famous crux."[69] The language is ironical and needs to be decoded. It is interesting that after his complaints of affliction by God (vv. 8-12) Job now returns to his friends, calling on them for help (vv. 21-22). The words of v. 20 relate to his physical pain and express his agony. Job may not necessarily experience his skin cleaving to his bones; this could be poetical language with the intention of expressing Job's pains, because the second part of the verse gives an indication that he had escaped the dreadfulness of his suffering.

Many scholars understand this verse as referring to Job's emaciation.[70] Clines argues against this understanding and brands it a "hasty confusion" based on Ps 22:18.[71] He argues that in Ps 22:18 the psalmist experiences emaciation, but that is not the case in the Book of Job. Job, he says, does not refer to any physical sickness; rather, what Job has experienced is a psychological attack. Therefore, Job's statement here should not be conceived in terms of exhaustion, dryness, or dehydration, such as was spoken of in chaps. 16–17.[72] Clines also

---

[68] Habel, *The Book of Job,* 302.

[69] Clines, *Job 1-20,* 450.

[70] See Driver and Gray, *The Book of Job,* 168; Rowley, *Job,* 170; Fohrer, *Hiob,* 315-16; Gordis, *The Book of Job,* 203.

[71] See Clines, *Job 1-20,* 430; Wolfers (*Deep Things out of Darkness,* 127) also agrees that v. 20 expresses not emaciation but survival: "I continue reluctantly to live."

[72] Clines, *Job 1-20,* 438.

argues that emaciation is not compatible with Job's desire in v. 26 and his longing in v. 27. He concludes:

> The conviction of vv. 25-26a and the unabated desire of vv. 26c-27b do not represent a radical and unmotivated shift of mood out of some deep despondency in earlier verses; rather we see set against one another, still at stalemate but now in a more equal struggle, the reality of divine hostility and reality of the human self-assurance.[73]

This verse is a figure of speech to call attention to Job's plight. He is isolated from the family, friends, and loved ones who were the "bones" that supported his life. Job feels that his support is gone and he no longer has strength.

The verb *dābaq* means "cling," "cleave," "keep close," that is, one thing clinging to another. According to Clines, an incorrect translation of *dābqāh* has found its way into some English Bibles.[74] Clines's argument stems from the research of E. F. Sutcliffe, who observes that it is normal for bone and flesh to cleave together.[75]

"Flesh" (*bāśār*) and "bone" (*'eṣem*) is a common collocation used to express familial relationships; when Eve is presented to Adam (Gen 2:23), when Laban addresses Jacob (Gen 29:14), when Abimelech addresses his mother's kinsfolk (Judg 9:2), when the tribes of Israel come to David at Hebron (2 Sam 5:1; 1 Chr 11:1), and when David addresses the elders of Judah (2 Sam 19:12-13), these terms are used together. It is possible to argue that the metaphor "flesh and bones" (English usage) has something to do with family, friends, and loved ones since in vv. 13-19 Job talks about family, friends, and loved ones; the verses that follow (vv. 21-22) are his cry to the friends, which indicates that Job is still within the context of family, friends, and loved ones. The metaphor of bone, flesh, and skin may thus possibly be a reference to family and loved ones. Janzen similarly suggests that,

---

[73] Ibid.

[74] See the translations of *NIB* and *NIV*, "I am nothing but skin and bones."

[75] E. F. Sutcliffe, "Further Notes on Job, Textual and Exegetical," *Bib* 31 (1950) 365-78, here 375-77.

because of the loss of both divine and human relationships, Job has to seek in himself companionship in order to keep his flesh and bone together.[76] Janzen thus considers bone and flesh as a reference to Job's own self.

"Flesh" and "bones" appear in Ps 102:6 "Because of my loud groaning my bones cling to my skin." The context here comes close to what we have in Job. Briggs and Briggs, using the example of Ps 102:6, state that when the body is dehydrated, the flesh may cleave to the bone.[77] Clines cites numerous emendations proposed with the example of Ps 102:6 in view; he believes the most acceptable emendation is to delete *bəʿôrî û* ("to my skin and") of v. 20, which is absent from Ps 102:6, but is not convinced about the emendation because it does not yield any meaningful interpretation.[78] Others delete *ûbibšārî* ("and my flesh"), but even this does not offer any help towards understanding the verse.[79]

Some scholars adopt LXX's version: "under my skin my flesh rots away" as a preferable reading of the first line of the verse.[80] The concept of rottenness of the bones is attested in Prov 12:4; 14:30; Hab 3:16. In Ps 31:11, the sufferer's bones "waste away" and in Ps 32:2, his bones are "worn out." Kisane adopts the entire version of the LXX and translates it as "In my skin my flesh rots away, and my bones come forth in (like) teeth" as the more preferable reading and thinks the corruption of the Hebrew occurred because the tradents of the Book of Job may have had been influenced by other texts, a special example is Lam 4:8b "their skin has shriveled on their bones; it has become as dry as wood; see also Ps 102:6: "because of my loud groaning my bones cling to my flesh." Bones may adhere to the skin (Lam 4:8) and to the flesh (Ps 102:6), but not to both at the same time.[81] Perhaps owing to

---

[76] Janzen, *Job*, 134.

[77] C. A. and E. G. Briggs, *A Critical and Exegetical Commentary on the Book of Psalms* (2 vols.; Edinburgh: T & T Clark, 1976) 2. 319.

[78] Clines, *Job 1-20*, 430.

[79] Fohrer, *Hiob*, 315-16; Budde, *Hiob*, 100. Given the problem it poses, *NEB* and *NAB* also delete *ûbibšārî*.

[80] Pope, *Job*, 143; Dhorme, *The Book of Job*, 279-80; Edward J. Kisane, *The Book of Job* (New York: Sheed and Ward, 1946) 122; Budde, *Hiob*, 100. In *The Jerusalem Bible*, *dābqāh* is translated as "rot."

[81] The *NRSV* translates the MT's *bāśār* as "skin" instead of "flesh."

the influence of Lam 4:8, the word "bone" was taken over to v. 20a and the verb "rotten" changed to "cleave." Kisane argues that the sentence means that Job's flesh is rotting away and that he is emaciated (see 7:5). He buttresses his claim with reference to Elihu's similar remark about the fate of a sinner afflicted by God:

> Their flesh is so wasted away that it cannot be seen;
> and their bones, once invisible, now stick out (33:21).[82]

But his interpretation is not convincing, especially in the light of the Syriac version. The Syr, "my skin and my flesh cling to my bones," gives a good rendering of the first line of the verse because under normal circumstances it is the skin and the flesh that adhere to the bone, not the other way around.

The flesh, the skin, and the bone make up the body. The flesh and the skin support the bones, even if they are broken or rotten. The sense of Job's complaint is that the disease has weakened him, that his bones have become dislodged from their proper position. He is no longer supported by his bones (Job 2:5; Gen 29:14; Lam 4:7).[83] The weakness of Job's bones is understood by Clines as an image of decay of vigor rather than the emaciation referred to in Ps 22:18.[84] Clines goes on to say that the alienation of family, friends, and the society "have weakened his spirit and sapped his vigor."[85] The reference is to a psychic reaction rather than a physical, visible state. Psalm 102:5-8 shows that the psalmist may have experienced loneliness like Job's isolation, which he expresses with the image of a lonely sparrow on top of a house:

> [5]Because of my loud groaning
>   my bones cling to my skin.
> [6]I am like an owl of the wilderness,
>   like a little owl of the waste places.
> [7]I lie awake;
>   I am like a lonely bird on the housetop.

---

[82] Kisane, *The Book of Job,* 122.

[83] Clines, *Job 1-20,* 451.

[84] For more on weak bones and skin, see ibid.

[85] Ibid., 452.

⁸All day long my enemies taunt me;
   those who deride me use my name for a curse.

Terrien understands *wāʾeṯmallǝṭāh* as "escape." He retains the cohortative form of the verb and explains that whereas adult teeth have no skin, the milk teeth of children do have a tissue underlying them. Since there is tissue underlying each milk tooth, he wonders if *wāʾeṯmallǝṭāh* could be a metaphorical reference to innocence. According to Terrien, Job's wish is: "Si seulement je pouvais m'échapper avec mon intégrité intacte!" ("If only I could escape with my integrity intact!").⁸⁶ And when Job survives, Terrien says of Job, "J'ai tout perdu, mais je me suis échappé vivant" (I have lost everything, but I have escaped alive).⁸⁷ All along Job has been fighting to restore his self-image and integrity. The integrity is his innocence that needs to be made known to his enemies. Clines, on the other hand, thinks the "escape" referred to by Job is from death, not from loss of integrity, as Terrien holds.⁸⁸ According to Clines, although Job's bones cleave to his skin and flesh, he has narrowly eluded death. The narrow margin of Job's escape, Clines explains, is expressed by the phrase *wāʾeṯmallǝṭāh bǝʿôr šinnāy* ("by the skin of my teeth").

In conclusion, the language of the verse is metaphorical so that we cannot say with absolute certainty what the meaning is. The most plausible understanding may be that it refers to Job's frustration caused by his physical state and the loss of family, friends, and loved ones who should have been a support for him just as bones are for the skin and the flesh. The verse does not refer to a distinct symptom of physical illness. The author of the book uses poetical language to add vivid coloring to his story, as in 6:12-13; 13:25, 27-28; 16:7-9; 17:7. We can say that 19:20 is one such way of presenting his story. It is possible that Job uses the words of this verse to let the friends know the seriousness of his plight before he addresses them in the next verses.

---

⁸⁶ Terrien, *Job*, 195 n. 3c.
⁸⁷ Ibid., 195.
⁸⁸ Clines, *Job 1-20*, 452.

F. Verses 21-22: Cry against Alienation from Friends

ḥonnūnî ḥonnūnî ʾattem rēʿāy

Have mercy on me, have mercy on me, you my friends;

kî yaḏ-ʾĕlôᵃh nāḡʿāh bî

for the hand of God has struck me.

lāmmāh tirdəpūnî kəmô-ʾēl

Why do you pursue me like God?

ûmibbəśārî lōʾ ṭiśbāʿû

Have you not had enough of my flesh?

This plea is against the unjust accusation of his friends. It is a call to the friends to reconsider their decision and show Job mercy. Social relationships demand that individuals in a society interact and behave in a meaningful way, but when there is a breakdown in social relationships, reciprocity on the part of societal members ceases. Job is met with hostility, he has been deserted by his family and friends, their former loyalty and respect has disappeared, and he has no one on his side; he needs to shout to friends for help.

V. 21

Job's cry is a sorrowful one. According to Dhorme, "What could be more vehement, more piercing than the twofold cry: Have pity on me, have pity on me!"[89] Clines thinks Job is pleading with his friends to stop their accusation.[90] Habel considers the plea a sarcastic remark and a mockery of his friends.[91] Pleading for mercy does not mean giving up his innocence before his friends and family but rather

---

[89] Dhorme, *The Book of Job*, 280.
[90] Clines, *Job 1-20*, 453.
[91] Habel, *The Book of Job*, 297.

seeking their support in his suffering. He begged for assistance from his servant, which the servant failed to give (19:16). Job needed human assistance and it was denied; he once again calls out to his friends, pleading with them to abandon their persecution of him. The phrase *ʾattem rēʿāy* ("you my friends") is emphatic and depicts the friends' failure to fulfill their duty as friends (6:14-17; 16:2).

"The friends" Job is addressing in this verse are the three friends, not the friends referred to in 19:13-19. The three friends were indeed close friends, who came to sit with him and sympathize with him in his time of sorrow (2:11-13). In course of their effort to show sympathy, they engaged Job in a dialogue that generated sharp disagreement between them. If Job calls now on these three friends for help, then his call is sarcastic because earlier on Job accused them of treason (6:15), insensitivity (6:27), stupidity (12:2-3; 13:2), lacking values (13:4), and practicing falsehood (13:7).

In their prejudice (13:7-9) they torment his life (16:2) with the intent of crushing him (19:2). Since Job made such remarks then, his plea now is meant as a mockery. Even directly after this plea for help, he utters words that threaten them should they continue to maintain their views (vv. 28-29).[92]

Internal evidence from the Book of Job shows that Job's call in v. 21 is addressed to his three friends. The term (*rēʿāy*) that Job used for the three friends in v. 21 appears in 2:11; 32:3; 35:4; 42:7, 10 but not in 19:13-19, which evidently places "the friends" referred to there in a different category. All the same, the friends mentioned in 19:13-19 were not loyal to him either because they contributed to his suffering or because of their alienation from him. They did not offer him any comfort. Despite the attitude of his three friends, they appear to be the best friends he has because they still stayed with him when others completely abandoned him. Job understands that God, not his friends, caused his situation; they add to his suffering because of their blind defense of God.

Job needs comfort, compassion, and consolation because God has engulfed him (4:5; 19:6, 8-12). The phrase *yaḏ-ʾĕlôªh* ("The hand of God") is an expression for the power of God (6:9; 10:7; 12:9; 13:21)

---

[92] Habel, *The Book of Job*, 302.

that embraces all the affliction that God has caused him.[93] Job never ceases to lament over the power of God and his domination of his life. He does not need the words of his friends any more because their words only increase his pain. He knows the friends do not have the strength to overcome God. He knows that their thoughts about him are wrong and unjustified (19:6). The appeal is not for them to fight God or stop what God has caused, but rather to stop adding to what he is suffering already. His friends are supposed to help Job bear what God has inflicted upon him, what Clines refers to as "the pitiless ferocity of God's violence."[94] Friends are supposed to be "shock absorbers" in times of crises. Here, the friends have made matters worst by attempting to execute divine justice.[95]

V. 22

The verb "pursue," "chase," "persecute" (*rādap*) is usually used in the context of enmity. God is said to pursue his enemies (Pss 35:6; 83:16), and now he pursues Job; Job has become God's enemy. The attitude of Job's friends made him question whether his friends have also turned against him and are pursuing him like God. Rather than coming to his aid, his friends join forces with God.

The following phrase *ûmibbəśārî lōʾ tiśbāʿû* ("Have you not had enough of my flesh?") refers to the attitude of his friends. The friends appear as wild beasts devouring his flesh. Probably, the phrase is a metaphor depicting how wild beasts devour their prey. If taken literally, it means to be satisfied with flesh (see 31:31); but since it is a metaphor, it suggests rather that the friends are killing him indirectly. Job's friends have become carnivores devouring him; just as in Psalm 22 the psalmist refers to his enemies as beasts about to devour his flesh (22:13, 16, 20-21). In Psalm 27:2, to devour someone's flesh is to cause the person harm.[96] In Akkadian and Arabic, to eat the flesh of someone means to accuse or slander the person (see also Dan 3:8; 6:25;

---

[93] "The hand of God has struck me" is an expression referring to Job's calamity. The hand of God is destructive here. In other parts of the Bible, it is used in connection with disaster, including illness (Pss 32:4; 39:11; 1 Sam 5:6; 6:3, 5).

[94] Clines, *Job 1-20*, 454.

[95] Terrien, *Job*, 196.

[96] Dhorme, *The Book of Job*, 281.

Ps 27:2; Eccl 4:5).[97] Ps 27:2 and these Akkadian and Arabic usages serve to elucidate the exact attitude of Job's friends here. The friends have become a pain in his flesh and have intensified his agony with their accusation and false justification of God.

Conclusion

Most of the descriptions in Job 19:13-22 are not meant to be taken literally since we are in the context of poetry; rather, these images are vivid descriptions of the plight of Job. For instance, Job's treatment as a stranger (v. 15), his repulsiveness to the wife and children (v. 17), his bones clinging to the skin and his escape by the skin of his teeth (v. 20), and his friends never satisfied with his flesh (v. 22), refer to the isolation and alienation he is going through.[98]

Social alienation occurs several times in the Bible, but most especially in the psalms, where in most cases God is not the cause of the alienation but is called upon to be the rescuer. The Book of Job is distinctive in that it describes the alienation of one single person and labels God as the cause of his alienation. Job's cry is that of a person God has blessed profusely (1:1-3), has allowed the accuser to torment (1:9, 21; 2:3, 7), and dealt with dreadfully by not responding to his cry for help (7:17-21). This presentation is evidently different from what we normally see of a sufferer in the psalms, where there is no bargain on the life of the psalmist as was in the case of Job.

---

[97] Gordis, *The Book of Job*, 203; Pope, *Job*, 143; Dhorme, *The Book of Job*, 281; Clines, *Job 1-20*, 454.

[98] Clines, *Job 1-20*, 449.

Chapter Five

Social Alienation in the Book of Psalms

This chapter concentrates on Psalms 22, 31, and 88 in connection with the theme of social alienation. The similarity between these psalms and the Book of Job will be discussed with particular attention to common literary features; that will be followed by literary, structural, and textual analyses of these psalms. [1]

I. Similarity between the Psalms and the Book of Job

The Psalter contains different types of psalms; for example: psalms of lament, thanksgiving, trust, and enthronement. The psalms of lament have an affinity with the Book of Job. Usually, lamentation occurs when life has turned worse for the individual or a group of people and they are displaced from their normal way of life. [2] The words of lament bemoan this problem. Sometimes the prayers or the words of lament have a psychosocial impact that can heal the supplicant socially and psychologically. In Psalms 22, 31, 88 and Job 19:13-22 the suffering is described by the individual involved.

A. The Choice of Psalms 22, 31, 88
Psalms 22, 31, and 88 can be seen as similar to Job 19:13-22 for the following reasons: the supplicants are isolated from their society and abandoned by their loved ones; they call on God to intervene; and where there is no visible enemy as the cause of the problem, God is blamed (Psalm 88). The psalmists and Job express trust in God and express dismay at their suffering. In Psalms 22 and 31, for example, the psalmists know who the enemies are and call on God to come to their aid; in Psalm 31, the psalmist even asks for the punishment of his

---

[1] All references to and quotations of the Hebrew text are taken from the *BHS*; the English translation of the Hebrew text will be taken from the *NRSV*.

[2] Brueggemann calls psalms of lament "psalms of disorientation" because the life of the psalmist is marked by disequilibrium, incoherence, and unrelieved asymmetry. See Walter Brueggemann, *The Message of the Psalms* (Augsburg Old Testament Studies; Minneapolis: Augsburg, 1984) 51.

enemies. In Psalm 88, God is blamed because God allowed the affliction of the psalmist. In the Book of Job, Job addresses God because God knows the truth of his plight and Job believes it is only God who can vindicate him.

The prayers of the psalmists and the complaint by Job are words of individuals in need. Whatever their original situation may have been, the suppliants experience some level of relief once they have unburdened themselves by externalizing their grief.

B. Features Common to Psalms 22, 31, 88 and Job 19:13-22

The laments of the psalmists and of Job are words of complaint and petition based on their experience of social ostracism. Their poetic features help express this social alienation. The unavailability of help and support from friends and loved ones lead to a search for God. This search is common to the psalmists and the author of Job. Their words follow a characteristic pattern:

1. A Statement of Shock

They express their shock over their situation in statements such as:

> Even young children despise me;
> > when I rise, they talk against me (Job 19:18)

> All who see me mock at me;
> > they make mouths at me, they shake their heads (Ps 22:8)

> I am the scorn of all my adversaries,
> > a horror to my neighbors,
> an object of dread to my acquaintances;
> > those who see me in the street flee from me (Ps 31:12)

> I am counted among those who go down to the Pit;
> > I am like those who have no help,
> like those forsaken among the dead,
> > like the slain that lie in the grave,
> like those whom you remember no more,
> > for they are cut off from your hand (Ps 88:4-5)

You have caused my companions to shun me;
>you have made me a thing of horror to them.
I am shut in so that I cannot escape (Ps 88:9).

2. Description of Mistreatment by Others

The sufferers complain against the attack of the enemy:

Many bulls encircle me,
>strong bulls of Bashan surround me;
they open wide their mouths at me,
>like a ravening and roaring lion (Ps 22:13-14)

For I hear the whispering of many—
>terror all around!—
as they scheme together against me,
>as they plot to take my life (Ps 31:14)

Your wrath has swept over me;
>your dread assault destroys me (Ps 88:17)

His troops come on together:
>they have thrown up siege works against me,
and encamp around my tent (Job 19:12).

3. A Cry for Help

In their desolation the speakers plead with God or loved ones to come to their aid. Their cry includes a declaration of innocence and reference to their need for attention from friends:

Have pity on me, have pity on me,
>O you my friends,
for the hand of God has touched me! (Job 19:21)

How long will you torment me,
>and break me in pieces with words? (Job 19:2).

A cry to God for help is usually introduced in these texts with exclamations, sometimes an invocation of God. The invocation shows the intimate relationship between God and the petitioner.[3] The supplicant questions the delay in God's intervention:

> My God, my God,
> > why have you forsaken me?
> Why are you far from helping me,
> > from the words of my groaning? (Ps 22:2)

> Be gracious to me, O LORD, for I am in distress;
> > my eye wastes away from grief, my soul and my body
> > also (Ps 31:10)

> Why do you cast me off?
> Why do you hide your face from me? (Ps 88:15).

The "why" questions are a reproach, while "how long" suggests the urgency of the help needed.[4]

---

[3] Westermann makes a distinction between "invocation" and "address" to God in the psalms. On the one hand, "invocation," he states, makes contact with God and acquires intensity because it comes from a distressed heart; for example, "My God, my God" (Ps 22:1) becomes a cry for help and indicates that something is amiss. "To call" means to draw attention, to invoke presence. So invocation suggests a separation between God and the supplicant and expresses a desperate yearning on the part of the supplicant to see God. On the other hand, an "address" is made to God not by use of his name but by means of a divine predicate; for example, "O Shepherd of Israel" (Ps 80:1). An address asks God to do something God is noted for, in this case to lead Israel, since God is a good shepherd. See Claus Westermann, *The Living Psalms* (trans. J. R. Porter; Grand Rapids: Eerdmans, 1989) 26-27.

[4] When one is afflicted the "why" question is a sign of his or her readiness for repentance and a renewed life if he or she has sinned, but if there is no sin involved then an explanation is needed for the suffering. See Samuel E. Balentine, *Prayer in the Hebrew Bible: The Drama of Divine-Human Dialogue* (Minneapolis: Fortress, 1993) 8. "How long," on the one hand, draws on the steadfast love of God, asking him for forgiveness and to come to the rescue. On the other hand, it is a complaint against God for the unnerving and incomprehensible experience that the supplicant is going through. See Claus Westermann, *Praise and Lament in the Psalms* (trans. Keith R. Crim and Richard N. Soulen; Atlanta: John Knox, 1973) 176-78.

4. Words of Motivation

The supplicants use words of persuasion to prompt God to act:

> Do you work wonders for the dead?
>> Do the shades rise up to praise you?
> Is your steadfast love declared in the grave,
>> or your faithfulness in Abaddon?
> Are your wonders known in the darkness,
>> or your saving help in the land of forgetfulness? (Ps 88:11-13)

> Have pity on me, have pity on me,
>> O you my friends,
> for the hand of God has touched me! (Job 19:21).

Sometimes, God's past deeds of deliverance are recounted with the recognition that the present problem is as nothing compared to what Yhwh has done in the past:

> Yet you are holy,
>> enthroned on the praises of Israel.
> In you our ancestors trusted;
>> they trusted, and you delivered them.
> To you they cried, and were saved;
>> in you they trusted, and were not put to shame (Ps 22:4-6).

5. Societal Isolation

The sufferers are isolated by their society:

> You have caused my companions to shun me;
>> you have made me a thing of horror to them.
> I am shut in so that I cannot escape (Ps 88:9; see also v. 19)

> But I am a worm, and not human;
>> scorned by others, and despised by the people.
> All who see me mock at me;
>> they make mouths at me, they shake their heads;

"Commit your cause to the LORD; let him deliver—
      let him rescue the one in whom he delights!" (Ps 22:7-9,
    see also v. 22)

For my life is spent with sorrow,
      and my years with sighing;
my strength fails because of my misery,
      and my bones waste away.
I am the scorn of all my adversaries,
      a horror to my neighbors,
an object of dread to my acquaintances;
      those who see me in the street flee from me.
I have passed out of mind like one who is dead;
      I have become like a broken vessel (Ps 31:11-13).

Also the entire passage of Job 19:13-22 is an example. Isolation brings with it feelings of shame, helplessness, pains, and self-pity.

6. State of Depression

The sufferers become depressed because they find themselves abandoned by God and loved ones or because help from God is delayed:

I am poured out like water,
      and all my bones are out of joint;
my heart is like wax;
      it is melted within my breast;
 my mouth is dried up like a potsherd,
      and my tongue sticks to my jaws;
      you lay me in the dust of death.
For dogs are all around me;
      a company of evildoers encircles me.
      My hands and feet have shriveled;
I can count all my bones.
      They stare and gloat over me;
they divide my clothes among themselves,
      and for my clothing they cast lots (Ps 22:15-19)

Be gracious to me, O LORD, for I am in distress;
> my eye wastes away from grief, my soul and body also.

For my life is spent with sorrow,
> and my years with sighing;

my strength fails because of my misery,
> and my bones waste away (Ps 31:10-11)

Wretched and close to death from my youth up,
> I suffer your terrors; I am desperate.

Your wrath has swept over me;
> your dread assaults destroy me.

They surround me like a flood all day long;
> from all sides they close in on me (Ps 88:16-18)

My bones cling to my skin and to my flesh,
> and I have escaped by the skin of my teeth (Job 19:20).

There is nothing more depressing than betrayal by friends (Job 19:19; Pss 31:12; 88:9, 19), especially if they join with enemies or become enemies themselves.

II. A Study of Social Alienation in Psalm 22

Psalm 22 has a distinctive character among the lament psalms because of its high intensity of feeling. It expresses anguish, recalls God's wonders, calls for rescue, and looks for God's universal reign. As in many of the lament psalms, the poet is derided for his fidelity and loyalty to God and his situation looks gloomy because God has abandoned him. The psalm gives a graphic and powerful description of a sufferer who trusts in God, but is forsaken by him and is left in the hands of his enemies; yet he continues with his plaintive cry and concludes with a hopeful promise of thanksgiving.

Although the reason for the persecution spoken of in Psalm 22 is unknown, it is possible that the psalmist was persecuted for his fidelity to God (v. 9). The poet is someone who, despite his desperate situation, still hopes in the saving power of God. The poet suffered alienation from members of the society that he interacts with.

A. Literary Analysis of Psalm 22

Psalm 22 begins with a lament (vv. 1-22) and ends with the promise of thanksgiving (vv. 23-32). Psalm 22 is a lament psalm with most of the typical elements of a lament, namely: an address to God, description of present need, plea for help, motivations for God's hoped-for intervention, and a vow to offer praise when the plea is granted. It is an individual prayer because it reflects personal affliction and calls on God to come to the psalmist's rescue.

The psalmist mentions his kin and a great assembly, but indicates that he was ostracized; the psalmist's enemies probably do not belong to the community of God's people because they say,

> "Commit your cause to the Lord;
>> let him deliver—let him rescue the one in whom he delights" (v. 9).

Some scholars, for example, Briggs and Briggs, and Hirsch, propose that the poet was an individual or the king praying on behalf of all Israel.[5]

The poet refers to powerful and rapacious people as "beasts" (vv. 13-14, 17-18, 21-22). In the literature of the ANE, animal imagery is often used to represent demonic forces or evil powers.[6] As evildoers, his enemies have no standing with God, because evil leads to destruction. The last figure of speech in the lament section leads into a hopeful future: "God has rescued me from the horns of the oxen" (v. 22).

The second half of the psalm (vv. 23-32), the praise section, is filled with the language of kinship and references to friendliness and communal life, which eventually lead to worship. While the first section reflects the persecution and antagonism suffered by the poet, the second section records the poet's reintegration and acceptance into the community. At the end of the psalm the poet expresses the hope of

---

[5] Charles A. Briggs and Emilie G. Briggs, *The Book of Psalms* (ICC; 2 vols.; Edinburgh: T & T Clark, 1976) 1. 190-201; Samson R. Hirsch, *The Psalms: Translation and Commentary* (New York: Philipp Feldheim, 1960) 159-69.

[6] J. Clinton McCann, Jr., "The Book of Psalms," *NIB* 4 (Nashville: Abingdon Press, 1996) 640-1280, here 763.

enjoying the company of his society and of extolling God in the midst of his community.

The repetition of the same words, "far" (vv. 2, 12, 20), "cry" (vv. 2, 6, 25), "trust" (vv. 5 [2x], 6), and "praise" (vv. 4, 23, 24, 26, 27) constitutes the theological thrust of the poem. This thrust is strengthened by words with equivalent meanings, for example, "God" (vv. 2 [2x], 3, 11) and "LORD" (vv. 9, 20, 24, 27, 28, 29, 31); and the frequency of their occurrence highlights the psalmist's need for God. The words "deliver" (vv. 5, 9, 21, 31), "save" (vv. 6, 22), "rescue" (vv. 9, 22), and "help" (vv. 2, 12, 20) express the psalmist's need of assistance. Because God has delivered his ancestors, the poet believes God will also deliver him (Ps 22:5).

B. Structural Analysis of Psalm 22

The psalm is divided into two parts: lament (vv. 1-22) and praise (vv. 23-32), with the lament itself being subdivided into two sections: vv. 1-12 and vv. 13-22. These are subdivided once again into smaller units: vv. 1-12 consist of vv. 1-6 and vv. 7-12 and include expressions of trust (vv. 4-6, 10-11), petition (v. 12), and complaint (vv. 1-3, 7-9).[7] Similarly, vv. 13-22 may be subdivided into complaint (vv. 13-16, 17-19) and petition (vv. 20-22). The following major divisions can be distinguished: invocation (vv. 1-3), personal lament (vv. 7-9, 15-16), and lament about the enemy (vv. 8-9, 13-14, 17-19). The lament section is followed by a narrative section of praise. The praise section, vv. 23-32, is subdivided into vv. 23-27 and vv. 28-32.

The structure noted above is marked by inclusions based on the psalmist's choice of words. For example vv. 1-22 are framed by "you do not answer" in v. 3 and "you answered me" in v. 22, vv. 1-12 by "why are you so far from helping me?" in v. 2 and "do not be far from me" in v. 12. Also, in vv. 13-22, the psalmist mentions animals both in v. 13 and again in v. 22. In the praise section, "I will tell of your name" in v. 23 is picked up by "and proclaim his deliverance" in v. 32.

---

[7] The inclusion of a review of God's past benefits is limited normally to communal laments; it is unusual in an individual lament. The psalmist lists God's past benefit in two ways: his dealings with his people (vv. 4-6) and his relationship with the psalmist (vv. 10-11). See also Westermann, *The Living Psalms,* 82.

C. Social Alienation in Psalm 22

The purpose of this section of our study is to explore social alienation in Psalm 22. I shall treat this topic under three different headings:

1. Social alienation results in the search for divine intervention;
2. The physical and psychological effects of social alienation;
3. The psalmist's desire to be reintegrated into society.

1. Social Alienation Results in the Search for Divine Intervention

The effects of abandonment by a society are a characteristic feature of some psalms of lament. The poet begins with a cry for help (v. 2) and words indicating the absence of God in his life.

a. The Silent God (vv. 1-3)

The expression of despair in prayers of lament is evoked by the feeling of the absence of God in the life of the sufferer. The petitioner addresses God by invoking his name in a cry "My God, my God," (v. 2) because his supplication has received no answer. The repetition of the invocation "My God" expresses the depth of the affliction of the psalmist.[8] Despite his suffering, his relationship with God continues. He still calls Yhwh "my God" and repeats this again in vv. 3 and 11. No matter how desperate the psalmist has become, he cannot deny the relationship.[9]

The repetition of the interrogation "why" in v. 2 expresses the poet's shock at God's silence whiles his deep distress is expressed by the verb "abandon." A plea for assistance always expresses a hope for redemption and reinstatement in one's own community. The word "far" (v. 2) reinforces the sense of abandonment of the psalmist. The word recurs again in vv. 12 and 20 and expresses the full force of the psalmist's experience of the absence of God. The theme of gods abandoning their worshipers is a common phenomenon in the ANE cultures.[10]

---

[8] Hans-Joachim Kraus, *Psalms 1-59* (Continental Commentary; trans. Hilton C. Oswald; Minneapolis: Fortress Press, 1993) 294.

[9] Westermann, *The Living Psalms,* 84.

[10] See Lambert, "The Poem of the Righteous Sufferer *Ludlul bēl Nēmeqi,*" *BWL,* 33 lines 43-44.

The verbal noun "roaring" likens the psalmist's cry to the roaring of a lion and gives a vivid picture of his affliction. The words "by day" and "by night" in v. 3 express the absence and the silence of God and suggest the long duration of the sufferer's pleading (see also Ps 88:1-3).[11] His cry "day" and "night" establishes the mood of anguish and isolation because there is "no answer" to his plea; as a consequence, he cannot have "rest."

Kraus notes that the psalmist's sense of abandonment springs from God's silence. However, as Kraus also points out, God's silence in psalms of lament does not lead the supplicant to renounce God but rather to cleave to God without rest until a solution is found.[12]

b. Motivation: Appeal to History (vv. 4-6)

God is "holy" (v. 4) and has no equal. God's holiness demands justice, as the psalmist realizes. Unfortunately, the psalmist is not experiencing the justice of God. God's holiness is far from him, alien to the psalmist. Yhwh, the God of Israel, no longer behaves as expected. Yhwh cared for the ancestors and so, the psalmist believes, God should care for him. His confidence grows as he recalls that it is Yhwh who delivered his ancestors in the past. The psalmist's present distress is contrasted with God's past glorious deeds of deliverance.

The phrase "our ancestors" in v. 5 indicates that the God of the poet is also a God of the whole community of Israel, which includes both the living and the dead. The poet's trust in God is based on what God has done in the past; it is because of his past glorious deeds that he is "enthroned on the praises of Israel," (v. 4). In the sacred poems of the ANE, poets petition their gods for assistance through acts of thanksgiving and praise, recounting the attributes of the gods.[13] The whole verse highlights the contrast between what God has done in the past and what he is not doing now.

---

[11] Kselman explains the absence of God in terms of both space and time. See John Kselman, "Why Have You Abandoned Me? A Rhetorical Study of Psalm 22," in *Art and Meaning: Rhetoric in Biblical Literature* (ed. David J. A. Clines, David Gunn, Alan J. Hauser; JSOTSup 19; Sheffield: JSOT Press, 1982) 172-98, here 183.

[12] Kraus, *Psalms 1-59*, 295.

[13] J. David Pleins, *The Social Vision of the Hebrew Bible. A Theological Introduction* (Louisville: Westminster John Knox Press, 2001) 419.

The verb "trust" is used twice in v. 5 and once in v. 6. It refers to the "our fathers" in v. 5 who trusted God and experienced his living presence in their lives through the wonders he worked for them in Egypt. That the deliverance from Egypt became a source of trust for Israel in the Lord is seen in many psalms (see Pss 78:12, 43-55; 106:9-12; 135:8-12; 136:10-22). The psalmist's confession of trust reveals his state of hopelessness in his situation and his hope that God will intervene as he did before.[14] One can identify three keywords in vv. 1-6: *pālaṭ* ("deliver," v. 5) or *mālaṭ* ("deliver," v. 6), *ʿānāh* ("answer," v. 3), and *bāṭaḥ* ("trust," vv. 5-6). These three words are used throughout the Psalter to express the psalmist's trust and dependence on God.

The psalmist uses personal address to emphasis his relationship with God. For example, vv. 2-3 have "you" and "I," vv. 4-6 are dominated by "you," vv. 7-9 by "I," while v. 5 has "our." In short, "I" (the poet) relates to "you" (God) because of "our" (ancestors). The poet addresses God as "holy," "king," and "savior" to motivate him to act accordingly.

2. The Physical and Psychological Effects of Social Alienation

His abandonment by the psalmist's society is evidenced in his physical appearance and affects him mentally. The poet's enemies are represented as beasts, and beasts are a threat to human life. Job, similarly, may imply his friends are beasts eating his flesh (Job 19:22).

a. Animal Imagery

Verses 13-22 depict the psalmist's enemies as dangerous beasts. The poet chiastically alternates human body parts and references to beasts:

> Vv. 13-14: beasts
> Vv. 15-16: body parts
> V. 17a: beasts
> Vv. 17b-19: body parts
> Vv. 21-22: beasts

---

[14] McCann, "The Book of Psalms," 762.

The progression of beast-human-beast-human-beast in the psalm's imagery is a good rhetorical reflection of the psalmist's emotional anxiety. The animal imagery presents the psychological and the sociological trauma that the psalmist went through and so enables the reader to sense the effect of social alienation on the psalmist.

The phrase "many strong bulls of Bashan" (v. 13) is a metaphorical expression referring to formidable enemies; in some the ANE texts "bulls" represent demonic forces.[15] Bashan was a fertile grazing plateau northeast of the Jordan and famous for its cattle (see Deut 32:14; Ps 68:16). The bulls of Bashan were deemed fierce, enormous, and dangerous.[16]

The psalmist used "roar" for himself in v. 2 and now uses the same term for his enemies in v. 14. But here the enemies "tear" as well. The poet has been stripped of his dignity as a human being because of isolation and torture. The poet tells of his misfortune but says not a word about personal faults that would have merited such torture and abandonment.

The dogs of vv. 17 and 21, Clifford observes, are not scavengers but hunting dogs, which are portrayed on ancient seals attacking human beings.[17] Such dogs usually moved in packs and so are called "an assembly of maltreaters."[18] The author also refers to his enemies as a pack of evildoers, similar to a pack of dogs.

b. Dehumanization (vv. 7-9)

This section features the social aspect of the poet's suffering and explains what the attitude of others means to the poet. He has been made comparable to a worm, to nothingness (cf. Job 25: 6). His enemies take advantage of his alienation and taunt him even more. The statement "they shake their heads" (v. 8) refers to the mockery of his enemies. The attitude of his enemies intensifies his suffering and makes him sink deeper into loneliness. The sufferer is perhaps being persecuted for his fidelity to God.

---

[15] Ibid., 763.

[16] Richard Clifford, *Psalms 1-72* (Abingdon Old Testament Commentaries; Nashville: Abingdon Press, 2002) 126; Robert Alter, *The Book of Psalms: A Translation with Commentary* (New York: W. W. Norton, 2007) 73.

[17] Clifford, *Psalms 1-72,* 126.

[18] Briggs and Briggs, *The Book of Psalms,* 1. 196.

c. Disintegration of Body Parts

The petitioner's physical agony is occasioned by suffering, which even though is internal pain may be described in terms of bodily sensations. The statements "I am poured out like water" (v. 15), "my bones are out of joint" (v. 15); and "my heart is like wax, it is melted in my breast" (v. 15) express the dissipation of his strength, the crumbling of the seat of his vital force, the weakening of the muscles of his body, and his psychological breakdown.[19] He is dried up like a potsherd (v. 16); his tongue adheres to his jaws. God has laid him "in the dust of death."[20]

d. Near-death Situation

In laments, death sometimes appears inevitable for the sufferer. In the case of this psalmist, his body is emaciated (v. 18). His bones are dislocated within his body. His enemies have divided his garments among themselves because they expect him to die (v. 19). A similar situation is echoed in a Mesopotamian hymn, which says: "The coffin lay open, and people already helped themselves to my valuables; before I was even dead, the mourning was already done." [21]

3. The Psalmist's Desire to Be Reintegrated into Society

The desire to be reunited to loved ones occasions the psalmist's plea to a higher authority for deliverance.

a. Complete Abandonment to the Power of God

The psalmist has confidence that God will save him. His trust in God is seen in the cry "my God, my God" (v. 2), which expresses his intimate relationship with God. His firm belief that it is only God who can save him, and will save him, is evident in his repeated plea for God to be near and not far away from him (vv. 2, 12, and 20).

---

[19] Terence Collins, "The Physiology of Tears in the Old Testament: Part II," *CBQ* 33 (1971) 185-97, here 191-94; Alter, *The Book of Psalms*, 73.

[20] The "dust of death" is another term for the netherworld, "Sheol." Sheol is a place for the dead where there is no worship of God. We shall see more references to Sheol in Psalm 88.

[21] Arthur Ungnad, *Die Religion der Babylonier und Assyrer* (Jena: Eugen Diederichs Verlag, 1921) 230, cited in Kraus, *Psalms 1-59*, 298.

The "horn" represents the power from which God has to deliver him (v. 22). The term "haste" in v. 20 shows the urgency of his need for rescue. Verse 23 is a turning point in the psalm.[22] The psalmist now no longer laments, but rather gives thanks to God.

b. The Vow as a Promise in Return for Deliverance

It is normal to give thanks for a favor received. The supplicant promises to make known the name of God after his deliverance (v. 23). His praise will be a testimony that his plea in vv. 2-3 has been heard. It is a common phenomenon in the Bible that people who are in distress make vows to bring offerings to God (Lev 7:11-18) when delivered. Such a vow to God is not to be understood as a bribe but rather as an acknowledgement of the relationship between God and the petitioner.[23] The promised payment of vows, McCann holds, "is a typical element of the prayers for help and songs of thanksgiving (see Ps 56:12; 61:8; 116:14, 18), and such payment apparently involved a thank offering and sharing of a sacrificial meal."[24] Yhwh is known to have done mighty deeds in the past, and now the psalmist will add his own story of deliverance to those already told of Yhwh. His gratitude is for his hoped-for reintegration with his brothers and sisters (v. 23) and his praise will resound from the community of worshipers (v. 26).

The singer announces the "the name" (v. 23) of Yhwh to the worshiping "assembly" (v. 23) because from "the name" of Yhwh came the power of his rescue.[25] Those who fear Yhwh always bow to him and those who will hear of the poet's deliverance will bow in praise of Yhwh and Yhwh's enemies will be ashamed. The "fear" (v. 24) of Yhwh (reverential fear) will be experienced among the "progeny" of Jacob or Israel (v. 24). God's deliverance will be heard not only by the psalmist's immediate friends and family but also by the whole of Israel and to the ends of the world (v. 28).

c. God's Provident Care for the Poor

God always cares for ʿānî ("the poor" or "the afflicted," v. 25), he is always with the afflicted (cf. Pss 9:13: 34:7; 35:10; 40:18;

---

[22] Alter, *The Book of Psalms*, 75.

[23] Kraus, *Psalms 1-59*, 299.

[24] McCann, "The Book of Psalms," 764.

[25] Kraus, *Psalms 1-59*, 299.

140:13); and the psalmist, having being afflicted himself, believes God has heard his plea. God does not despise (v. 25) what human beings despise (v. 7).[26] The confidence that God has heard his plea is the reason for the psalmist's praise. If God could be the cause of the psalmist's death (v. 16), then God is the source of his praise as well (vv. 25-26) because his life depends on God. The poet has come to a new understanding of God's silence. God was present in his suffering. God did not "hide his face" (v. 25) from his faithful one (v. 25), so God will save him and his praise will be a response to God's deliverance because he is trustworthy (v. 26). The verb *sātar* ("hide" or "conceal") is used (v. 25) to express God's absence and is an important way of suggesting God's withdrawal from someone that is commonly used in psalms of lament in the Bible (cf. Pss 27:9; 69:18; 88:15).

Those who seek the Lord will find him. The sufferer has become a living sign that calls other sufferers to trust in God. The "poor" are the faithful ones, the persecuted, the sick, the needy, the lowly, or people in the same category as the psalmist himself (v. 27). The expression, "May your hearts live forever" (v. 27), directed to the assembly, implies that God gives life to all those who seek him. They will enjoy a life of nearness to God at all times.[27]

d. The Universal Reign of God

The whole earth will be united in praise of God (v. 28). God is the creator of the world and rules the world; his governance will be remembered and all the earth will "return" to him (v. 28). Then the poet will regain his status among those of his social class.

The word "brother" (v. 23) and the phrase "all the families of nations" (v. 28) are generic expressions for human society. All human beings will worship the Lord because the Lord is king and the world belongs to him (v. 29). According to Isaiah, God's sovereignty is to be acknowledged by the entire human race (cf. Isa 24:14-23; 25:1-3; 43:12-23) because of who he is.

All the living, even those yet to be born (vv. 31-32), will acknowledge the good deeds of God and word will be passed on from

---

[26] Clifford, *Psalms 1-72*, 128.
[27] Kraus, *Psalms 1-59*, 300.

generation to generation; even those who have gone down to the dust (v. 30) will praise God. Verse 30 looks beyond Sheol. The dead have no access to God and do not praise him (see Pss 6:6; 88:11-13), but after the barrier between them is broken, then the dead will praise God. The mention of the living, those yet to be born, and the dead all giving praise to God, is suggestive of the African family system in which the family consists of the living, those yet to be born, and the dead.

God's presence in the affliction of the sufferer is a help for understanding God, human life, and human death. Since the poet is one of God's own faithful, he believes that God will deliver him as a lesson to all sufferers that God does not abandon his faithful sufferer but abides with him.[28] The poet will not hesitate to call on the dead to praise God because they had praised him in their lifetimes.

III. A Study of Social Alienation in Psalm 31

This psalm is an individual lament that expresses an unshakable affirmation of trust in God. The psalm teaches personal and total surrender to God. God came to the aid of the petitioner to save him from all the lies, slander, and oppression that he suffered at the hands of his enemies (v. 8). The saddest portion of the psalm concerns the psalmist's abandonment by his family and friends. It is difficult to differentiate between his loved ones and enemies because both groups behaved equally badly toward him.

A. Literary Analysis of Psalm 31

The psalm opens with words that give a summary of the whole psalm (vv. 1-3), words that are similar to those of Ps 71:1-3. Psalm 31 can be divided into two distinct parts: lamentation (vv. 1-19) and thanksgiving (vv. 20-25). The lament section describes the severity of the poet's distress and explains how he was marginalized by his enemies and loved ones. It consists of statements of trust (vv. 3, 4-9, and 15-16) and petitions (vv. 1b-2, 10-14, and 17-19). The thanksgiving section concludes the psalm and extends an invitation to loyalty and love of God.

---

[28] McCann, "The Book of Psalms," 766.

The poet seeks God's intervention three times (vv. 1-6a, 9a-13, and 16-18) and three times he expresses the joy of deliverance (vv. 6b, 8-9b, 22-23). These three instances of petition and expression of joy for deliverance divide the psalm into three separate segments. Each section of petition and celebration of deliverance creates tension. This tension McCann refers to as "the persistent reality of the life of faith."[29] Faith is essential in order to endure torments from an enemy while hoping that God will come to the rescue. The poet makes a special plea against his enemies in vv. 18-19; in a similar manner, Job warns his friends of the future consequence of their attitude (Job 19:28-29).

The nature of the affliction the psalmist suffered is not mentioned, but the psalm does refer to the fierce opposition he suffered (vv. 8, 12, 14, 16, 19). Since his trust is in God, mockery of him is mockery of God and his shame is God's shame. God must deliver him from his shame. The poet appears confident (vv. 1-4) despite his persecution (vv. 9-16). The progressive profession of trust in the psalm is a lesson of trust in God. The psalmist is happy that Yhwh heard his plea (v. 23). The poet encourages his hearers to give thanks for his deliverance and to hold fast to the Lord (v. 25).

The psalm explains how the life of an individual can be weakened and devastated through abuse by enemies (vv. 10-11, 13) and the turning away of friends and loved ones (v. 12). His enemies slandered the psalmist with their lies (vv. 19-20) and planned to murder him (vv. 5, 14) while his friends avoided him. He has lost his social identity; his life was in danger.[30] He has to seek assistance and his only hope of refuge is in God (v. 6).

The remarkable feature in this psalm is its use of the words *ṣəḏāqāh* ("righteousness," v. 2), *ʾĕmeṯ* ("faithfulness," v. 6), *ḥeseḏ* ("steadfast love," vv. 8, 17, 22), and *ḥānan* ("mercy," v. 10).[31] These words concern God's own attributes. The psalmist makes four appeals

---

[29] Ibid., 802.

[30] Alec Basson, "'Friends Becoming Foes': A Case of Social Rejection in Psalm 31," *VE* 27 (2006) 398-415, here 398.

[31] These words are often used in times of joy and sorrow. In times of joy, they are used to praise the mighty deeds of God; in time of sorrow, they are used by petitioners to strengthen their faith in God and seek his help. For example, the psalmists use them in their request for forgiveness of sin (Psalm 51), for deliverance from enemies (Psalm 6), and as the source of their praise of God (Psalm 5).

in succession to these attributes: God's "steadfast love" (vv. 8, 17, 22), "faithfulness" (v. 6), "righteousness" (v. 2), and "mercy" (v. 10) in his affliction.

The poet's choice of words for the urgent deliverance he seeks include deliverance (vv. 2, 3, 9, 16), rescue (v. 3), salvation (vv. 3, 17), and redemption (v. 6). The deliverance can come only from God. The psalmist uses "LORD" ten times (vv. 2, 6, 7, 10, 15, 18, 22, 24 [2x], 25) because the LORD is his "refuge" (vv. 2, 3, 4, 5, 20), "fortress" (vv. 3, 4), and "rock" (vv. 3, 4), who has to deliver him from "shame" (vv. 2, 18 [2x]). No one takes delight in shame and God has to deliver him for the sake of his "steadfast love" (vv. 8, 17, 22). The poet uses "trust" (vv. 7, 15) to voice his confidence and entrust his life (my life: vv. 6, 11, 14) into God's hands because he believes in his "righteousness" (vv. 2, 19). The psalm is "the act of self-surrender to Yahweh." [32]

B. Structural Analysis of Psalm 31

This psalm, as already mentioned, is divided into two main sections: lament (vv. 1-19) and thanksgiving (vv. 20-25). The lament (vv. 1-19) is subdivided into vv. 1-6a, 6b-9, 10-16, and 17-19. Each of the lament subdivisions begins with a petition (vv. 1, 10, 17) and ends with a thanksgiving (v. 6b, 8-9, 15-16, and 20-25). The psalm moves between lament and thanksgiving, each section giving the impression that the sufferer has come to the end of the recitation of his sufferings (vv. 6b, 8-9b, 22-23) only to initiate another lament (vv. 10-18), until finally the psalm ends with a thanksgiving (vv. 20-25).

The petitions in the lament (vv. 1-3, 10-14, 17-19) are interwoven with words of trust (vv. 4-9 and 15-16). But basically we can say that vv. 1-6 are about trust in God, vv. 7-8 are a resolution to praise God, vv. 9-18 give the reason for the psalmist's praise, vv. 19-22 are the praise itself, while in vv. 23-24 the psalmist summons his hearers to join in his praise. This structure is marked by shifting themes and the repetition of words.

C. Social Alienation in Psalm 31

I shall study the text under the following headings:

---

[32] Kraus, *Psalms 1-59*, 367.

1. The dire need for divine intervention as a result of social alienation;

2. Physical and psychological description of the psalmist's social alienation;

3. The need to redeem one's social image.

1. The Dire Need for Divine Intervention as a Result of Social Alienation

An individual alienated by members of society resorts to a power higher than those members. Those who believe in God seek his attention.

a. Faith and Trust in the Salvation of God (vv. 1-3)

The phrase *ḥāsîtî* ("I seek refuge," v. 2) is an expression of submission and self-surrender by the supplicant; at the same time it is an affirmation of trust. The phrase is commonly used in lament psalms, for example, at the opening of Psalms 7, 11, 16, and 71. The words "refuge" (v. 2), "place of safety" (v. 3), and "stronghold" (v. 3) are synonymous terms that allude to the strength of God and to the protection he gives to his faithful ones. The petition at the beginning of the psalm calls for a bond of protection between the psalmist and Yhwh. The solid nature of the bond is symbolized by the use of the metaphor "rock." The phrase *ḥāsîtî* often goes with *ṣûr* ("rock," v. 3; see Pss 18:3, 32, 47; 19:15; 28:1) and *selaʿ* ("cliff," "rock," v. 4; see Pss 18:3; 42:10).[33]

The psalmist avers that it is only God who can take away his "shame," as stated in vv. 2, 18. Shame is a major theme in the lament language of the Bible (cf. Job 19:13-19; Jer 23:40). The following phrases "incline your ear to me" (v. 3) and "rescue me speedily" (v. 3)

---

[33] The word *ṣûr* ("rock") appears 74 times in the Hebrew and twice in Aramaic (Dan 2:35, 45) in the MT. It occurs 24 times in the Psalms and 6 times in the Book of Job. See Heinz-Josef Fabry, "צוּר," *TDOT*, 12. 311-21. The synonym of *ṣûr* is *selaʿ*. The word *selaʿ* appears 63 times in the OT. See E. Haag, "סֶלַע," *TDOT*, 10. 270-77. "Rock" appears several times in the Bible and especially in the psalms to express the assured safety one finds in God. See Fabry, "צוּר" *TDOT*, 12. 315, 317-21.

express the urgency of the poet's need for rescue from shame. [34] The plea is reinforced by the imperative "incline" and its purpose is to move God to action. Words that evidence the poet's sole dependence on and need for God for deliverance are *pālaṭ* ("deliver," v. 2; cf. Ps 22:5, 9), *nāṣal* ("rescue," v. 3; cf. Ps 7:2), and *yāšaᶜ* ("save," v. 3; cf. Ps 7:2). These are synonymous terms used together to reinforce the poet's plea for salvation.

b. An Appeal for God's Guidance (vv. 4-6)
The poet asks God to deliver him "for the sake of your name" (v. 4). The failure of his fellow human beings to support and guide him leads to his request for the Lord to "lead" and "guide" him (v. 4). God alone can be trusted. These two words "lead" and "guide" usually occur together, although their meaning is similar.

McCann notes that "take me out" (v. 5) is a reminiscent of the life-altering exodus experience of the Israelites. The verb *yāṣāʾ*(go out) is used a number of times in Exodus (see Exod 13:9, 14, 16; 18:1; 20:2); here the poet is requesting a personal exodus for himself from his affliction. God responded to the cry of Israel in Egypt (cf. Exod 3:7, 17) and delivered them. The psalmist's cry is based on God's past activity of liberation; he believes he will be liberated.[35]

The word "net" (v. 5) is an element of the imagery used to describe the wicked activities of the enemy (cf. Pss 9:16; 10:10; 25:15; 35:8; 57:7; 140:6; Job 18:8). The psalmist pleads with God to free him from the trap set for him by his enemies (v. 5) and entrusts his life to the care of God (v. 6; cf. Pss 9:13-16; 25:15; 140:2-6) because he sees God as the source of stability, protection, and victory.

The word *rûah* designates the "breath of life" and the "potential for life"; the psalmist's vitality is what he has placed in the hands of God. The hand symbolizes God's power. The petitioner's confidence in his deliverance is based on Yhwh's faithfulness in redeeming his faithful ones (see Exod 34:6) because he is a "faithful God" (v. 6). The psalmist's exclamation "you have redeemed me" (v. 6) is based on his trust in God's past deliverance (cf. Pss 25:22; 26:11). In the past (v. 1), God delivered his ancestors. Clifford observes that "have

---

[34] Alter, *The Book of Psalms*, 105.
[35] McCann, "The Book of Psalms," 800.

redeemed" when said of Yhwh is an expression of a "habitual act" that describes the psalmist's present relationship with God; because God always redeems, the psalmist will be redeemed.[36]

c. Affirmation of Trust in God (vv. 7-9)

This section constitutes a hymn of thanksgiving. The poet affirms his loyalty to God in opposition to his enemies, who are against God (v. 7). His enemies will experience the wrath of God and will not achieve their aim of putting an end to his life. The petitioner rejoices and exalts because God has seen his misery (v. 8). God is the source of his joy and his enemies will be ashamed. The poet has placed his life in God's hand (v. 6) and now he affirms his confidence that God will not hand him over to his enemies (v. 9). God provided a secure and broad open place (v. 9) for him as opposed to the narrow spot that the enemies created for him.

2. Physical and Psychological Description of His Social Alienation

This section elucidates the nature of the psalmist's alienation: the cruelty of his society, the shunning by his family and loved ones, and the violent persecution by his enemies.

a. Effects of His Alienation (vv. 10-11)

The psalmist reintroduces his plight with a detailed description of the depth of his affliction by his enemies and his consequent abandonment by loved ones. The urgency behind his request is expressed with the imperative "be gracious to me" (v. 10). He calls on God for mercy; his eyes, body, and soul are wasting away; his physical distress has intensified. He sees his power of life diminishing; his death is near.

He has been in this sorrowful state for an extended period of time (v. 11). His strength is gone (v. 11) and his bones are out of joint (v. 11); he has been "sighing" (v. 11) day and night.

---

[36] Clifford, *Psalms 1-72*, 162.

b. Abandonment by Friends and Neighbors (vv. 12-14)

These verses recall the shame from which the psalmist asked God to deliver him in v. 2. He is socially ostracized; no one sympathizes with him. The petitioner has become a "scorn" (v. 12) for his enemies, a social outcast. His appearance is a dreadful sight to his neighbors, and to his friends he became an object of horror and a threat (v. 12); when they see him, "they flee" (v. 12). Most people have friends to rely on in times of sorrow. When one's trusted friends turn against one in a time of need, it can be very devastating.

He is forgotten and smashed like a clay vessel (v. 13). The verb "forget" (v. 13) features prominently in laments. To forget is to abandon. The poet is assumed to be dead; it is only the dead who are forgotten. The expression "forget," together with a "broken vessel," best describes the poet's wretched condition. He has started experiencing death and his life has become as useless as a broken vessel. His uselessness to society is seen in the reference to the enemy conspiring to take away his life (v. 14). The psalmist encounters violence on two fronts: abandonment by his friends and neighbors and attack by his enemies; he is alienated.

3. The Need to Redeem One's Social Image

The sufferer has to regain his position in the society. The desire of a sufferer to redeem his image may take different forms. He may examine himself to determine if there is any guilt that might have provoked his plight. Job is a typical example of such a response when he reexamines his whole life and finally makes his case for vindication. The poet pleads with God to reverse his shame and disgrace (v. 17). He knows what is ahead of him; he overheard the plot of his enemies but is powerless to fight against them. He seeks the protection of God against his enemies and asks for vengeance (vv. 18-19).

a. Resignation to the Will of God (vv. 15-17)

Mention of the deadly conspiracy in v. 14 is followed by the psalmist's affirmation of trust in God, comparable to that in vv. 6-9. He uses both the proper name of God, "Yhwh" and the general divine name "God" in the same verse (v. 15). In combination, the two forms highlight the poet's commitment to God. The poet ends the verse with the acclamation of trust "You are my God" (v. 15) such as one finds in Ps 22:11.

The poet commits his present and future life into the hands of God and pleads for deliverance from his enemies (v. 16). The "hand" (v. 16) represents the power of God.[37] He pleads with God to deliver him from the hands of his enemies (vv. 9 and 16). He is helpless and his longing for God's intervention is seen in the expression "let your face shine on your servant" (v. 17). The psalmist's appeal here is for the gracious blessings and friendly presence of God (v. 17). God has to show his face for the sake of his *hesed* ("goodness," "kindness," v. 17) because the poet has entrusted his entire life into his hands.

b. Vengeance on His Enemies (vv. 18-19)

The psalmist wants vengeance against his enemies so that the enemies may feel the power of God (v. 18). He had appealed against the shame that his enemies intended for him; now he wants God to shame them. The psalmist not only wishes their shame but also that they find that place in Sheol (v. 19) which they wished for him (v. 14). God will, he hopes, silence his enemies' lies (v. 19) and seal their lips in Sheol. Perhaps the enemies bear false witness, which would explain why their lips have to be sealed to keep them from telling more lies. God will prevent any further contempt or scorn on the enemies' part and will exercise his power against these enemies. The psalmist, on the other hand, will not be silenced; he will continue to love and praise God for his faithfulness (v. 24).

c. Praise of God's Ultimate Goodness (vv. 20-25)

The psalmist sings praise to God, as is typical in psalms of lament. The exclamation expressed in the phrase "O how abundant is your goodness" (v. 20) opens a new section. The psalmist says God is kind to those who fear him (v. 20) and proclaims God's goodness.[38] The praise concerns God's provident care; God has delivered the psalmist from his alienation. The second colon of v. 20 recalls God's

---

[37] McCann, "The Book of Psalms," 801.

[38] The above exclamation adds feeling to the litany of God's blessings and expresses the intensity of this feeling. See Luis Alonso Schökel, *A Manual of Hebrew Poetics* (trans. Adrian Graffy; Rome: Editrice Pontificio Istituto Biblico, 2000) 152.

great goodness to the psalmist, which is seen and heard by all the people.

The psalmist believes God's deliverance will add to God's glory. God protects and guides those who fear him from their enemies by keeping them in his presence, "in the shelter of your presence" (v. 21). God's protection as recounted in v. 21 recalls the poet's reference to God in vv. 2-3 as a place of refuge and a rock.

The psalmist blesses God because he has experienced his steadfast love. God has made him into a fortified city. "To bless the Lord is to acknowledge his divine blessing publicly."[39] In times of suffering, it is possible to think God has abandoned one, but God is always present with his faithful ones, even in their deepest suffering. When the psalmist called, God answered him (v. 23). Finally, the poet attributes his deliverance to God's faithfulness. He is always faithful and loyal to those who love him (v. 24). The psalm confirms that one's life is safe in the hands of God.

The poet's faithfulness and dependence on God are rewarded with protection, respect, recognition, and the identity that all human beings seek and deserve. His restoration enabled him to be reintegrated into his society. God has removed the shame he had experienced. He thought he was alienated completely (v. 23), but now he experiences the divine help which abounds for all who seek God. He speaks of God's goodness because he has experienced it.

IV. A Study of Social Alienation in Psalm 88

Psalm 88 has a very distinct character among the psalms of lament because of its high intensity of feeling and the severity of the complaint of the sufferer.[40] The psalm is a prayer concerning abandonment by God: the justice of God has failed.[41] Clifford considers the psalm as "the most anguished and least hopeful lament in

---

[39] Clifford, *Psalms 1-72,* 163.

[40] McCann, "The Book of Psalms," 1027.

[41] Walter Breuggemann, *The Psalms and the Life of Faith* (Minneapolis: Fortress Press, 1995) 106.

the Psalter."[42] For Brueggemann the psalm is "an embarrassment to conventional faith."[43] The psalm is pervaded with words that show the dreadfulness of the psalmist's suffering. The language of the psalm is that of someone whose life is on the verge of ending (vv. 1-3, 10, and 14) and who calls urgently for divine intervention. It is urgent that God do his saving work before it is too late.

The poet is separated from society and forgotten by God. He sees the threat of death looming over him. Such a threat accounts for the poet's use of words associated with death. He complains about how death separates people from God. He asks to be rescued from death and blames God for his suffering, just as Job blames God for causing his alienation from family, friends, and loved ones (Job 19:13).

A. Literary Analysis of Psalm 88

The psalm offers no hope from beginning to end. It expresses a need for God that supersedes any other of life's essentials. The poet does not mention personal enemies, but speaks only of his intense suffering. The psalmist is not identified and the actual cause of his suffering is not mentioned; indeed, the only information we have about the psalmist in the psalm is that his plight began when he was young (v. 16). Two verses, vv. 9 and 19, express the psalmist's complaint that God is responsible for his suffering. Like Job, the psalmist is helpless, and one might expect his plea to God would evoke a response from God. But God still remains silent.

The psalmist cried out to God for help on three separate occasions, vv. 2, 10, 14, which provide a threefold division to the psalm. Each cry is followed by words that show that every possible means for finding help has been exhausted without any result. The psalm is filled with emotions of hopelessness; almost every sentence has a connection to death. Brueggemann calls the psalmist's experience "'the dark night of the soul,' when the troubled person must be and must stay in the darkness of abandonment, utterly alone."[44]

The first section (vv. 2-10a) registers the psalmist's suffering and his complaints about his unheeded plea. The second section (vv.

---

[42] Richard Clifford, *Psalms 73-150* (Abingdon Old Testament Commentaries; Nashville: Abingdon Press, 2003) 86.

[43] Brueggemann, *The Message of the Psalms*, 78.

[44] Ibid.

10b-13) continues with a complaint about God as the cause of the psalmist's suffering. It also highlights the theme of God's abandonment with its rhetorical questions. The third section (vv. 14-18) ends with the psalmist recapitulating his suffering, thus recalling the first section. For example "cry out" appears in vv. 2, 3 and 9 and in vv. 14 and 19; "my prayer" occurs in vv. 3 and 14; "day" occurs in vv. 2 and 18; and "darkness" appears in vv. 7 and 19.

The characteristic features of this psalm resemble those of Psalms 6, 22, 31, 38, and 41. In addition to its parallelism with those psalms, the poet's situation is reminiscent of the story of Job or the suffering servant of Isaiah 53. With the Book of Job, the psalm shares a common theme that is evident in the use of similar vocabulary, for example, *dāʾăbāh* ("faintness," "failure of mental energy"—v. 10 and Job 41:14), *rəpāʾîm* ("shades," "ghosts"—v. 11 and Job 26:5), *ʾăbaddôn* ("destruction," "ruin," "Abaddôn"— v. 12 and Job 26:8; 28:22; 31:12), *nōʿar* ("youth," "early life"—v. 16 and Job 33:25; 36:14), and *ʾēmāh* ("terror," "dread" —v. 16 and Job 20:25).[45]

The death-saturated nature of the psalm has led some scholars to suggest that it was probably written in the depths of the exile when the people were really suffering and were living in a hopeless situation.[46] The psalmist uses figures of speech to express his death-like experience. The psalmist's death language is intriguing. The psalm expresses its preoccupation with death in words or phrases such as, "Sheol" (v. 4), "pit" (vv. 5, 7), "shades" (v. 11), "die" (vv. 6, 11); "perish" (v. 16), "the land of forgetfulness" (v. 13), "darkness" (vv. 7, 13, 19), "grave" (vv. 5, 6, 12), "deep" (v. 7), and "Abbadon" (v. 12). These words and phrases are synonymous and suggest the poet's proximity to death. Such assertions are not uncommon; they appear in other psalms as well (Psalms 6, 28, 30, 143; Job 26:6). Each section of the psalm contains a Hebrew root for darkness. Darkness pervades the experience of the psalmist.[47] In the Book of Job, the word "darkness" (Job 15:22; 18:8; 20:26) or its synonyms "shadow" and "gloom" (Job

---

[45] Briggs and Briggs, *The Book of Psalms*, 1. 243-44.
[46] McCann, "The Book of Psalms,"1027; see also Briggs and Briggs, *The Book of Psalms*, 1. 244-48.
[47] McCann, "The Book of Psalms," ibid.

131

3:5; 10:21-22) become the equivalent of death. These words are used often to refer to the idea or place of death.

The psalmist believes that a response from God will alleviate his plight. He addresses "Yhwh" four times (vv. 2, 10, 14, 15), seeking his "presence" (vv. 2, 3, 14), but with no response. The psalmist, even though he is dying, holds on to God insistently; and despite his harsh words regarding God's unresponsiveness, he maintains his faith in God.

B. Structural Analysis of Psalm 88

The psalm is structurally divided into three sections, each introduced by a form of a verb for calling out (vv. 2-10a, 10b-13, and 14-18).[48] Sections 1 and 3 both focus on the personal suffering of the psalmist. Sections 1 and 3 start with a cry to the Lord (v. 2 and v. 14) and both end with mention of abandonment by friends and neighbors (v. 10a and v. 19).

Section 2 highlights the theme of God's abandonment and contains rhetorical questions. These questions are of two types: those containing words that describe the affliction of the psalmist: "death" and "shades" (v. 11), "grave" and "Abaddon" (v. 12), "darkness" and "the land of forgetfulness" (v. 13); and those containing words that describe the character of God's saving action: "wonders" and "praise" (v. 11), "steadfast love" and "faithfulness" (v. 12), "wonders" and "saving help" (v. 13).

C. Social Alienation in Psalm 88

I shall now study the text under the following headings:

1. Divine absence results in suffering;
2. The effect of social alienation on the life of the poet;
3. The psalmist's desire to be reintegrated into society.

---

[48] Clifford, *Psalms 73-150*, 87; Hans-Joachim Kraus, *Psalm 60-150* (Continental Commentary; trans. Hilton C. Oswald; Minneapolis: Fortress Press, 1993) 192; Breuggemann, *The Message of the Psalms*, 78.

1. Divine Absence Results in Suffering

a. The Silent God (vv. 1-3)

The psalm opens on a tone of intimacy but also with an urgent appeal for rescue. The psalmist addresses God as the one, who saves, "O LORD, God of my salvation," (v. 2); he expresses his unshakable trust that God will save him. This attribute of God has its roots in Exod 15:2 and is repeated in other psalms (cf. Pss 68:21; 89:27). The intention of the address is to move God to action. The psalmist affirms "salvation" as a fundamental attribute of God and voices his own loyalty to God in the formula *yhwh* *ʾĕlōhê* *yəšûʿātî* ("O LORD, God of my salvation"). Both "day" and "night" he cries to God in his "presence," pleading for his intervention (v. 2); yet God remains silent. The frustration caused by God's unresponsive character is a major problem for this supplicant.

b. Reason for the Cry for Help (vv. 4-6)

The psalmist's cry in vv. 4-6 is similar to Job's cry:

> Even when I cry out, 'Violence!' I am not answered;
> I call aloud, but there is no justice (Job 19:7).

The psalmist received no answer to his plea and God fails to intervene to justify him. The urgency of his plea is expressed in the metaphor "my soul is full of troubles" (v. 4), and this is the reason for his cry.

The words "Sheol," "pit," "deep," and "grave" used in these verses express the poet's isolation and his struggle against death. No one comes back from the place of the dead (cf. Eccl 9:5-6; Job 10:20-21), and so he needs to be delivered now. God has the power to restore life. The phrase "going down to the pit" (v. 5) is a common expression for those who are destined for death (cf. Pss 28:1; 30:4; 143:7; Isa 38:18; Ezek 31:14-16; 32:18, 24-30). "The Pit," Brueggemann notes, "is not final judgment or fiery place of punishment. It is only beyond the range of communion."[49]

---

[49] Brueggemann, *The Message of the Psalms,* 79.

The verb *gāzar* ("cut off," v. 6), used with "hand," indicates the poet has been cut off from the power of God. The verb "cut off" is used in the account of the
"Servant of Yhwh" in Isa 53:8 and for the exile in Ezek 37:11. In these cases, the verb expresses the absence of the power of God. The verb *gāzar* is followed by mention of grave and tomb in Isa 53:9. Similarly, in Ezekiel, the word *qeber*, "grave," is found in the same context (Ezek 37:12) as it is in this psalm. These examples suggest that the one who is cut off from God no longer has God's protection and is as good as dead.

The dead are not remembered by the living and they can neither speak with the living nor praise God because they are cut off from the care of God.[50] The psalmist has no strength to fight, and his place of sleep is in Sheol, which means he is counted among the dead (v. 5; see also Job 33:22; Pss 22:19; 107:18; Prov 2:18; 5:5; 7:27). To be in Sheol is to be "released" to the land of the dead.[51] The psalmist is cut off from society and now sees himself cut off also from God. He has no one to appeal to but to remind God of his appalling fate (v. 6). The fate of the sufferer is intensified because he is "in the depths of the Pit, in the regions dark and deep" (v. 7). In v. 6, the psalmist uses the verb *zākar* ("remember") with its deep theological connotations. The theology behind *zākar* is that God neither forgets nor forsakes his faithful ones because he always "remembers" (Exod 3:7); here, however, the psalmist feels himself forgotten.[52]

2. The Effect of Social Alienation on the Life of the Poet

The effects of social alienation are spiritual, physical, and psychological. Spiritually, the psalmist's trust in God is shaken because

---

[50] Kraus, *Psalms 60-150*, 193.

[51] Clifford, *Psalms 73-150*, 88. Sheol is a place of God-forsakenness, of separation from God where no earthly life exists. It is featured frequently in the Book of Job; for example, Job pleads with God to allow him to enjoy some comfort before entering Sheol (Job 10:18-22) and acknowledges the power of God over Sheol (Job 26:5-6).

[52] In the words of Clifford, "The verb *to remember* is important in the Psalter. It does not mean to recall what had been forgotten, but to make a past event present by describing it" (*Psalms 1-72*, 23). The OT uses the verb ("remember") to make present the covenant God made with Abraham, Isaac, and Jacob (Deut 8:18).

his prayers are not being answered; physically, his eyes are wasting away and he is shut in; psychologically, he is disturbed because of the threat of death.

a. God the Cause of His Suffering (vv. 7-8)

The absence of God has resulted in the psalmist's woeful experience of pit and darkness (Ps 88:7, 13, 19; see Ps 143:3; Lam 3:6). The words *məṣôlāh* ("deep," v. 7), *ḥēmāh* ("heat," "kindle," v. 8), and *mišbār* ("water of the sea," v. 8) are mythological and describe the action of the chaotic waters where no life exists. The words recall the destruction of Pharaoh and his army beneath the waves of the sea (Exod 15:4-5).

b. Abandonment by Friends (vv. 9-10, 19)

The psalmist accuses God of causing his friends to abandon him. The poet twice mentions his abandonment by loved ones (vv. 9 and 19). This adds to his pathetic situation. The friends who could support him failed to do so. The reason they abandoned him is not mentioned. Unlike Job, who is said to be repulsive (Job 19:17), there is no explanation given why the psalmist was alienated by his friends (vv. 9, 16-18). There are numerous cases in the Bible where people are ostracized by friends and loved ones (cf. Job 19:13-19; 30:9-15; Ps 31:12; Jer 11:18-20; 12:6). In this psalm, there is no reference to any hostility on the part of the friends who seriously seem not to desire to be in his company.

The psalmist is caged in and cannot escape; he is cornered and wishes to be released from his suffering (v. 9).[53] His eyes have grown dim and do not see well because of his agony. The shedding of tears day and night may have caused his eyes to become swollen. The poet resorts to prayer "I spread out my hands to you," petitioning God to deliver him (v. 10).

---

[53] Kraus notes that in Babylon to heal the sick is to free the victim from fetters. He believes that the psalmist may be expressing the same idea in this verse (Kraus, *Psalms 60-150*, 194).

3. The Psalmist's Desire to Be Reintegrated into Society

Every human being seeks identity and recognition in his or her society. Socially alienated persons long to be reintegrated into society. Reintegration makes the person feel accepted and secure in society. To be reintegrated after having been alienated is always a struggle; and for this reason the psalmist, who has suffered for a long time (v.16) and been condemned by his society, believes it is only God who can deliver him. The desire to be exonerated is greater when the person has been falsely accused.

a. Six Rhetorical Questions Concerning the Place of the Dead (vv. 11-13)

The questions in this section become more urgent because the poet still wants to live and give praise to God. There is no praise for Yhwh in the world of the dead nor remembrance of his mighty deeds. It is only the living who praise God. The poet recalls the wonders God has done; such wonders are not done in Sheol and no one would see them there and so give praise to God. But because God's wonderful deeds were life-saving events, God is praised for them (vv. 11 and 13). The recipients of God's deliverance praise him not in Sheol but among the living (v. 12). The psalmist likewise wants to praise God among the living rather than among the dead, where there is no opportunity to do so (v. 13).

The psalmist appeals to three divine attributes: *ḥeseḏ* ("steadfast love," v. 12), *'emûnāh* ("fidelity," v. 12), and *ṣəḏāqāh* ("righteousness," v. 13). God is known by these attributes and the psalmist expects Yhwh to manifest them. The psalmist's rhetorical questions themselves call for negative answers, as the poet is aware; however, they are also questions that encourage stronger faith and hope; they appeal for life and ask for reintegration into society.[54]

---

[54] Clifford, *Psalms 73-150*, 87. The questions reveal an unremitting, undeterred quest for life, which the petitioner believes Yhwh, and he alone, can give. The bitterness of death is the absence of life with God, which includes praise and worship of God. The unanswered question in this psalm is the "way" of God's absence from the sufferer.

b. A Plea for God's Intervention (vv. 14-19)

The depth of the poet's abject situation does not prevent him from crying again to God. The complaints are all personalized, with emphasis "but I," (v. 14). They call for imminent action in the restoration of life to the psalmist. The section highlights God's distance, beginning with a plea, similar to the one in vv. 1-3, seeking the presence of God. The psalmist offers his prayers "in the morning," idiomatically "every morning" (v. 14), [55] and expects an answer.

Verses 14-15 contain three verbs that are typically used in OT prayers for help. They are *šāwaᶜ* ("cry out," v. 14), *zānaḥ* ("cast off," "reject," or "spurn," v. 15), and *sātar* ("hide" or "conceal," v. 15).[56] These words suggest God's passivity in the face of the psalmist's call. God's inaction means continued suffering for the psalmist, who will continue to suffer from his sickness or from his enemies.[57] The psalmist's affliction is as though the waves of the sea were battling against him (v. 17-18), and there is no one to rescue him. God has cast him off and hides his face from him (v. 15).

The psalmist's plight started in his youth and he has become desperate because his affliction still remains (v. 16; see also v. 9). Just as Job was besieged by God (see Job 6:4; 19:7, 12), so also is the psalmist (v. 17; see also Ps 42:8). He is trapped in the net; he has no option but to give up, because he has no chance of escape (v. 18). Rejected by friends and loved ones in society (vv. 9, 19), his sole companion is darkness.

The psalm ends with *maḥšāḵ*, a word for darkness, with no sign of hope for deliverance. The psalmist's presentation of his case is

---

[55] On the idiomatical expression "in the morning," see Alter, *The Book of Psalms,* 310; see similar examples in Pss 46:6; 90:14; 143:8.

[56] The recurrence of these words highlights the psalmist's affliction and how dependent human beings are on God to deliver them. For *šāwaᶜ* ("cry for help"), see Pss 5:3; 18:42; 22:25; 28:2; 30:3; 31:23. For *zānaḥ* ("cast off," "reject" or "spurn"), see Pss 43:2; 44:10, 24; 60:3, 12; 74:1; 77:8; 89:39. For *sātar* ("hide" or "conceal"), see Job 13:24; Pss 13:2; 22:25; 27:9; 30:8; 44:25; 69:18; 102:3.

[57] The sick, the persecuted, and the economically deprived are considered the poor of Yhwh and Yhwh comes to their aid (cf. Pss 9:14, 19; 10:9, 14; 22:25; 40:18; 41:2-3; 70:5; 72:12-14). It is expected that Yhwh will respond to the psalmist, but the psalmist has had no response.

dramatic and a lesson to all who suffer; even though there is no response from God, one has to keep waiting and believing that God will answer in his own time. This is a situation in which faith faces real life situations. Even though the poet realizes his abject situation, he continues to seek deliverance. To be silent and not speak is to lose one's identity as one of Yhwh's faithful. Even if God is unresponsive, the petitioner needs to continue to present his petition. There may be situations in which there is no answer, yet faithfulness demands complete abandonment to God.

Conclusion

The psalms demonstrate how true human happiness rests in God. Just as Job seeks vindication from God, so the psalmists cry to God to deliver them. God is the creator and the sovereign ruler of the world and all that exists belongs to him. The psalms teach us that life may not be what we think; one needs perseverance in the face of difficulties. Job endured and was vindicated. We see numerous demonstrations of faith in the psalms; the more the supplicants are tortured by their enemies, friends, and loved ones, the more intense becomes their desire for God to intervene. The three psalms we studied agree with the Book of Job in assuring us that God wields the ultimate power in life and that deliverance depends on him. Loyalty and fidelity to God can be a cause of pain, but one has to endure them for the sake of one's relationship to God.

The cry to God in prayers of lament is based on trust in God's steadfast love that endures forever. Kraus notes, "Worship in the OT is not a natural and magical renewal of life, no dramatically engineered importation of power, but an encounter with the Lord of all of life."[58] Worship is an act of thanksgiving to God, who gives life to those who call on him. For his creation, therefore, where there is life, there must be praise.[59] For God's faithful, worship is part of human existence (see Isa 38:9-20) and so long as one is alive, worship is due to God.

God's silence calls for increased faith and loyalty in those who seek his presence. The continuous repetition of the psalmists' call to

---

[58] Kraus, *Psalms 1-59*, 70.
[59] Claus Westermann, *The Praise of God in the Psalms* (trans. Keith R. Crim; Richmond: John Knox, 1965) 160-61.

God to answer and deliver, as in the Book of Job, indicates a remarkable depth of faith. The purpose of the plea is to restore disintegrated life. The psalms and the Book of Job open new possibilities for understanding and accepting human life and death. In this regard, we see life as consisting not only in self-fulfillment with pleasure but also encompassing disappointments and unpleasant situations. Such situations should be endured with trust and full dependence on God, who knows us from birth (cf. Job 10:8-19; Ps 22:10-11). It is in suffering that we need support and encouragement from one another, even to the extent of sharing in the other's sufferings. In the psalms, just as in the Book of Job, there is no human help for the sufferer, however. The psalms show the alienation of the psalmists from their fellow human beings and hence their appeal to God for help.

Although we are people created in the image of God, life can be a struggle; and every human being struggles to live, no matter how burdensome life appears. Psalms 22, 31, and 88 give us shining examples of this struggle.

Chapter Six

The Response of the Sufferer: Job's Words about Alienation of Family, Friends, and Loved Ones

The problem of suffering is common to all humanity. The suffering of the innocent caused by the powerful is very common. In the Bible, God's own laws prescribe protection for the needy. In many cases the psalms do so as well; and the prophets denounce oppression of the poor and the needy. While some suffer through their own fault, it is not always so. Job is an example of an innocent sufferer.

When there is a disaster, the first thought is to rationalize the cause of the problem. Both the victim and the loved ones begin to seek understanding of the problem. When a solution is found to the problem, there is peace; but if a solution is not found a different result is possible. Instead of friends sympathizing with the unfortunate situation and assisting the victim, they may prefer to look for a reason for the problem. Where there is no explanation for the suffering, the victim and loved ones are left in total uncertainty. Such would be the case with Job's wife, family, and friends, but the friends were convinced that sin was the cause of his suffering. This conclusion Job rejected.

The victim seeks a reason for the suffering and questions his relationship with God, if he happens to be a religious person. If the victim faults himself, then pardon is sought; if not, an appeal is made to God to remedy the situation. Such is the case with Job: he questions his way of life and having found no wrongdoing, seeks exoneration from God.

This chapter will be divided into three sections:

a) The expression of disbelief and the intensification of the sufferer's pain. This section deals with the bitterness and frustration faced by Job because of the betrayal and withdrawal of family, friends, and loved ones.

b) Conceptual attitudes of society towards a sufferer. This section deals with social factors that blinded and prevented society from supporting Job, a suffering member who is considered by the society as a deviant and the effect these social factors had on Job, the sufferer.

c) The fight for the integrity: the rebound of the suffering Job. This section describes the positive attitude that Job needed in order to persevere and emerge victorious from his social alienation. This positive attitude includes reflection on past experiences in life (Job chaps. 29–30), examination of conscience (chap. 31), and presentation of one's defense; in Job's case, this even involves taking an oath (27:2-6).

I. The Expression of Disbelief and the Intensification of the Sufferer's Pain

It is shocking and frustrating when one's way of life changes for the worse. The sufferer who has been afflicted with a calamity evaluates his situation. This is especially necessary when the person is isolated by society. When the sufferer is responsible for his suffering he looks for a remedy, but Job has not done any wrong. He is shocked to learn what has happened to his family and his well-being. His first reaction is to rise, tear his robe, shave his head, and fall to the ground and worship (Job 1:20). Job, like any other pious person, calls to mind his way of life, reflects on his lifestyle, but finds that he has done nothing wrong. His piety is described in the first two chapters of the book. He asks the reason for the sudden turn of events in his life and especially why he has been abandoned.

Job's rejection by his family and friends intensified his suffering and worsened his situation. The reader is aware, as Job is not, that his plight was initiated in the heavenly court. Job claims that God is besieging him ("he bursts upon me again and again; he rushes at me like a warrior," 16:14), and he accuses God of being responsible for his plight. But he also accuses society of the same offense ("as through a wide breach they come; amid the crash they roll on," 30:14). The same root is used in different forms in both cases: the verb *pāraṣ* ("break through") and the noun *pereṣ* ("bursting forth") occur in 16:14 and in 30:14. The family and loved ones have caused Job harm, just as God has done.

The harm caused by society is serious because although Job cannot see God, the society he does see refuses to give him any help.

Even if Job were suffering for his sins, he would need the support of his wife, family, and friends. The extreme pain occasioned by their lack of affection and support reaches its climax in chap. 19. If it were up to God and Satan alone, Job's suffering would have been less. The pressure occasioned by abandonment by his family and loved ones (19:13-19) adds exponentially to his suffering (19:21-22).

A. The Family as a Constituent of the Society

The ancient Israelite family was comprised of the father, his wife or wives, children, their married sons with their wives and children, and servants.[1] Individual families constitute the society in which they play a major role; without the family, the society ceases to exist because it is its members that assume responsibility in society. Society, through the process of socialization, encourages individuals of its various families to embrace social rather than personal interests. Whatever the individual in the family learns from socialization is what he or she will live in society. Through this arrangement society becomes more powerful and more important than the individuals who make it up. Putting society before the individual may result in suffering for some of its members.

The honor of a family member reflects honor for the whole family and, similarly, dishonor of a member of the family reflects dishonor on the whole family. Job brought disgrace on his family because of his calamity and subsequently lost his authority over his household (19:16). The consequent abandonment by his family may have been occasioned by their fear of sharing his suffering (cf. 2 Sam 21:1). Social relationships are an integral part of living a good life, and Job's rejection by his family, friends, and neighbors is tantamount to declaring Job dead.

1. Job's Alienation by His Wife and Household

The family is the primary support for any human being. Job's first encounter at the beginning of his suffering was with his wife, who advised him to curse God and die (Job 2:9).[2] This was the very

---

[1] de Vaux, *Ancient Israel: Its Life and Institutions*, 8.

[2] The MT has *bārak* ("bless," 1:5, 11; 2:5, 9) instead of *qālal* ("curse"). But *bārak* is used here as an euphemism, to avoid using an offensive verb with reference to God. It cannot be determined whether it is a scribal substitution or the author's

intention of the accuser, who expected Job to curse God, as his words to God make clear: "But stretch out your hand now, and touch all that he has, and he will curse you to your face" (1:11; see also 2:5). Job's answer to his wife foils the accuser's intention (2:10). His insistence on his innocence reveals his integrity. The sufferer should not be alienated on account of his physical condition. Even if a person appears repulsive, he should not be abandoned, as Job was when he became repulsive to his wife and children (19:17). A spouse should continue to show marital love for the afflicted spouse. Unfortunately, Job's wife did not do so. Job's own servant disobeyed him (19:16) and his guest and maids behaved as if they did not know him (19:15). His kindred forgot about him and made no effort to behave as relatives should. His own friends also ostracized him (19:19). Job was left completely alone.

2. Kinship Neglect as a Failure of Family Responsibility

A kinship group consists of families and is sometimes called *šēḇeṭ* ("tribe") or *mišppāḥāh* ("clan") in the OT. A tribe is an autonomous group of families who may be descended from a common ancestor. A tribe may be called by the name or surname of that ancestor; in the Hebrew Bible it is sometimes preceded by the word *ben-* ("son of"). The members of the tribes are bonded together by the blood relationships they share, and are considered brothers and sisters (Judg 9:2; 1 Sam 20:29; 2 Sam 19:13). The clans are ruled by the heads of families, *zəqēnîm* ("elders"). The individual grows to maturity interacting with this kinship group and through the social process gains social experience as a member of this ancestral group. An individual cannot experience oneself outside one's kinship group. Job belonged to an ancestral group and interacted with them from the time he was born. These are the people who rejected him; social rejection is kinship violation and dishonor.

Kinship denotes close family relations. Their social behavior becomes a language for the kinship group. The kinship relationship,

---

own usage. For the use of *bārak* to soften harsh language in a text, see 1 Kgs 21:10, 13; Ps 10:3. See also Clines, *Job 1-20*, 3; Habel, *The Book of Job*, 78; Dhorme, *The Book of Job*, 4-5; Gordis, *The Book of Job*, 13.

Cross notes, generates legal, political, and religious institutions.[3] Legal, political, and religious institutions form the basis of the Israelite community. Such a basis demands that the society defend and protect a member, whereas Job's kindred deserted him. Relatives have the obligation to help and protect one another (Job 17:3).[4] When an entire group turns against a fellow member, the victim finds it almost impossible to change his or her perception of life, to use intellectual abilities, manifest physical prowess, and a host of other things. "To forsake a fellow kinsman in times of affliction violates the kinship principles, and turns amity into non-amity."[5]

The failure of friends to help in time of need is mentioned in several places in the Bible (see, e.g., Ps 55:13-15) and in other ANE texts. For example, in the *Egyptian Dispute between a Man and His Ba*, the sufferer expressed his dissatisfaction with his friends:

To whom shall I speak today?
Brothers are mean,
The friends of today do not love....

To whom shall I speak today?
The criminal is one's intimate,
The brother with whom one dealt is a foe.

To whom shall I speak today?
The past is not remembered,
Now one does not help him who helped.

To whom shall one speak today?
Brothers are mean,
One goes to strangers for affection.

To whom shall I speak today?
Faces are blank,

---

[3] Frank M. Cross, *From Epic to Canon: History and Literature in Ancient Israel* (Baltimore: John Hopkins University Press, 1998) 3.

[4] de Vaux, *Ancient Israel: Its Life and Institutions,* 11, 22.

[5] Ibid., 406.

Everyone turns his face from his brothers....

To whom shall I speak today?
None are righteous,
The land is left to evil doers.

To whom shall I speak today?
One lacks an intimate,
One resorts to an unknown to complain.
To whom shall I speak today?
No one is cheerful,
He with whom one walked is no more.

To whom shall I speak today?
I am burdened with grief
For lack of an intimate.

To whom shall I speak today?
Wrong roams the earth,
And ends not.[6]

The sufferer in the Egyptian text laments the attitude of his friends because he has to go to strangers, hoping that they will extend the help he really expected from his friends. In Job's case, however, there was no help from strangers, either; those he encountered pretended not to recognize that he needed help. The disloyalty of family and friends adds insult to injury for him.[7]

---

[6] Miriam. Lichtheim, trans., *Ancient Egyptian Literature: A Book of Readings: The Old and Middle Kingdom* (3 vols.; Berkeley: University of California Press, 1973) 1. 163-67, here 166-67. See also Lambert, "The Poem of the Righteous Sufferer *Ludlul bēl Nēmeqi*," 35.

[7] Basson, "'Friends Becoming Foes'," 406.

B. Job's Alienation by Friends and Society

1. The Three Friends of Job

It is a common practice to sympathize with a friend or neighbor who encounters problems and to help the person. Job was visited by his three friends Eliphaz, Bildad, and Zophar. They heard of their friend's misfortune and came to sympathize with him. They were so moved with pity that they sat with him for seven days in silence (2:11-13). Their argument with Job began after Job's conscious reflection on his situation (chap. 3). The conversation turned out to be a psychological trauma for Job because no reason could be given for his suffering. They all believed in the doctrine that good people prosper and wicked people suffer, "deed and consequence" (15:17-35), so the friends concluded that Job must have done something wrong. Religion, as perceived by Job and his friends, is that which gives joy, well-being, peace, prosperity, serenity, and enthusiasm for life to all those who believe and are righteous. Therefore, so long as they continue to be good and worship their God, their well-being in this world is assured.

Jacques Vermeylen observes that in the Book of Job the supposedly wicked character of Job holds a central place in the eight speeches of his friends, with the exception of chap. 25, which contains only five verses; Vermeylen asks "Mais pourquoi cette insistence presque obsédante? Quelle est la fonction de ce thème dans leurs discours?" (But why almost this obsessing insistence? Which is the function of this theme in their speeches?). According to Vermeylen, there is still more to be researched about how Job's friends consider him.[8] His friends' attitude reflects not only the "deed and consequence" belief, but the entire social concept they inherited from their society.

The argument, which was begun by Eliphaz in chap. 4, continues until chap. 31. Chapters 4–31 are poetic and are composed mainly of Job's defense and his friends' accusations that he had sinned. They contain legal words rather than the familiar sapiential words that one expects to find in wisdom literature. The content is legal because

---

[8] See Jacques Vermeylen, "Le Méchant dans les Discours des Amis de Job," *The Book of Job* (ed. W. A. M. Beuken; Leuven: Leuven University Press, 1994) 101-27, here 101.

Job is accused and is forced to defend himself.[9] The argument with his friends is characterized by impatience on the part of both Job and his friends. To his friends Job's argument seems to undermine the foundations of society (18:4). The movement of the argument shows that Job and his friends cannot agree about whether Job is innocent (10:7; 16:17). Job is convinced that he is innocent, while his friends believe that no mortal can be righteous before God (4:17-19). The following are some of the allegations of his friends.

Eliphaz reminds Job of the concept of "deed and consequence" and blames Job for failing to accept the consequence of his evil deeds (4:1-6). It is only fools who are visited by adversity (5:2-5). Job should mind what he says (5:6-7) and stop justifying himself, since he still remains mortal. It is known that evildoers suffer and the righteous prosper (15:17-35). It is insane for Job to criticize God (15:11-13); how can he, a mortal, present himself before God (15:14-16)? No pious person ever receives punishment (22:1-4). Job's punishment is a result of his wicked and oppressive treatment of the poor, the widow, and the orphan (22:5-9). His suffering is the consequence of such wickedness (22:10-11). God punishes only evil people (22:12-30). Once again, Eliphaz advises Job to ask for forgiveness, so that he can regain his former life (22:21-30).

The second friend, Bildad, increases the pressure on Job, blaming him for accusing God of injustice (8:3). Bildad tells Job to repent and ask for forgiveness because evil deeds have far-reaching consequences and it is only wicked people who come to a bad end (18:8-21). He also says that if Job is innocent, it could be his children who sinned (8:4). Unless Job changes his attitude, he will continue to suffer and will die in the process, leaving no inheritance.

Zophar, the third friend, is more radical than the others. He rebukes Job for his impassioned speeches, which will not win him any favor. He accuses Job of being a liar and a hypocrite (11:1-5). He admonishes Job to become wise before God reveals his guilt (11:5). The happiness of the wicked is short-lived; it blossoms like a flower, but withers at the end of the day. No matter how successful and powerful the wicked become, inevitably they will perish (20:1-11).

---

[9] Clines, *Job 1-20*, 437.

Their evil deeds become a source of misfortune and their happiness, like a sumptuous meal, becomes poison which eventually kills them (20:12-16). Divine wrath crushes the criminal and destroys his family; on judgment day the wicked will be condemned by both heaven and earth (20:22-29).

The three friends of Job created difficulties for him. They unduly chastised him and put unnecessary pressure on him, hoping to encourage him to repent. One may not blame the friends; they meant well, wanting to help Job to regain his good life, but they were wrongly indoctrinated. They were convinced that Job must listen to them and stop his senseless defense. For his friends, there is only one thing for him to do, namely, to be converted and thus to reenter the category of good people whose lot is completely different from that of the wicked. Their attitude of mistrust made Job more disappointed, depressed, and isolated. He felt isolated because he was considered impious, a liar, and a hypocrite.

In the world of Job's friends it was believed that no human being exists without sin (4:17), and those sins are punishable in this world (18:18; 20:6-8). Punishment is a chastisement that God sends to discipline evildoers and to encourage them to live good lives (5:12-14, 17-19). It should therefore be unnecessary for a sufferer to question why he or she is suffering, as Job does. Job is supposed to keep quiet, suffer his punishment, and repent of his sins. However, Job, in his conscience, knows that he has not committed any crime. Job's reaction to the role society has imposed on him is a cry of vengeance against his enemies:

> May my enemy be like the wicked,
>   and may my opponent be like the unrighteous (27:7).

Job, aware of his total rejection, warns his friends to change their attitude or face the consequences (Job 19:28-29).

Job expresses anger and warns his friends (Job 19:28-29) because of their ignorance and faulty judgment (16:1-5). Job regards their arguments as unreasonable and senseless (6:6-7). Animals of the field, birds of the air, plants, and fish of the sea know that God has caused his misfortune, but his friends could not (12:7-9). They should give him support, but they have become disloyal, betrayed his friendship, accused him falsely, and abandoned him. He concludes that it is impossible to rely on his friends (6:14-23). He challenges them to prove his guilt, if they think he has sinned (6:24-30). Job does not want to deal with his friends any more, he advises them to keep silent— that will be their wisdom (13:5)! It is disappointing and hurtful for a sufferer who expects support from loved ones, but instead receives bitter accusations and condemnations. On this Dhorme remarks "there is nothing so distressing as desertion by one's friends and relatives (13-14); but when the most intimate bosom friends and confidants become enemies and detractors it spells the extremity of affliction." [10] To agree with his friends would be to give up his integrity, his very essence, the only treasure he has left. Job will not profane himself in the name of friendship; that would be against his integrity.[11] Although the friends insist that no human being can be innocent before God (4:17), Job regards their accusations as evidence of their religious deficiency (25:4).[12]

Job prefers to deal with God, because human judgments are not always just, as he has experienced in the case of his friends. That is why he longs to see God and seeks his intervention. As the story unfolds, one perceives an increase in Job's faith in God and a corresponding decrease of faith in his friends (9:32-35; 16:19-21; 19:25-27). Job's friends intended to be a conscience for Job, but they had become so overzealous that their attempt to influence him was overbearing. When society is not well informed or does not understand a religious teaching, its attitudes can involve serious consequences.

2. Job Ridiculed by Children and Lesser Members of Society

A sufferer who is isolated by society as a deviant enjoys no respect within the society. In Job's case, even neighborhood children, the innocent members of society, free of social bias, make fun of and insult him (19:18). The outcasts of society make fun of him because he has become an outcast among the outcasts.[13] Job recounts how he is scorned and dishonored by people without worth, people whose parents are worthless, poverty stricken, and despicable (30: 1-3). Job's

---

[10] Dhorme, *A Commentary on the Book of Job*, 279.
[11] Clines, *Job 1-20*, 647.
[12] Terrien, *Job*, 192.
[13] Habel, *The Book of Job*, 419.

language is a sign of his hate for what they are doing to him. He is "held in contempt by the contemptible."[14] He compares them to dogs and calls them fools, people without repute. They sing songs to mock him (12:4; 30: 9); his eyes pour out tears to God, hoping that his redeemer will maintain his right with God (16:20-21). Lawlessness in society is blamed on the elders in the society because they are responsible for teaching the young ones. For the young ones to mock an elder of Job's caliber shows how much he has lost touch with his society and the young ones who should accord him respect.

Job's society "abhors" him and keeps a "distance" from him (30:10; see also 19:13, 19).[15] Job cannot ignore their provocation (17:2). Job hates his isolation, but because of their hostile attitude he prefers that they keep their distance. The outcasts rob him of his honor.[16] Socially, Job still deserves his honor, but because of his affliction they deny him his social status, that is, his "nobility" (30:15) that gives him self-esteem, confidence, and power to feel human. For Job, their attitude is an assault against him (16:7-10) and their intent is to disgrace him; he has been cast into the mud and put on a level with dust and ashes (17:2; 30:18-19). Job sobs with pain at his treatment; dismay and shuddering seizes his flesh as he thinks of his predicament (21:5). At this point of alienation the sufferer turns to serious decisions about his life because the life he now experiences within society is unfair.

3. Job's Frustration with Life

Every individual desires a happy life and to live a rewarding life in society. Job was a philanthropist. He brought many servants and guests into his house and fought for the cause of the poor and the needy. His world consists of his family, friends, and loved ones, but they have become hostile to him. Job has inherited the fate of the wicked and he is ostracized. His servant will not answer his call (19:16) and the guests he brought to his house pretend not to know him

---

[14] Carol Newsom, *The Book of Job. A Contest of Moral Imaginations* (New York: Oxford University Press, 2003) 189.

[15] These same words ("abhor" and "distance") are also used to describe his alienation by his family and friends in 19:13, 19.

[16] Clines, *Job 1-20*, 1004.

(19:15). His life has been poured out, he is exhausted with grief and pain; if he speaks, his pain is not assuaged, and if he refrains, the pain does not depart from him (16:6). He needs counsel and comfort; but his friends with whom he takes counsel abandon him (19:19).

Job's initial anger is registered in chap. 3 where he "laments the destiny that gives him life";[17] he curses the day of his birth. Job's affliction causes him to hate the world that has alienated him from loved ones. The curse, in fact, is a rhetorical gesture that shifts his aggression and unloads it onto the day of his birth.[18] The transfer of aggression is a healthy way of preserving oneself psychologically. That day should have prevented Job's birth, and is to be punished by being deprived of light (3:4) because that day allowed Job to see the light.

In his abandonment, Job laments and asserts that he will never experience anything good again in life (7:7) because his spirit is broken, his plans are thwarted, and he cannot fulfill his heart's desire any more; his days are past and extinguished, his grave is ready and waiting for him (17:1, 11). Life has become loathsome; he knows he is blameless but, given his affliction, he doubts if he still has true knowledge of himself (9:21).

4. The Broken Bond of Unity between Job and His Society

Members of society have a bond that unites them. Solidarity is evident when Job's friends come to sympathize with him in what Weber terms as "communalization" of social relationships.[19] The result of this kind of social behavior leads to emotional attachment among the participants. Communal social relationships exist because members of the society share similar qualities and are found in similar situations and as a consequence have a common behavior pattern. The visit by Job's three friends is motivated by this bond. They sat with him in silence (2:11-13) and "the silent sharing of suffering is a manifestation of fellowship."[20]

---

[17] Gordis, *The Book of God and Man*, 11.
[18] Newsom, "The Book of Job," 366.
[19] Weber, *Basic Concepts in Sociology*, 91-93.
[20] Gutiérrez, *On Job: God-Talk and the Suffering of the Innocent*, 7.

Significantly, the friends subsequently speak with one mind, as if they had conspired against Job. None of his friends perceives the problem from Job's viewpoint. Religion is spiritual in character, but it also has a moral dimension. I have argued that the friends push the "deed and consequence" concept too far, ignoring the mysterious aspect of God, thereby straining the bond that exists between them and Job.

The kind of relationship that developed between Job and his family and Job and his friends after his misfortune is referred to by Weber as "struggle."[21] Weber explains that to the extent that the behavior of one party is oriented toward making its will prevail against that of another party, there is a struggle. If the struggle does not involve physical violence, then it is a nonviolent struggle; this is the case in the Book of Job. Job struggles within himself because of his mysterious affliction; he also struggles against alienation by family and loved ones.

The desire for stability and continuity in a society sometimes renders it reluctant to review its social values, some of which may have become negative values which need to be changed. When institutions in a society are disrupted, people may suffer, and their suffering may lead to social disorder. If the disruption is for the good of the society then their suffering is worthwhile; if it is not beneficial to the society, their suffering can be destructive. Change is seen as a threat not only to society as a whole but also to the individuals in it. As a result, there is little desire to review the negative aspects of existing social structures and social institutions.[22] Job became a victim in a society that did not want to change its concepts about life. I will now review some of the conceptual ideas of Job's society that led to his alienation.

II. Conceptual Attitudes of Society towards a Sufferer

Society has conceptual attitudes towards its members. Most of these attitudes are inherited through the process of socialization. Socialization identifies an individual with his or her society and in that

---

[21] See Weber, *Basic Concepts in Sociology*, 85.
[22] On existing social structures and institutions, see Ritzer, *Sociological Theory*, 11-12.

process the individual is shaped by the objectives of the society; consciously or unconsciously, the individual represents and expresses those values.[23] Parents and elders of the society usually impart wisdom to the young; for this reason Ben Sira invites the uneducated to lodge in his house of instruction to learn wisdom (Sir 51:23).

Effective socialization depends upon what society holds as its objective. If what society holds as its objective is defective, the members of the society grow up with a defective mentality. In the case of Job's society religion is a primary objective. Job becomes integrated into his society with full religious knowledge. He takes the attitudes of others as his own because that enables him to fit into the social environment in which he and other individuals interact.[24] As a consequence, Job received from his society the misinterpreted concept of "deed and consequence" which he embraced until he became its victim.

The process of socialization is intended to enable individuals to develop behavior that is acceptable. Job's society sees in his affliction an indication of unacceptable behavior. The yardstick for judging acceptable and unacceptable behavior needs to be well defined. People who are disloyal receive no compassion from society. For Job's society, when a person suffers mysteriously, such suffering is viewed as a divine scourge. Thus, Job's suffering is thought to be sent by God. Socialization that is defective can have grave consequences.

The author of the Book of Job realizes the problem that socialization has caused because of misinterpreted concept of "deed and consequence" in his society. The society believes that only wicked people suffer and thus pushes "deed and consequence" beyond all reason. The author uses Job and his society to unveil and correct the negative attitude of his own society.

A. The Reasons for Job's Social Alienation

The reader is aware that Job is innocent (1: 1-12; 2:1-7). Job's friends are not aware of this; they only know that the once honorable and respected man has become an object of shame.

---

[23] Berger, *The Sacred Canopy*, 15.

[24] For more on personal attitudes and interaction, see George H. Mead, *Mind, Self and Society* (ed. Charles W. Morris; Chicago: University of Chicago Press, 1934) 47.

1. Job's Bodily Defects

The second trial of Job by the accuser involved bodily affliction (2:1-10). Job's deteriorating body results in social consequences. In 19:17, Job says,

> My life is repulsive to my wife;
> I am loathsome to my own children,

while earlier he stated,

> My flesh is clothed with worms and dirt;
> my skin hardens, then breaks out again (7:5).

The physical appearance of Job has changed. This change may have been responsible for the taunts, mockery, and jeering that he received from society. As a diseased person he has to be separated from other members of society because his infirmity affects the ordered structure of the society and endangers the group.[25]

As Basson notes, society sees its purity to consist in the bodily cleanliness of individuals. Basson says, "Whereas whole bodies were regarded as ideal and pure, unwhole bodies were considered impure and dangerous because they violated the structured arrangement of the social order."[26] Corporeal identity gives meaning to the individual in society and is essential for social acceptance. Individuals with bodily defects are considered socially dead; they have no privileges in the society since they no longer live within the boundaries of social protection.[27] Israelite society put laws in place for regulating infectious skin diseases (Lev 13:2-59) such as that which marked the deformed body of Job.[28]

---

[25] Meir Malul, *Knowledge, Control and Sex: Studies in Biblical Thought, Culture and Worldview* (Tel Aviv: Archeological Center Publications, 2002) 440.

[26] Alec Basson, "Just Skin and Bones: The Longing for Wholeness of the Body in the Book of Job," *VT* 58 (2008) 287-99, here 296-97.

[27] H. Viviers, "The 'Body' and Lady Wisdom," *OTE* 18 (2005) 879-90, here 801.

[28] Basson, "Just Skin and Bones," 290.

Job's infection leads to rejection by his family, friends, and loved ones.[29] Rejection of an infected person by society is a means of protecting the society from pollution.[30] The expulsion of an infected person reflects the collective consensus of society that aims at a society without defects. Job is defective and isolated, and has to fight his enforced separation. Basson explains the fate of Job and the reason for his vehement desire for vindication:

> An investigation into the situation of Job illustrated that physical completeness was indeed a prerequisite for social inclusion and participation in the various social institutions. Because of his impure body, Job was abhorred and treated as an outcast. Unwhole bodies thus have social implications. Job's lament about his physical affliction is therefore not just a complaint about the pain caused by aching wounds but a desire for a whole and pure body, for only then will he be allowed access into the realm of kin relations in which his identity is embedded.[31]

Job seeks for healing and reacceptance by his community.

Job's exclusion from his social environment affects his spiritual life. Job suffered both social and spiritual isolation. In his frustration, he addresses God:

> If I am wicked, woe to me!
> If I am righteous, I cannot lift up my head,
> for I am filled with disgrace and look upon my affliction
> (10:15).

No matter what Job says, his friends claim that the affliction evidenced by his physical appearance is visited only upon evil people. Accordingly, the only remedy for him is to renounce his sins and ask for forgiveness. On the one hand, if he accepts his situation as the friends encourage him to do, then he is a sinner; but such acceptance of

---

[29] Dhorme, *A Commentary on the Book of Job,* 274.

[30] Jon L. Berquist, *Controlling Corporeality. The Body and the Household in Ancient Israel* (New Brunswick, NJ: Rutgers University Press, 2002) 20.

[31] Basson, "Just Skin and Bones," 297.

guilt by the innocent Job will not take away his suffering. On the other hand, if he dissents, then he risks questioning the justice of God; this he does, in fact, in his remark to God, asking him to tell him how he has sinned (7:20). Job's isolation is a disgraceful and a shameful humiliation. The harsh judgment by his loved ones is probably because Job has become a public shame.

2. Dishonor and Shame

Social isolation of a member of society is a dishonor and a shame to the person. Job complains about the dishonor that his family and loved ones have heaped upon him (19:13-22). Honor and dishonor are crucial human values that determine the life of the individual. Dishonor is considered a punishment for the wicked and occasions mockery, humiliation (2 Chr 30:10; Isa 57:4; Jer 20:7; Lam 3:14), and shame. An individual seeks honor from society and society confirms what the individual has deserved: either honor or dishonor. The social esteem of the individual is conferred by society.

Honor and dishonor can be inherited or achieved, inherited through ancestry or societal status or achieved through one's own personal efforts. Honor promotes cohesion among group members while dishonor creates division among group members.[32] Acceptance into a social group is deemed an honor, rejection by the group dishonor. Job recounts his good days when he believed God's blessing was upon him (Job 29:1-5). He received honor and respect from the members of society for all his good deeds of charity (Job 29:7-17); he was like a tree planted by the waterside (Job 29:18-25; cf. Ps 1:1-3). Honor is a principal component of social happiness. Now, however, Job's privileged status appears to be lost because he is being mocked with gross disrespect by the very people who honored him previously (Job 30:1-15). They spit in his face, an expression of very strong contempt (Job 17:6; 30:10).[33] Dishonor leads to low self-esteem, as the victim is rejected and abandoned.

---

[32] Basson, "Friends Becoming Foes," 409.
[33] Clines, *Job 1-20*, 395.

156

B. The Cause of Job's Social Alienation

Religious societies serve as conscience for the individual members of the society. Their purpose is to strengthen members and bring those who have gone astray back to God. Society does this job effectively because every member of a religious community serves as conscience to the others. Religious misunderstanding by his society is the cause of Job's social alienation.

1. Religious Consciousness and Its Impact on Job's Society

Developing the religious consciousness of its members is a priority for all religious societies. The story of Job is intended to purify the understanding of the "deed and consequence" concept in the author's society. The story of Job essentially attempts to correct the wrong notion that only the wicked suffer.

The religious experience of members of a society is the sum of the individual members' experiences of the divine. The society helps the individual to maintain such experiences and to keep the faith and share it with other members of the society. Through this interaction, the individual becomes capable of living in the society. The author of the Book of Job realizes the harm that the misinterpreted "deed and consequence" concept is causing in his society. The author thus presents Job, a faithful person (Job 1:5, 8) who deals generously with friends and strangers alike and provides for the needy (Job 29:11-17), but is nevertheless plagued by suffering. The story makes it clear that Job's affliction is wrongly attributed by his friends to evil done by him.

Every social institution is distinguished by the particular convictions of its members. "Deed and consequence" was an embodiment of normal religious teaching, a conviction shared by the whole society. The idea, once formulated, is inherited and passed on to others. This inherited idea creates relationship. This social relationship is what Weber refers to as aggregation.[34] Aggregation, Weber states, is the result of an agreed balance of interests which is motivated by rational value judgments, which may be, although not necessarily, adopted by mutual consent. If the consent is value-oriented, it may be based on faith, which requires a commitment on the part of all

---

[34] Weber, *Basic Concepts in Sociology*, 91.

157

individuals in the society, and if it is goal-oriented, then it is with the hope that the other party will live up to it.[35]

In the society portrayed in the Book of Job, "deed and consequence" concept suggests an obligation binding all members to pursue goodness. Job's society, like any other society, is responsible for concepts prevailing in the society. Its members contribute and uphold its course. It is the responsibility of society members to ensure that the prevailing concepts are strictly followed because all of them are affected by those concepts and because the welfare of the society is at stake; whatever the society upholds as good is taken to heart by all members.

2. The Problem with Religious Observances and Its Consequences on Job

Human beings are religious by nature and their religious life is social in character. Religious influences, sociologically speaking, are twofold: a positive or cohesive integrating influence, and a negative, destructive, or disintegrating influence.[36] Since religion deals with good and evil, negative religious influences can lead members of the society into unfortunate situations with regards to religious beliefs, norms, rites, and values. As Durkheim asserts, religious beliefs are understood by society from the viewpoint of the sacred and the profane.[37] These beliefs have a binding effect on the members of the society and unite them as they share their common life.

Religious beliefs relate to the nature of the sacred. In fact, rites are rules of conduct which prescribe how a member of the society must behave in relation to sacred things.[38] Good and evil are in opposition to each other, and the members of the society know the difference between the two. To Job's society, his predicament identifies him as an evildoer, and so Job is told to renounce his evil deeds in order to regain his former position in society.

---

[35] Ibid.

[36] Ibid., 35-36.

[37] Durkheim, *The Elementary Forms of the Religious Life*, 52. See also idem, *Durkheim on Religion*, 112-18.

[38] Durkheim, *The Elementary Forms of the Religious Life,* 56.

3. Misinterpretation of Religious Ideas and Its Effects on Job

Religious zeal can lead members of a society into unfortunate misinterpretations of religious ideas. "Deed and consequence" was a collective idea of Job's society. Its application had serious consequences and involved sanctions that resulted in Job's alienation. Social alienation deprives an individual of his identity and strips him of self-esteem and the ability to control his life.

The reason some members of the Israelite community went to extremes in interpreting "deed and consequence" may possibly have been due to the exile, because much emphasis is placed on "deed and consequence" in many of the books written after the exile. Israel in exile reflected on its fidelity and attributed its downfall to religious failure. Strict observance of the law, people hoped, would recover the favor they formerly enjoyed with God. The author of the Book of Job did well to bring to the attention of his people how they had overstretched the understanding of the concept "deed and consequence."

C. The Effects of Social Alienation on Job's Life

1. Job's Society Fails to Identify with Job

An individual in society develops his or her identity from the society through socialization. A society creates its own environment for its members to live in. In that environment, they experience one another as one people and this provides identity for the individuals of the society. Human identity leads to human formation. Berger notes three fundamental moments of formation: externalization, objectivation, and internalization. [39] According to Berger, an

---

[39] Berger identifies human formation from the perspective of Karl Marx. Although I do not accept his explanation in full, his ideas on externalization, objectivation, and internalization are helpful for my discussion. According to Berger, "Externalization is the ongoing outpouring of human beings into the world, both in the physical and the mental activity of men. Objectivation is the attainment by the products of this activity (again both physical and mental) of a reality that confronts its original producers as a facticity external to and other than themselves. Internalization is the reappropriation by men of this same reality, transforming it once again from structures of the objective world into structures of the subjective consciousness. It is through externalization that society becomes a human product. It is through

empirically adequate view of society can only be arrived at if these three moments are understood together.

Job identified externally with his society by interacting with its members; he pursued the objectives of the society; he internalized them and expressed them in his piety and care for the poor and needy. Individuals in society cannot be identified outside the environment to which they belong because they grow up exercising the ideals of the society. This is why society makes a point of controlling the activities of its members so that every member can reflect the image of the society. Because of Job's affliction, he no longer reflected the conceptual image of the society.[40]

Society makes the individual members who they are by making them aware of their objectives in life. When individuals perform good deeds in society, they enjoy positive societal attention because such acts are recognized as good by the society. Similarly, an individual who engages in an unacceptable type of behavior is scorned by society because such actions affect the group in an adverse manner. Job enjoys good social status until his fall (29:8-10, 21-25). He was applauded by the society for his good deeds (29:11; 31:31-32). But society is also viewed in terms of the conditions of its members and so Job's misfortune became a disgrace to the society.

2. Job Deprived of Social Consciousness

Social and individual consciousness is necessary for any society to exist. Where this consciousness is absent, the society suffers. Job's society acted in haste in condemning him because of their preconceived ideas. To be aware of society is to be aware of the individual members. Social consciousness and self-consciousness cannot be separated from each other because no one can conceive of himself or herself without reference to others in a social context.

The individual and the society are concomitants; that is, neither can be accorded temporal priority over the other.[41] Society becomes a

---

objectivation that society becomes a reality *sui generis*. It is through internalization that man is a product of society." See further Berger, *The Sacred Canopy,* 4.

[40] A society that examines its social life produces a healthy society for all its members. See Berger, *The Sacred Canopy*, 9.

[41] Calvin J. Larson, *Major Themes in Sociological Theory* (New York: David McKay, 1973) 92.

mirror by which members come to know themselves because society is the world in which they exist.[42] Cooley points out that "self and society are twin-born, we know one as immediately as we know the other, and the notion of a separate and independent ego is an illusion."[43] Job cannot refer to himself without his society because the society has given him his image; but he does not see himself as society does. The attitude of Job and his loved ones are different products of the same society. It is important that a society be conscious of its actions and their consequences.[44]

3. Job's Social Rejection Is Social Death

Social rejection is social death. The kinship structure provides an environment that binds all members of the kindred group together. Social affiliation is very important for the existence of the individuals of a society because without interaction, individuals cease to exist. Such social affiliation serves as a lifeline for the individual members of the society. A person who lives outside the society is socially dead because the person is deprived of the companionship and protection of the group. When Job is denied social affiliation, he sees his life ebbing away (17:1-6) and ending as maggots in the grave (17:13-16). Instead of dwelling with his family and friends, Job looks to Sheol as his house (17:13). A similar rejection is expressed by the psalmist, who cries out:

> I have passed out of mind like one who is dead;
> I have become like a broken vessel (Ps 31:13);

this poet is socially ostracized and is considered dead to the society, just as Job is.

Social death may lead to physical death. Physical death is an evil; it destabilizes the society. Society is not always aware of the

---

[42] Halbwachs makes good observations on how an individual visualizes himself or herself as an objective real self in the society. For more information, see Maurice Halbwachs, *Les Cadres Sociaux de la Mémoire* (Paris: Presses Universitaires de France, 1952).

[43] Charles Horton Cooley, *Social Organization: A Study of the Larger Mind* (New York: Schocken Books, 1962) 5.

[44] Social consciousness and self-consciousness are in the mind and thus the interpretation of behavior is in the mind of individuals. See Larson, *Major Themes in Sociological Theory*, 92.

social death it may cause its members. In Job's case, initially, his social death led him to prefer physical death. Job believes that if he had been aborted or still-born, it would have been better for him. He would have enjoyed the peace of death and the calm of Sheol (3:11-19), but here on earth, he is suffering. He seeks justification, but dreads the presence of God:

> See, he will kill me;
> > I have no hope;
> but I will defend my ways to his face (13:15).

He has reached that point which sociologists refer to as "marginal situation," which is the point of abandoning one's life.[45] When all hope of clinging to life is exhausted, the sufferer has no choice, but to submit to the grave (Job 17:13-16). Of course, already in the earlier chapters (3:11, 13, 16; 7:7-21) Job has lost his desire for life because of his excruciating pain. The statement,

> Who is there that will contend with me?
> > For then I would be silent and die (13:19)

expresses Job's depressed situation. Such was the point to which his social alienation had led him.

However, Job's social death has not led to his physical death. Physical death as a solution to Job's problem disappears when he realizes that the best thing for him to do is to seek the face of God, even if that will cost him his life (cf. Job 13:13-17). He wishes that his claim of innocence be written down in order that future generations will be aware of his side of the story (19:23-24); he expects that he will be vindicated by the time he sees God in the flesh (19:25-27). Physical death, he believes, is clearly not the answer to his problem because it comes to the poor and the rich alike, as well as to the righteous and the wicked; he clearly prefers trying to prove his innocence during his lifetime. Because physical death is not annihilation, Job hopes he will be vindicated; even if he is in Sheol, his innocence will be known by all

---

[45] See Berger, *The Sacred Canopy*, 22-23.

who will later hear of his case. Job understands how society perceives him, so his only remedy lies with God who must acquit him before his detractors.

D. Job's Frustration with God

Job's frustration with God is due to God's silence. He accuses God of causing the alienation of his family, friends, and loved ones (19:13). But prior to his direct accusation of God as the agent of his alienation in 19:13-22, Job had made several statements expressing his dissatisfaction with God. Job was living in peace until God interfered with his life. His ill-treatment is summarized in these lines,

> I was at ease, and he broke me in two;
> > he seized me by the neck and dashed me to pieces;
> he set me up as his target (16:12).

His affliction caused his enemies to insult him by striking him on the cheek (16:9-10).

Job knows he is innocent and that the only one who can vindicate him is God (17:3-4; 30:20-23), and so he keeps calling on God, appealing to his justice (10:2-3) even as he claims that God does not repay the unrighteous or punish them or their children (21:18-26).

Job knows very well God has power and that he cannot face him and win his case (9:14-21; 11:7-9). However, he also looks for consolation from his society and cries to his friends,

> Have pity on me, have pity on me,
> > O you my friends,
> for the hand of God has touched me! (19:21).

No mortal can challenge God or deserve an answer from God (9:2-3, 28; 10:13; 42:2), but Job dares to seek an answer from God (10:1-3; 23:1-4) because he believes that he cannot do more than he has already done to prove his innocence. He had appealed to God for mercy (9:15) and now appeals to his friends to show him mercy as God does not (19:22). Job expects God to execute justice (10:4-7; 13:13-23; 16:18-22) and warns his friends against their false accusation (19:28-29). He wonders if all his past glory was just a ploy by God to make fun of him and afflict him later (10:12-17; 19:6-12). He likewise wonders whether God counts him as one of his enemies (7:12; 13:24; 19:11).

III. Job's Fight for Integrity: The Rebound of a Sufferer

This section constitutes an important part of my discussion of Job's social alienation. Job's society has failed him. Society becomes a mirror for individuals to judge themselves; however, society may be wrong in its judgment and in such cases it is up to individuals to vindicate themselves. Job's integrity is at stake (*tām*, "man of integrity," "blameless," "complete"—Job 1:1); God also emphasized Job's integrity (Job 1:8). The fight for one's integrity is important because integrity lives beyond the grave.

A. The Need for Self-identity

Personal identity is essential because it gives self-awareness. Without self-awareness individuals may become what society conceives them to be, and so long as individuals do not arrive at self-awareness, they remain what society thinks of them. When the individual realizes that society thinks badly of him yet tries to vindicate himself, society may react because the individual's understanding differs from its own. Job has a problem to deal with. The problem he faces is "a well-informed conscience that finds itself guiltless"[46] but is accused by others as guilty. Job defends himself and holds fast to his integrity without yielding to what society thinks of him. This personal insistence on one's convictions is what gives identity to every human being.

Job knew he was considered an evil person by his society, yet he also knows that he is righteous and calls for justice to be done. He seeks a court proceeding and takes an oath to show his sincerity—a strong reaction to the charges leveled against him (27:2-6). A good assessment of oneself will demand a critical inquiry into one's life story, and in Job's case this includes the good times (chap. 29) and the bad times (chap. 30).

---

[46] Alexander Di Lella, "An Existential Interpretation of Job," *BTB* 15 (1985) 49-55, here 52.

1. Job Swears an Oath (27:2-6)

Job speaks out with vigor in the face of God's silence and affirms his innocence and integrity (27:2-6). He swears an oath to affirm his innocence and stresses his determination to maintain that innocence. Andersen calls these verses "the punch-line" and Habel refers to them as "a catalytic action" in the narrative plot to evoke God's action. [47] The verses serve as a summary of Job's thoughts as expressed earlier in 21:34 and 24:25. Job defends his justice (v. 2), his integrity (v. 5), and his righteousness (v. 6). This is what he says:

> As God lives, who has taken away my right,
>> and the Almighty, who has made my soul bitter,
> as long as my breath is in me
>> and the spirit of God is in my nostrils,
> my lips will not speak falsehood,
>> and my tongue will not utter deceit.
> Far be it from me to say that you are right;
>> until I die I will not put away my integrity from me.
> I hold fast my righteousness, and will not let it go;
>> my heart does not reproach me for any of my days
> (27:2-6).

These verses represent the climax of Job's statements in the book and prepare for 31:35, the conclusion of Job's defense of his integrity and innocence.[48] Job addresses God because he is the "ultimate custodian of justice, the impartial punisher of all perjury." [49] God needs to answer him. Job is making an appeal to God against injustice. Job's oath has been interpreted in several ways.[50] His bitterness does not

---

[47] Andersen, *Job*, 219; Habel, *The Book of Job,* 380.

[48] The idiom "as God lives" at the beginning of the oath is the standard oath formula in the OT; see 1 Sam 3:17; 14:39, 45.

[49] Andersen, *Job*, 220.

[50] Fohrer understands Job's statement as asserting that God should not live if Job's words are not true (*Das Buch Hiob,* 379-80); see also Habel: "Job's oath is the last resort of a desperate victim" (*The Book of Job*, 379); Hartley: "If Job's statement is false, God will activate the curse on Job" (*The Book of Job,* 369). Gordis thinks there is profound irony in Job's speech, because he lived an upright life but is now being dealt with unjustly. The God to whom Job is appealing is identical with the

allow him to acknowledge God as God deserves. He accuses God of two offenses: God has denied his right and made his life bitter (27:2).[51] For God to deny him justice means that God has denied himself because justice is one of God's attributes and it is wrong to deny justice to the needy (Deut 24:17; 27:19; 1 Sam 8:3; Isa 40:27).

The oath is a proof of Job's innocence; as long as he is alive (27:3) Job will pursue his justification. Job's reference to the life-giving force *nəšāmāh* ("breath," 27:3) and *rûᵃḥ ʾĕlôᵃh* ("spirit of God," 27:3) is an indication of his continual dependence on God for life and subsequent vindication. Hartley notes that the oath represents a parenthetic statement by Job that God is the source of his life.[52] Job will not say anything untruthful (27:4). It is out of place for him to agree with the assertion of his friends that he has committed evil when he knows that he has not (27:5). The declaration *ḥālîlāh llî* ("Far be it from me") is a self-imprecation, which would amount to sacrilege, if Job is lying (see 1 Sam 24:7; 2 Sam 20:20).[53]

Job's oath is a testimony of one who has expended all his vigor pursuing vindication and whose oath is his last effort. His oath is not a curse against God (27:6).[54] Job's boldness and self-surrender in the oath is expressed with eightfold repetition of "my," plus "me" and "I" three times each in five verses (27:2-6). The conditional nature of the oath is articulated by the triple *ʾim* ("if") clause in 27:4-5, while the three negatives in 27:5-6 express his determination. Job's integrity underlies his firm insistence on his innocence; his "conscience" (*lēbāb*)

God who wronged him (Gordis, *The Book of Job*, 287); see also Wolfers: "The oath asserts a stubborn reconciliation between faith in God and a reality which is incompatible with all he is supposed to stand for. In psychoanalytical terms it might be described as a resolution of the collective human oedipal conflict" (*Deep Things out of Darkness*, 427).

[51] For the word "bitter," see also 3:20; 7:11; 10:1; 13:26; 21:25; 23:2. According to Andersen, the most arresting feature of Job's oath is reference to God as the one "who has taken away my right" and "who has made my soul bitter" (Andersen, *Job*, 220). The verse expresses Job's trust in God.

[52] Hartley, *The Book of Job*, 369.

[53] Habel, *The Book of Job*, 380.

[54] To lie under oath is to destroy one's own integrity. For more on the oath and its moral implications, see Janzen, *Job*, 183-84.

does not convict him of anything (27:6).[55] The hiphil of the verb *ḥāzaq* ("hold fast," see also 1:3, 9) is a sure indicator that Job will not give up his integrity. The vengeance that his friends expect to come upon him he asserts will befall them. Job is not the wicked person they think he is (27:7-10). Job will teach them the wisdom and the knowledge of God that they fail to recognize (27:11-12).

2. Job's Respect and Honor in His Society (29:1-25)

In times of misery it is helpful to look back to good times past. Job looks back to his glory days in the society, when God watched over him, and his children were around him (29: 1-5). In his affliction, Job now thinks that God no longer watches over him (v. 2).[56] Job's comments (vv. 1-5) are prompted by the fact that he no longer has honor in society; and so it is with all human beings who in time of sorrow think that God has abandoned them. Job now recounts the respect and honor that he received when he appeared in the city gate (v. 7); all conversations ceased as he approached, the young men withdrew and the old rose to their feet to accord him respect (v. 8). The nobles refrained from speaking and covered their mouths (v. 9), while the princes became dumb (v. 10) because of Job's status (vv. 21-24).[57] Honor among males is a necessity; Clines says, "Typical for a male in his society, the principal ingredient in his social happiness was that of honor, the regard paid to him by other males."[58]

Job was a savior to the underprivileged in the society (vv. 12-16) and protected them from being bullied (v. 17); this answers Eliphaz's charges of Job's insensitivity to his society (22:6-9). Job was praised for his good deeds and society is a witness to those deeds. His

---

[55] See Job's other references to his innocence in 1:8; 2:3, 9; 4:6; 9:20-22; 27:5; 31:6.

[56] Job does not know that God still cares for him. God told Satan not to touch his life in 2:6; God is in absolute control of Job's life. Job's thought about himself as suffering innocently is not different from that of many others who suffer innocently or who suffer mysteriously.

[57] In words of de Vaux, "These are men of influence and position who can no doubt be called 'nobles' and in a broad sense, but they do not form a nobility in the proper sense of a closed classto which one belongs by birth, which enjoys certain privileges and owns a large part of the land" (de Vaux, *Ancient Israel: Its Life and Institutions,* 70).

[58] Clines, *Job 1-20,* 985.

prominence in society came about because of his concern for the needy (v. 14). Good deeds call for blessings and long life.[59] His honor gave him power like the bow (v. 20) and made his fellow counselors listen to him and wait on his counsel (vv. 21-22). Job was never previously challenged; it is an abomination that his three friends have now challenged him, unlike his associates at the city gate, who became speechless at his wisdom (v. 23). Job was like a king (v. 25).

3. Loss of Honor and Respect (30:1-31)

Job's glory days are over and all he can do is mourn; he depicts his sad situation with three exclamations "and now!" (vv. 1, 9, 16), which open the three divisions of chap. 30 that recount his woes of mockery and torture by society.[60] Job's greatest lack is of honor and respect. Honor is the worth of any individual in society.[61] Honor gives approval and recognition, but Job is now receiving shame and ridicule even from people without respectable parents (vv. 1-3). Job is an elder in his society (29:7-10) and had occupied a prominent position in society.[62] The elders make the laws of the society and attend to the well-being of the community. They transmit wisdom to the young through socialization and the young are bound to respect the older members of the community (Lev 19:32).

Job's language in vv. 1-9 is an expression of his anger against his mockers. The useless of society now have power to mock him. For Job, there has been a planned attack upon him (vv. 12-14); his reputation is blown away as the wind scatters the chaff, and his prosperity disappears like a cloud (v. 15).

---

[59] Anthony R. Ceresko, *Job 29-31 in the Light of Northwest Semitic: A Translation and Philological Commentary* (BibOr 36; Rome: Biblical Institute Press, 1980) 24-25.

[60] Ibid., 35.

[61] See J. Plevnik, "Honor and Shame," *Biblical Social Values and Their Meaning: A Handbook* (ed. J. J. Pilch and B. J. Malina; Peabody, MA: Hendrickson, 1993) 95-104, here 96.

[62] The affairs of the land are in the hands of the elders who were known as *hazəqnîm*, "elders," literally, "bearded ones" (1 Kgs 21:8, 11; Prov 31:23). *śārîm*, "nobles" (Job 29:9; Prov 8:16) were family heads who sat at the gate to take counsel for the good of the society. They had great influence. These groups of people formed a sort of council for every Israelite town (1 Sam 30:26-31).

Job is exhausted with grief and pain (v. 16); his tormentors do not sleep and so deprive him of sleep (v. 17). Job is disgraced and humiliated; his shame, disrespect, and grief are poetically expressed by the statement about his being picked up and cast into the mud (vv. 18-19). He is singled out as a victim (v. 21) who is made to ride on the wind only to be brought down in shame like the wicked (v. 22). His maker's intention is to return him to dust, to the house where the living go after death (v. 23). Job comforted people, but has no one to comfort him (v. 24). He is deformed and this accounts for his gaunt appearance (vv. 28-31).[63] Job has lost his dignity and power.

4. Loss of Control

Job realizes he has lost control of his life. Personal awareness enables individuals to realize when they have lost control and power; a necessary redirection must come into play if those individuals are to regain power and control. Socialization gives empowerment that enables the individual to function in his or her society. When an individual loses that power, fear and anxiety may set in. Job wanted to regain his status, but realized that it was impossible. He has one choice: to fight for his integrity rather than die; but this demands a deliberate examination of conscience.

B. Job's Rebound: Declaration of Innocence and the Quest for Justification

In chapter 30, Job expressed his sense of isolation. In chap. 31 he subjects himself to a rigorous scrutiny with reference to various possible sins, including greed, cheating, adultery, idolatry, extortion, self-complacency, abuse of servants, and neglect of the poor, the widow, and the orphan. Having judged himself not guilty, he requests the bill of his indictment and takes God to court.

---

[63] Collins explains that the external affliction causes internal distress which produces a physiological reaction from the intestines that affects the whole body. See Terence Collins, "The Physiology of Tears in the Old Testament Part I," *CBQ* 33 (1971) 18-38, here 18.

1. Job Exonerates Himself Regarding Assorted Vices (31:1-31)

Job, in the courtroom of his mind, examines his relationship with God and his neighbors in terms of a series of vices, some of which he has been accused by Eliphaz, Bildad, and Zophar (15:20-36; 18:8-21; 20:4-29; 21:17; 22:10-11), who told Job that what he is experiencing is the outcome of his evil deeds. For example, the children of the wicked perish (27:14) and his children died (1:18-19); a good person enjoys his or her wealth (27:17); and even though Job enjoyed his earlier days (29:2-25), these did not last long because the wicked perishes in the midst of his riches (27:18-19). If the wicked continues to live, his life will be full of suffering and pain (27:20-23), and Job is experiencing both. All these charges Job has heard and now he has to prove himself innocent of them. Gordis calls chap. 31 a "confession of integrity."[64]

a. Sins of Desire (31:1-4)

Job made a resolution to control his eyes, so that sensual attraction would not entice him to sin (v. 1); all human beings are accountable for their actions (v. 3). Job is angry because he led a pure and holy life; his righteousness surpasses that of any mortal (1:1, 5), but he is undergoing the suffering destined for the ungodly (v. 4; see also 16:11; 18:21; 27:7). From the statement in v. 4,

> Does he not see my ways,
> and number all my steps?

It might appear that Job is making a mockery of God's justice; but as Terrien notes, Job has no intention of doing this.[65] Job is simply passionate about his innocence.

b. Job's Defense of His Loyalty (31:5-8)

Job asserts his loyalty to God. The deeds of every individual stand under the eyes of God for judgment (v. 5; see also 23:10).[66] He

---

[64] According to Gordis, chap. 31 reflects at every turn the ideals of justice, equity, reverence, and consideration for the weak, enjoined by the Torah and the Prophets. See Gordis, *The Book of God and Man*, 215.

[65] Terrien, *Job*, 256.

[66] Clines, *Job 1-20*, 1015.

never walks in falsehood. Job has no sin of desire or of action.[67] The heart is the place of consent for both good and evil deeds, and he probes his heart and finds himself worthy (v. 7). He asks to be weighed in a balance to ensure that God knows he is just (v. 6). Job puts his own life at risk, asking perdition for himself if he has done any evil (v. 8).

c. Adultery (31:9-12)

Job claims to be innocent of adultery. Because adultery is a social shame, Job did not look with lust at women and did not lie in wait for other women (v. 9); if he had done that, he says, let the consequence be that other men go into his wife (v. 10) or let him and his property be annihilated (v. 12). Terrien speaks of adultery as an infringement of someone's property, the consequence of which is very severe.[68]

d. Attitude towards Slaves (31:13-15)

Job treats his slaves fairly because they have rights like any other human being (v. 13). Slaves are also created by God (v. 14) and must be respected by others (v. 15). Job asserts he has given no cause for a slave to complain. He affirms the oneness of humankind and the uniqueness of the creator and that wealth and social status have never influenced him in his dealings with others.[69]

e. Relationship with the Underprivileged (31:16-23)

The underprivileged include the poor, the widow, the naked, the homeless, and the orphan. Eliphaz had accused Job of oppressive behavior towards them and alleged this as the reason for his present suffering (22:5-11). God punishes only evil people (22:12-20). Eliphaz also said Job stripped his kinsfolk naked, let them go hungry, and denied the right of the needy (24:6-9). Job now denies these charges of selfish behavior.

Job defends himself against accusations of any form of greed, avarice, and cheating (v. 17). Job never withheld anything from the needy (v. 16); he was a social person and provided for the needy. Since

---

[67] Dhorme, *A Commentary on the Book of Job,* liii.

[68] Terrien, *Job,* 257.

[69] Ceresko, *Job 29-31 in the Light of Northwest Semitic,* 126.

his youth he has been a father to the fatherless (v. 18) and a guide to the widow. He clothed the naked (v. 19-20) and protected the defenseless (v. 21); if he was ever violent toward any such, let him be stripped of his strength (v. 22). Job knows of the sanction against depriving the needy (v. 23).

f. Trust in Wealth or False Gods (31:24-28)

Job never took pride in his own wealth but rather always relied on the power of God. Sin for Job is not only an external act but also the inner disposition of the person. Job never trusted in his wealth although he had an abundance of property; his trust is in God, even though wealth gave him social honor and power (vv. 24-25). Job further asserts he was not enticed to worship any heavenly bodies such as the sun and the moon and thereby to worship a false god (vv. 26-28).

g. Wishing Evil to Enemy (31:29-30)

Job has not rejoiced at the fall of his enemy (v. 29) nor has he ever cursed that person (v. 30).

h. Hospitality (31:31-32)

A good reception for a guest was regarded as a sacred obligation in the ANE and so hospitality is highly esteemed as a virtue.[70] Job is known as a generous host to strangers, and people in the community testify to that (v. 31). Those who lodge under his tent dine at his table and eat meat (v. 31). He opens his door to resident aliens and passers-by who seek a place to spend the night (v. 32).[71]

[i. Sin against the Land (31:38-40)

Job defends himself against any accusation concerning his land. If Job has taken undue profit from the land or cheated the people who work for him on the land (v. 39), then let his land become useless (v. 40ab).][72]

---

[70] de Vaux, *Ancient Israel: Its Life and Institutions*, 10: "The Hebrew family is scarcely complete without the stranger;" see Clines, *Job 1-20*, 1028.

[71] Clines, *Job 1-20,* 1029.

[72] Verses 35-37 and 40c appear to be the intended ending of chap. 31. There is no general consensus as to where vv. 38-40ab belong, but it is certain that vv. 38-40ab do not form the conclusion of chap. 31. The position of these verses has been a

j. Hypocrisy (31:33-37)

These verses declare Job's faithfulness to his conscience. He has not sinned and has nothing to hide (vv. 33-34). He challenges God to charge him, to expose his guilt (v. 35). He will proudly wear the indictment on his shoulder (v. 36) and will not hesitate to lay it bare for all to see. Job calls on God to answer him; this is his final appeal (v. 37).

With these words of avowal Job concludes his self-examination (v. 40c). He judges himself not guilty of any of the charges and challenges God to refute his claim to innocence.

2. Job's Demand for Justification

In 27:4, Job promised,

> My lips will not speak falsehood,
> and my tongue will not utter deceit;

based on this promise, he conscientiously recounts his part of the story to the court (chaps. 29–31). Job is very sure of his innocence and, confident of having proved himself innocent, he now asks for judgment. "Here is my signature! Let the Almighty answer me!"(31:35). Job summons God to court. Job is the only human being to take God to court in the OT. The word *tāwî* ("my signature or my mark") is a proof of innocence.[73] The combination of the two words *tāwî* and *sēper* ("scroll"), normally connotes the idea of a writ of divorce (Deut 24:1) or bill of sale (Jer 32:10-15), but in Job's case it

---

source of controversy among scholars. Most scholars agree that the verses have been displaced from their original position, but where that might be is the problem. Pope relocates them after v. 8; Budde after v. 12; Duhn, Dhorme, and Kissane after v. 32; Gordis, Clines, and Fohrer after v. 34. Habel retains the verses in their MT position and views vv. 1-3 and vv. 38-40ab as the outer frame of Job's oath based on traditional covenant motifs; this underscores the fact that Job's oath is grounded on past commitment, Habel, *The Book of Job*, 428. These few examples show that vv. 38-40ab present a problem in their MT position.

[73] Wolfers, *Deep Things out of Darkness*, 441.

constitutes his bill of indictment.[74] Job will publish his accuser's indictment for all to see.

C. Personal Responsibility

Humans are gifted with intelligence and free will; they know what actions they plan to take and the probable consequences of the actions. They are thus responsible for their actions and their consequences. Even one who has lost power and control in society continues to be responsible for maintaining his or her integrity. Some people in a state of anomie may commit suicide or begin to abuse drugs, alcohol, sex, or engage in some other kind of evil. Some may even attack others in the name of revenge, but this only makes the problem worse. Job, although he may have wished for death, did not attempt suicide or do violence to others.

For a better society human behavior must be oriented toward positive goals. Job maintains his focus as a respected individual and reminds his friends that he is not a simpleton; the fact that he is arguing against their charges means he has the same knowledge and wisdom as they. Job has not abused his God-given talent, as the friends insisted he has. Godliness means not only faithfulness to God but also to neighbors because virtue is measured with reference not only to God but also to neighbors who profit from one's good deeds (22:2-3). [75]

D. Wisdom Inaccessible for Humans

Wisdom is essential for living a worthy life. Although Job accepts the concept of "deed and consequence," he has become critical of society's understanding of it and its implementation. Knowing very well that there is no way he can convince them of his innocence, he looks forward to God for vindication:

> Look, my eye has seen all this,
>> my ear has heard and understood it.
> What you know, I also know;

---

[74] Job's statement of protest (31:35) started when God became his legal opponent. Job has made challenges, accusations, and protestations claiming his integrity: 9:15-16, 21;10:2; 12:4; 13:3, 15-16, 18-22; 16:17, 19; 19:25-27; 23:4-7, 10-12; 27:2-6, all of which he now finally makes public here in 31:35.

[75] Dhorme, *A Commentary on the Book of Job,* xlv.

I am not inferior to you.
But I would speak to the Almighty,
and I desire to argue my case with God (13:1-3).

Job calls his friends "worthless physicians" and an embodiment of "whitewashed lies" (13:4), mocking them for presenting themselves as full of wisdom (12:2) because he realizes the adverse effect the incorrect interpretation of the "deed and consequence" concept has on society. Job's words in 12:13-25 describe how the wisdom of God operates in the human world; this passage gives us a clue about how Job understands God's activity in creation. God is independent of his creatures and his creatures cannot manipulate him. God has the power to do what he wills; he involves himself in human affairs, dismantling normal social institutions and wreaking havoc on human affairs. Job has to wait on God for his justification; he cannot fight God. God does not act according to the principle of "deed and consequence"; rather, he operates in a manner that is beyond human comprehension. Job's friends believe they know the principle on which God acts, but Job, with his unhappy experience of suffering, knows that the principles on which God acts are not known to humans because God does what he wants and has his own reasons for doing so.

The poetic interlude in chap. 28 comes at a point in the book at which both Job and his friends have missed the mark of true wisdom. The poem demonstrates the difficulty involved in the attainment of wisdom by human beings. It expands on the true nature of wisdom and the mystery of knowledge. Verses 1-11 describe how human beings can find precious stones and metals and the extent to which they have to go to do so. But wisdom is a precious thing that cannot be found by such effort. Verse 12 raises an important question which can be taken as a central theme of the book:

But where shall wisdom be found?
And where is the place of understanding?

Verses 13-22 deny that humans know where to find wisdom and how to acquire it; it is inaccessible to them. It cannot be purchased (vv. 15-19). The author asserts that only God understands the way to wisdom and knows its place because he created the universe (vv. 23-27). Thus, it is only God who can impart wisdom (28:28). In the light of the overall concern of the book, the author may be saying here that the problem of innocent suffering is beyond human comprehension.

E. Job's Alienation Indicates the Need for Evaluation of Societal Ideas

There is need to assess the relevance of new ideas in a society. A new idea in a society creates a new world in which old concepts and institutions may lose their meaning and *raison d'être*.[76] Changes may occur in the following ways: the old order may give way to a new order, old ideas may be reinterpreted, or a completely new set of ideas may arise. New ideas come into being because what was previously held is seen to be deficient, as in the case of the "deed and consequence" concept. However, there is need to assess new ideas carefully before they are accepted.

It is also clearly a good practice to revisit the laws, rules, and norms of the society after a period of time. Society is so strongly attached to its ways that there is hardly any inclination to reevaluate its practices. The laws of a society command obedience from its members. However, there is danger that a given law may have outlived its usefulness. When individuals who have internalized these laws speak in public, it is the society that speaks through them because those individuals accept its laws and represent the society. As a consequence, such individuals need to be well-oriented. Individuals with an objective different from that of their society would not receive a hearing by the society's members. The society of Job had been fully indoctrinated with the idea that wicked people suffer and so Job was considered wicked because he was suffering. His claim that he is innocent would not be accepted by society.

In his *Elementary Form of Religious Life*, Durkheim notes that collective representations are the product of cooperation within the society dating to an earlier period.[77] Such collective representations arise because the individuals in the society have come to one mind and a common position. The concept arrived at thus represents what they believe has been proved through their experience and thus this

---

[76] Wach, *Sociology of Religion,* 35-36.
[77] Durkheim, *The Elementary Forms of the Religious Life,* 22, 29.

knowledge is beyond the thought of one mind. "Deed and consequence" was accepted as a consensus by Job's society because they saw in it a motive to encourage individuals to do the right thing.

To recognize the concept as defective demands purification, both psychologically and sociologically. The problem of Job's society is that their perception affected their social lives. Clines observes,

> It is not the social order in itself that bothers Job; it is what that says about innocence and what it says about his own personal worth. For Job, the worst thing is the loss of reciprocity, of speaking and answering, the human interchange that arose from the social network surrounding Job and that in every hour of Job's life proved his worth and indispensability to his family and community.[78]

The need to evaluate ideas comes to the forefront here since the society may not be conscious of its action, in this case, its action against Job. Job's affliction does not mean he should be rejected by society. Job's despair results from his calling out and getting no response (5:1; 9:16; 12:4; 13:22; 14:15; 19:7; 23:5; 30:20). Job's alienation arises because his society believes his affliction is a divine scourge, in accord with the concept of "deed and consequence." The truth or falsity of such ingrained ideas may be difficult to establish through observation alone. In cases such as this, one might need to look to some external signs to prove the truth or falsity of an idea. For example, the fact that righteous people in the society suffer and wicked people appear to prosper suggests that there are problems with the "deed and consequence" idea. Thus, Job's mysterious misfortune and his insistence on his righteousness signal the need of his society to reevaluate their thoughts about him and their concept of "deed and consequence."

---

[78] Clines, *Job 1-20*, 447.

Conclusion

A just person fights with confidence and defends his justice until the end. The energy to fight injustice is expressed in the social action of going beyond rejection and the resultant shame and dishonor until one is vindicated. Job's attitude in the book shows his intimate union with his God, a union built on mutual love. His aggressive attitude towards God, insistently urging God to answer him, reveals his understanding of God. His family, friends, loved ones, and neighbors, who represented his society, thought they had done their best to help him, but they lacked the wisdom that the Book of Job teaches.

Chapter Seven

Social Alienation: A Lesson from the Book of Job

This chapter presents a brief summary of each chapter and the principal conclusions reached in each. The chapter also raises the conscience of people about how to avoid actions that alienate and how to help those who are socially alienated.

The book brings to light how societies past and present have often tended to use a misconceived religious concept to socially isolate afflicted persons, thus causing them unnecessary suffering. In Job 19:13-22, the author describes the alienation Job suffers from his society. There is nothing more disheartening than the turning away of family and close friends in a time of great distress. The Book of Job does not condemn Deuteronomic principles of punishment for the wicked, but criticizes the manner in which his family, friends, and loved ones applied this concept to the case of Job.

Although his friends advise him to repent in order to bring an end to his suffering (22:21), Job cannot do this because he considers himself blameless. Many people likewise suffer in society and their lone voice is not heard. The misconception that led to Job's social alienation is also experienced in other sectors of social life like politics, economy, health, and prejudice. Before presenting a general conclusion, it is worth considering a summary of the previous chapters.

I. An Overview of the Chapters

Chapter One
This chapter gives a general introduction and explains the purpose of the research.

Chapter Two
This chapter analyzes the terms "Social Alienation" and "Human Suffering" and sets forth the methodology of the subsequent chapters. The term "social" has to do with human beings living together as a group, and "alienation" in this context has to do with separation of an individual from society at large. This often happens

when an individual member has been judged as a nonconformist according to the norms of the society. No human being can exist without a society, and no society can exist without the individuals of that society, since they depend on each other. Therefore this chapter emphasizes the need for objectivity in the rules that govern social behavior, rules that do not deprive individuals of their proper place in society, such as happened in the case of Job.

In the treatment of social alienation, the social concepts of Emile Durkheim and Max Weber, sociologists who laid the foundation for understanding social conduct were used.

Human suffering is next treated in the context of social alienation with specific reference to religion, its causes and effects in Israel and Mesopotamia. The Bible presents the fall of Adam and Eve in the garden as the beginning of human suffering. In the ANE poetic literature no fewer than seven works on suffering have been found in Egypt, Babylonia, and Sumeria. The gods were believed to impose punitive measures for sinful actions. Suffering was believed to be the consequence of sinful action. But, in three typical Mesopotamian stories, righteous sufferers describe their suffering, the mystery surrounding the cause of this suffering, and the possible end to the suffering.

When an individual experiences suffering, the initial reaction is to seek a reason for the suffering, and the pain is intensified when no reason can be found. The reason for suffering sometimes lies with the human quest for what an individual values most in life. Value systems in a society are institutionalized in norms and become rules for life. The one who fails to conform to the normative order has to suffer the consequences. Hence, conformity or nonconformity with an established normative order has its consequences.

Chapter Three

This chapter presents an overview of the Book of Job, including authorship, purpose, literary style, theology, its nature as wisdom literature, the concept of "deed and consequence" connection, and a history of research on Job 19. The Book of Job bears the title of its hero, Job, a pious man blessed with wealth and a family. God calls Job's piety to the attention of the accuser, who doubted Job's faithfulness and obtains permission to put him to the test. The book is the story of the test and its consequences. The book is unique and has a universal significance because it addresses the suffering of the innocent, the nature of God, and God's relationship with created human beings. The book calls into question the popular belief that good people always prosper and evil people always perish. This study shows that Job's problem was in the area of theodicy but, additionally, in the failure of his society to accept him. Job's expression of social alienation reaches its peak in Job 19:13-22.

The concept of "deed and consequence" supposes that every human action has its reciprocal reaction. What a person enjoys or suffers is the direct consequence of his or her previous actions. This means that the individual has no one else to blame for his or her misfortunes. The conviction that good acts produce good consequences and evil acts evil consequences is not strictly a wisdom teaching. The idea had been in existence for quite some time and was adopted as part of wisdom teaching. As already noted, this conviction was not simply an Israelite belief but rather a universal one.

Earlier studies on the Book of Job have mentioned social alienation, but none has dealt with Job's family, friends, and loved ones as responsible for his alienation and the resulting intensification of his suffering. However, many scholarly treatments of chap. 19 have brought out vividly Job's social neglect and his vehement desire to reintegrate into his society. The whole of chap. 19 is discussed in order to put Job 19:13-22 in a wider context. The following scholars, whose works have dealt most effectively with this chapter, are discussed in chronological order: Francis Andersen, Robert Gordis, Marvin Pope, Norman Habel, John Hartley, David Clines, Carol Newsom, James Wharton, and Samuel Terrien.

Chapter Four

This chapter provides an exegesis of Job 19:13-22, treating the total breakdown of Job's social network and his struggle for reintegration into society, offering a translation of the text that draw on four versions (Hebrew, Syriac, Greek, and Latin). The chapter also surveys diverse scholarly opinions that reveal Job's abject societal situation and the effects that social alienation has on him. The treatment of the immediate context (chap. 19 as a whole) reveals that it is not only God and his council who are against Job (19:6, 8-12) but also his family, friends, and loved ones (19:13-22), a situation that Job blames on God.

The literary analysis takes into consideration the social system of the ANE and examines the text as poetry. The structural analysis presents the division on which the verse–by–verse analysis of 19:13-22 is based.

Job's lament begins with vv. 13-14 and ends with vv. 18-19, thus placing domestic factors at the center of his lament (vv. 15-17). After his litany of isolation in 19:13-19, Job appeals to his friends (19:21-22), but to no avail. Job warns them of an impending judgment in which he will be vindicated.

The integral character of 19:13-22 is evident from the framework of the argument and the repetition of terms of mourning. The segment lists social intimates who have rejected, deserted, or disowned Job and moves from loved ones in his household to loved ones and others outside his home. What Job experiences is sociological and psychological violence. The passage is the climactic expression of Job's suffering.

Chapter Five

This chapter also speaks of social alienation elsewhere in the Bible, specifically in the Psalter. Psalms 22, 31, and 88 are chosen for study and are studied under the following headings: literary, structural, and textual analyses in the context of social alienation. The chapter describes the similarity between these psalms and the Book of Job, with particular attention to common literary features. These psalms share the theme of social alienation with the Book of Job.

Chapter Six

This chapter examines Job's response to his suffering and social isolation, particularly his disappointment at his abandonment by family, friends, and loved ones; it also analyzes Job's frustration at God's silence. Job believes he is suffering unjustly, and so seeks exoneration by God.

The friends, Eliphaz, Bildad, and Zophar, pit Job against God, arguing that Job's sin must have provoked his suffering. In this they betray attitudes inherited from society, attitudes that prevent them from supporting a suffering member such as Job. Some elements of human life, such as religion, need special attention because they are based on faith and on practices often thought to be beyond being questioned or challenged. However, if those practices or beliefs on which they are based are faulty, society's implementation of them becomes harmful. According to one of the religious concepts of his society, Job's suffering is the result of wrongdoing. His society thinks he needs reconciliation with God for a past evil deed, but Job is convinced he has no such need.

Job, before his affliction, was a respectable person, but he lost his dignity because of his affliction. Job did not give in to the pressure of the friends or the society because he believed that he was righteous. All Job has left is his integrity, and his integrity demands that he tells the truth. Job's defense is to take an oath proclaiming his innocence (31:5-34, 38-40ab) and to insist that God answer him (31:35-37, 40c).

That God asked Job to intercede for his friends is a sign that errors can occur in social relationships. The divine speeches finally provide a criterion by which one can judge the theological perspectives of both Job and his friends. The Book of Job carries a lesson for today's society because even today people suffer because of the false attitudes of others.

II. Conclusion

Job 19:13-22 and Psalms 22, 31, and 88 have three lessons for their readers. First, that no matter the hardship one encounters through social neglect by family, friends, loved ones, and enemies, the sufferer must not abandon his or her trust in God and must not let go his or her dignity and integrity. Second, that the sufferer should not resort to violence as his or her response to social neglect; Job never did that. Third, that those who do not suffer should show concern to those who suffer, help them, and not condemn them as evildoers.

In conclusion, human life may involve enduring humiliations and suffering, but persistence and perseverance is required. A sufferer must not let go his or her dignity or integrity in the face of injustice. The righteousness of a person resides in the heart. Members of the sufferer's society may not accept the sufferer's self testimony, as was in the case of Job, but the sufferer needs to pursue justice and persevere until the end as seen in the Book of Job. Job regained his honor after enduring his suffering. Defeat comes when the sufferer surrenders dignity and integrity. Today, there are many who suffer like Job in society because society does not believe their story. More tolerance and patience are needed in dealing with people who become victims of mysterious suffering.

Social alienation in religion as in the Book of Job still happens today. Some of the evils of today include: condemnation of those who question religious laws, sexual and racial discrimination during worship, violence against other members of society who do not profess the same faith, and denial of employment to applicants who do not share the same faith with the employer. These inhuman actions cast a slur on God's goodness, love, compassion, and mercy. The Book of Job teaches an aspect of religious growth, namely that people, who were nurtured in a particular situation in the past, can live in the present with a different situation of life because social life is dynamic and not static. This religious growth entails changing religious and social concepts when a concept is realized to have been wrongfully implemented and is causing undue suffering to the members of the society, or abandoned when that concept has outlived its usefulness in the society.

The Book of Job teaches that God's wisdom is sometimes incomprehensible to mere human understanding. God is not a custodian of rigid principles that causes undue suffering. God's unresponsiveness does not mean the sufferer is unfaithful. God is unique and deals with his creatures individually. Fidelity to God is not for external reward and no human work merits special favor from God. Job's frustration with God is caused by the guilt his society placed on him. Every individual of a society believes what society teaches and Job believed in the concept of "deed and consequence" until he became a victim. It is to be noted that God did not justify Job's suffering or make any attempt to assuage his suffering. God addressed Job as Job deserved in the book —an address which indicated that suffering is not a negative factor in human life. God allowed Job's affliction, but does not alienate *him* from his society. It is *the society* that alienated *him* on the grounds of a religious belief, a belief that had been misconstrued.

Bibliography

A. Biblical Studies

Dictionaries and Lexicons

Botterweck, G. Johannes, Helmer Ringgren, and Heinz-Josef Fabry ed. *Theological Dictionary of the Old Testament.* 14 vols. Trans. John Wills. Grand Rapids: Eerdmans, 1972, 1977.

Brown, Francis, Samuel R. Driver, and Charles Briggs. *Hebrew and English Lexicon.* Peabody, MA: Hendrickson, 1999.

Danker W. Frederick, ed. *A Greek-English Lexicon of the New Testament and Other Early Christian Literature.* 3rd ed. Chicago: University of Chicago Press, 1979.

Jenni, Ernst, and Claus Westermann. *Theological Lexicon of the Old Testament.* 3 vols. Trans. Mark E. Biddle. Peabody, MA: Hendrickson, 1997.

Koehler, Ludwig, and Walter Baumgartner. *The Hebrew and Aramaic Lexicon of the Old Testament.* Study ed. 2 vols. Trans. M. E. J. Richardson. Leiden: Brill, 2002.

Liddell, G. Henry, Robert Scott, Henry Stuart Jones, and Roderick McKenzie. *A Greek-English Lexicon.* 9th ed. With a Revised Supplement. Oxford: Clarendon Press, 1996.

Smith, J. Payne. *A Compendious Syriac Dictionary.* Eugene, OR: Wipf and Stock Publishers, 1999.

Commentaries

Alter, Robert. *The Book of Psalms a Translation with Commentary.* New York: W. W. Norton, 2007.

Andersen, Francis I. *Job: An Introduction and Commentary.* TynOTC 3. Downers Grove, IL: InterVarsity, 1976.

Brown, E. Raymond, Joseph A. Fitzmyer, and Roland E. Murphy, eds. *NJBC.* Englewood Cliffs, NJ: Prentice Hall, 1990.

Briggs, A. Charles, and Emilie G. Briggs. *A Critical and Exegetical Commentary on The Book of Psalms.* ICC. 2 vols. Edinburgh: T & T Clark, 1976.

Budde, Karl. *Das Buch Hiob.* Göttinger HKAT 2 vol. Göttingen: Vandenhoeck, 1913.

Clifford, Richard. *Psalms 1-72.* Abingdon Old Testament Commentaries. Nashville: Abingdon Press, 2002.

_____ *Psalms 73-150.* Abingdon Old Testament Commentaries. Nashville: Abingdon Press, 2003.

Clines, J. A. David. *Job 1-20.* WBC 17. Nashville: Thomas Nelson, 1989.

_____ *Job 21-37.* WBC 18A. Nashville: Thomas Nelson, 2006.

Davidson, Andrew Bruce, and H. C. O. Lanchester. *The Book of Job.* CBSC. Cambridge: Cambridge University Press, 1937.

Dhorme, Édouard. *A Commentary on the Book of Job.* Trans. H. Knight. London: Nelson, 1984.

Driver, R. Samuel, and G. B. Gray. *A Critical and Exegetical Commentary on the Book of Job.* ICC 14. Edinburgh: T & T Clark, 1958.

Duhm, Bernhard. *Das Buch Hiob erklärt.* KHCAT. Tübingen: Mohr, 1897.

Fohrer, Georg. *Das Buch Hiob.* KAT 16. Gütersloh: Gütersloher Verlagshaus, 1963.

Good, M. Edwin. *In Turns of Tempest: A Reading of Job with a Translation.* Stanford, CA: Stanford University Press, 1990.

Gordis, Robert. *The Book of Job. Commentary, New Translation, and Special Studies.* New York: Jewish Theological Seminary, 1978.

Habel, C. Norman. *The Book of Job.* OTL. Philadelphia: Westminster, 1985.

Hartley, E. John. *The Book of Job.* NICOT. Grand Rapids, MI: Eerdmans, 1988.

Hesse, Franz. *Hiob.* ZBAT 14. Zurich: TVZ Theologischer Verlag, 1978.

Hirsch, H. Samson. *The Psalms: Translation and Commentary.* New York: Philipp Feldheim, 1960.

Horst, Friedrich. *Hiob.* BKAT 16/1. Neukirchen-Vluyn: Neukirchener Verlag, 1968.

Janzen, J. Gerald. *Job. Int.* Atlanta: John Knox Press, 1985.

Kisane, J. Edward. *The Book of Job*. New York: Sheed and Ward, 1946.

Kraus, Hans-Joachim. *Psalms 1-59*. Continental Commentary. Trans. Hilton C. Oswald. Minneapolis: Fortress Press, 1993.

_____ *Psalms 60-150*. Continental Commentary. Trans. Hilton C. Oswald. Minneapolis: Fortress Press, 1993.

McCann, J. Clinton, Jr. "The Book of Psalms." In *NIB* 4. Nashville: Abingdon Press, 1996. Pp. 640-1280.

MacKenzie, R. A. F. "Job." In *JBC*. Ed. R. E. Brown, J. A. Fitzmyer, and R. E. Murphy. Englewood Cliffs, NJ: Prentice-Hall, 1968. Pp. 511-33.

Newsom, A. Carol. "The Book of Job." In *NIB* 4. Nashville: Abingdon Press, 1996. Pp. 319-637.

Pope, H. Marvin. *Job*. AB 15. Garden City, New York: Doubleday, 1979.

Reyburn, D. William. *The Book of Job*. UBS Handbook Series. New York: United Bible Society, 1992.

Rowley, Harold Henry. *Job*. NCB. London: Oliphants, 1978.

Strauss, H. *Hiob: Band 2: 19:1-42,17*. BKAT 16, 1. Neukirchen/Vluyn: Neukirchener Verlag, 2000.

_____ *Hiob: Band 2: 32,1-37,24*. BKAT 16, 2A. Neukirchen/Vluyn: Neukirchener Verlag, 2000.

Terrien, L. Samuel, and Paul Scherer. "Job." In *IB* 3. Ed. G. Buttrick. Nashville: Abingdon, 1954. Pp. 877-1198.

Terrien, L. Samuel. *Job*. CAT 13. Deuxiéme édition actualisée. Geneva : Labor et Fides, 2005.

Weiser, A. *Das Buch Hiob*. ATD 13. Göttingen: Vandenhoeck & Ruprecht, 1968.

Wharton, A. James. *Job*. Westminster Bible Companion. Louisville: Westminster, 1999.

Whybray, R. Norman. *Job*. Readings—A New Biblical Commentary. Sheffield: Sheffield Academic Press, 1998.

Wilde, de A. *Das Buch Hiob:* Eingeleit et, übersetzt und erläutert. OTS 22. Leiden: Brill, 1981.

Other Books

Alter, Robert. *The Art of Biblical Poetry*. San Francisco: Basic Books, 1985.

Anderson, W. Bernhard. *Understanding the Old Testament*. 4th ed. Englewood Cliffs, NJ: Princeton University Press, 1966.

Aufrecht, E. Walter. *Studies in the Book of Job*. Society of Religion Supplements 15. Waterloo, ONT: Wilfred Laurier University Press, 1985.

Avigad, Nahman, and Benjamin Sass. *Corpus of West Semitic Stamp Seals*. Jerusalem: Israel Exploration Society, 1997.

Balentine, E. Samuel. *Prayer in the Hebrew Bible: The Drama of Divine-Human Dialogue*. Overtures to Biblical Theology. Minneapolis: Fortress, 1993.

Berlin, Adele. *The Dynamics of Biblical Parallelism*. Bloomington: Indiana University Press, 1985.

Berquist, Jon L. *Controlling Corporeality. The Body and the Household in Ancient Israel*. New Brunswick, NJ: Rutgers University Press, 2002.

Beuken, W. A. M., ed. *The Book of Job*. BETL 114. Leuven: Peeters, 1994.

Bloom, H. *The Book of Job*. New York: Chelsea, 1988.

Boadt, Lawrence. *Reading the Old Testament. An Introduction*. New York: Paulist Press, 1984.

Bradley, George Granville. *Lectures on the Book of Job*. Oxford: Clarendon Press, 1888.

Brueggemann, Walter. *The Message of the Psalms*. Augsburg Old Testament Studies. Minneapolis: Augsburg, 1984.

_____ *Old Testament Theology: Essays on Structure, Theme, and Text*. Ed. P. D. Miller. Minneapolis: Fortress Press, 1992.

_____ *The Psalms and the Life of Faith*. Minneapolis: Fortress Press, 1995.

_____ *Theology of the Old Testament: Testimony, Dispute, Advocacy*. Minneapolis: Fortress Press, 1997.

Bryce, E. Glendon. *A Legacy of Wisdom: The Egyptian Contribution to the Wisdom of Israel*. Lewisburg, PA: Bucknell University Press, 1979.

Ceresko, R. Anthony. *Job 29-31 in the Light of Northwest Semitic: A Translation and Philological Commentary.* BibOr 36. Rome: Biblical Institute Press, 1980.

Clements, E. Ronald. *Wisdom in Theology.* Carlisle: Paternoster, 1992.

Clifford, Richard. *Creation Accounts in the Ancient Near East and in the Bible.* CBQMS 26. Washington, DC: CBA, 1994.

_____ *Wisdom Literature.* Nashville: Abingdon Press, 1998.

Cosgrove, H. Charles. *Appealing to Scripture in Moral Debate. Five Hermeneutical Rules.* Grand Rapids: Eerdmans, 2002.

Course, E. John. *Speech and Response. A Rhetorical Analysis of the Introductions to the Speeches of the Book of Job (Chaps. 4-24).* CBQMS 25. Washington, DC: CBA, 1994.

Crenshaw, L. James. *Old Testament Wisdom: An Introduction Revised and Enlarged.* Louisville: Westminster, 1988.

Cross, M. Frank. *From Epic to Canon: History and Literature in Ancient Israel.* Baltimore: John Hopkins University Press, 1998.

Dalley, Stephen. *Myths from Mesopotamia: Creation, the Flood, Gilgamesh and Others.* New York: Oxford University Press, 1989.

Driver, R. Samuel. *An Introduction to the Literature of the Old Testament.* New York: Meridian Books, 1960.

Duquoc, Christian, and Casiano Floristán, ed. *Job and the Silence of God.* Concilium. Religion in the Eighties 13. New York: Seabury, 1983.

Ebach, J. *Hiobs Post. Gesammelte Aufsätze zum Hiobbuch, zu Themen biblischer Theologie und zur Methodik der Exegese.* Neukirchen-Vluyn: Neukirchener Verlag, 1995.

Ellison, H. L. *From Tragedy to Triumph. The Message of the Book of Job.* Grand Rapids, MI: Eerdmans, 1958.

Fohrer, Georg. *Studien zum Buche Hiob.* BZAW 159. Berlin: Walter de Gruyter, 1983.

Foster, R. Benjamin. *Before the Muse: An Anthology of Akkadian Literature.* 2 vols. Bethesda, MD: CDL, 1993.

Girard, R. *Job: The Victim of His People.* Trans. Yvonne Freccero. Stanford: Stanford University Press, 1987.

Gordis, Robert. *The Book of God and Man: A Study of Job.* Chicago: University of Chicago Press, 1965.

Gutiérrez, Gustavo. *On Job: God-Talk and the Suffering of the Innocent.* Trans. M. J. O'Connell. Maryknoll, NY: Orbis, 1987.

Heater, Homer, Jr. *A Septuagint Translation Technique in the Book of Job.* CBQMS 11. Washington DC: *CBQ,* 1982.

Jastrow, Morris, Jr. *The Book of Job: Its Origin, Growth, and Interpretation.* Philadelphia: Lippincott Company, 1920.

Janzen, Waldemar. *Old Testament Ethics. A Paradigmatic Approach.* Louisville: Westminster, 1994.

Job, John. *Job Speaks to Us Today.* Atlanta: John Knox, 1977.

Keel, Othmar. *The Symbolism of the Biblical World. Ancient Near Eastern Iconography and the Book of Psalms.* Trans. T. J. Hallett. Winona Lake, IN: Eisenbrauns, 1997.

King, L. Philip, and Lawrence E. Stager. *Life in Biblical Israel.* Louisville: Westminster John Knox, 2001.

Lambert, G. William. *Babylonian Wisdom Literature.* Winona Lake, IN: Eisenbrauns, 1996.

Levenson, D. Jon. *Creation and the Persistence of Evil: The Jewish Drama of Divine Omnipotence.* Princeton, NJ: Princeton University Press, 1988.

Lévêque, J. *Job et son Dieu I: Essai d'Exégese et de Théologie Biblique.* Paris: Librairie Lecoffre, 1970.

Lichtheim, Miriam, trans. *Ancient Egyptian Literature: A Book of Reading.* 3 vols. Berkeley: University of California Press, 1973.

Lugt, Pieter van der. *Rhetorical Criticism and the Poetry of the Book of Job.* OTS 32. Leiden: Brill, 1995.

Maag, Victor. *Hiob: Wandlung und Verarbeitung des Problems in Novelle, Dialogdichtung und Spätfassungen.* FRLANT 128. Hft. Göttingen:Vandenhoeck & Ruprecht, 1982.

McGarry, Cecil. *The Christian Meaning of Human Suffering.* Nairobi: Paulines, 2000.

Miskotte, H. Kornelis. *When the Gods Are Silent.* Translated with introduction J. W. Doberstein. New York: Harper & Row, 1967.

Mitchell, S. *The Book of Job.* San Francisco: North Point, 1987.

Morgan, F. Donn. *Wisdom in the Old Testament Traditions.* Atlanta: John Knox, 1981.

Malul, Meir. *Knowledge, Control and Sex: Studies in Biblical Thought, Culture and Worldview.* Tel Aviv: Archeological Center Publications, 2002.

Newsom, Carol. *The Book of Job. A Contest of Moral Imaginations.* New York: Oxford University Press, 2003.

Otto, Ruldolf. *Das Heilige.* Munich: Beck, 1963.

Parker, Simon, ed. *Ugaritic Narrative Poetry.* Trans. Mark S. Smith. Atlanta, GA: Scholars, 1997.

Perdue, G. Leo, and W. C. Gilpin, eds. *The Voice from the Whirlwind: Interpreting the Book of Job.* Nashville: Abingdon, 1992.

_____ *Wisdom in Revolt: Metaphorical Theology in the Book of Job.* JSOTSup 112. Sheffield: JSOT Press, 1991.

Pfeffer, I. Jeremy. *Providence in the Book of Job.* Portland: Sussex Academic Press, 2005.

Pleins, J. David. *The Social Vision of the Hebrew Bible. A Theological Introduction.* Louisville: Westminster, 2000.

Pritchard, J. B., ed. *Ancient Near Eastern Texts Relating to the Old Testament.* 3rd ed. Princeton, NJ: Princeton University Press, 1969.

Rad, von Gerhard. *Wisdom in Israel.* Trans. J. M. Martin. Nashville: Abingdon Press, 1972.

Robinson, H. Wheeler. *Corporate Personality in Ancient Israel.* Philadelphia: Fortress Press, 1980.

Schökel, Luis Alonso. *A Manual of Hebrew Poetics.* Trans. Adrian Graffy. Rome: Editrice Pontificio Istituto Biblico, 2000.

Smith, M. S. *The Early History of God: Yahweh and the Other Deities in Ancient Israel.* San Francisco: Harper & Collins, 1990.

Skehan, W. Patrick. *Studies in Israelite Poetry and Wisdom.* CBQMS I. Washington, DC: CBA, 1971.

Steck, H. Odil. *Old Testament Exegesis: A Guide to the Methodology.* Trans. James D. Nogalski. Atlanta: Scholars Press, 1995.

Stevenson, B. William. *The Poem of Job: A Literary Study with a New Translation.* London: Oxford University Press, 1947.

Thiel, E. John. *God, Evil, and Innocent Suffering. A Theological Reflection.* New York: A Herder, 2002.

Ungnad, Arthur. *Die Religion der Babylonier und Assyrer.* Jena: Eugen Diederichs Verlag, 1921.

Vaux, de Roland. *Ancient Israel. Its Life and Institutions.* Grand Rapids: Eerdmans, 1997.

Westermann, Claus. *The Praise of God in the Psalms.* Trans. Keith R. Crim. Richmond: John Knox, 1965.

_____ *Praise and Lament in the Psalms.* Trans. Keith R. Crim and Richard N. Soulen. Atlanta: John Knox, 1973.

_____ *Der Aufbau des Buches Hiob.* ATD 13. 2nd ed. Stuttgart: Calwer, 1977.

_____ *The Structure of the Book of Job: A Form-Critical Analysis.* Trans. Charles A. Muenchow. Philadelphia: Fortress Press, 1981.

_____ *The Living Psalms.* Trans. J. R. Porter. Grand Rapids: Eerdmans, 1989.

Wiesel, E. *The Trial of God: A Play in Three Acts.* Trans. M. Wiesel. New York: Schocken, 1979.

Wilcox, J. T. *The Bitterness of Job: A Philosophical Reading.* Ann Arbor: University of Michigan Press, 1989.

Wilson, A. John, trans. "A Dispute over Suicide." In *ANET* 405-7.

Wolfers, David. *Deep Things out of Darkness. The Book of Job Essays and A New English Translation.* Grand Rapids, MI: Eerdmans, 1995.

Wright, Nicholas Thomas. *Evil and the Justice of God.* Downers Grove, IL: InterVarsity Press, 2006.

Zuckerman, Bruce. *Job the Silent: A Study in Historical Counterpoint.* New York: Oxford University Press, 1991.

Articles

Aimers, J. Geoffrey. "The Rhetoric of Social Conscience in the Book of Job." *JSOT* 91 (2000) 99-107.

Basson, Alec. "'Friends Becoming Foes': a Case of Social Rejection in Psalm 31." *VE* 27 (2006) 398-415.

_____ "Just Skin and Bones: The Longing for Wholeness of the Body in the Book of Job." *VT* 58 (2008) 287-99.

Batto, F. Bernard. "The Sleeping God: An Ancient Near Eastern Motif of Divine Sovereignty." *Bib* 68 (1987) 153-77.

Bechtel, L. M. "Shame as a Sanction of Social Control in Biblical Israel: Juridical, Political and Social Shaming." *JSOT* 49 (1991) 47-76.

Begg, T. Christopher. "Comparing Characters: The Book of Job and the Testament of Job." In *The Book of Job*. Ed. W. A. M. Beuken. Leuven: Leuven University Press, 1994. Pp. 435-45.

Bergman, Jan, Helmer Ringgren, and H. Haag, "בֵּן." *TDOT* 2. 145-59.

Blumenthal, David. "A Play on Words in the Nineteenth Chapter of Job." *VT* 16 (1966) 497-501.

Brenner, A. "Job the Pious? The Characterization of Job in the Narrative Framework of the Book." *JSOT* 43(1989) 37-52.

Brueggemann, Walter. "A Neglected Sapiential Word Pair." *ZAW* 89 (1977) 234-58.

Clines, J. A. David. "Why Is There a Book of Job and What Does It Do to You if You Read It?" In *The Book of Job*. Ed. W. A. M. Beuken. Leuven: Leuven University Press, 1994. Pp. 1-20.

Collins, Terence. "The Physiology of Tears in the Old Testament: Part I." *CBQ* 33 (1971) 18-38.

_____ "The Physiology of Tears in the Old Testament: Part II." *CBQ* 33 (1971) 185-97.

Di Lella, Alexander. "An Existential Interpretation of Job." *BTB* 15 (1985) 49-55.

Fabry, Heinz-Josef. "צוּר." *TDOT* 12. 311-21.

Fohrer, Georg. "The Righteous Man in Job 31." In Fohrer, *Studien zum Buche Hiob*. Berlin: de Gruyter, 1983.

Freedman, N. David, and J. Lundbom. "בֶּטֶן." *TDOT* 2. 94-99.

Gese, Hartmut. "Wisdom Literature in the Persian Period." In *CHJ*, 4 vols. Ed. W. D. Davies and L. Finkelstein. Cambridge: Cambridge University Press (1984) 1. 189-218.

Haag, E. "סֶלַע." *TDOT* 10. 270-77.

Hartley, D. John. "From Lament to Oath: A Study of Progression in the Speeches of Job." In *The Book of Job*. Pp. 79-100. Ed. W. A. M. Beuken. Leuven: Leuven University Press, 1994.

Hermission, Hans-Jürgen. "Gott und das Leid. Eine alttestamentlich Summe." *Theologische Literaturzeitung* 128 1, (2003) 3-18.

Holman, J. "Does My Redeemer Live or Is My Redeemer the Living God? Some Reflections on the Translation of Job 19, 25." In *The Book of Job*. Ed. W. A. M. Beuken. Leuven: Leuven University Press, 1994. Pp. 377-81.

Irwin, W. A. "Job's Redeemer." *JBL* 81 (1962) 217-29.

Kellermann, Diether. "גּוּר." *TDOT* 2. 439- 449.

Kessler, R. "Die Welt aus den Fugen. Natur und Gesellschaft im Hiobbuch." In Witte, Markus (Hg.), *Gott und Mensch im Dialog. Festschrift für Otto Kaiser zum 80.Geburtstag. Bd. 2.* (BZAW 345). Berlin: de Gruyter 2004. Pp. 639-54.

Koch, Klaus. "Is There a Doctrine of Retribution in the Old Testament?" In *Theodicy in the Old Testament*. Ed. J. L. Crenshaw. Issues in Religion and Theology 4. London: SPCK, 1983. Pp. 57-87.

Knellwolf, U. "Hiobs Nächster. Frage und Antwort, Klage und Trost." NZST 45 (2003) 263-75.

Kselman, John. "'Why Have You Abandoned Me' A Rhetorical Study of Psalm 22." In *Art and Meaning: Rhetoric in Biblical Literature*. Ed. David J. A. Clines, David Gunn, Alan J. Hauser. JSOTSup 19. Sheffield: JSOT Press, 1982. Pp. 172-98.

Kutsch, E. "Text und Textgeschichte in Hiob XIX: zu Problemen in V. 14-15, 20, 23-24." *VT* 32 (1982) 464-84.

Lacocque, André. "Job or the Impotence of Religion and Philosophy." *Semeia 19* (1981) 33-52.

Martin-Achard, R. "גּוּר." *TLOT* 1. 307-10.

Mettinger, N. D. Trygve. "The God of Job: Avenger, Tyrant, or Victor?" In *the Voice from the Whirlwind: Interpreting the Book of Job*. Ed. L. E. Perdue and W. C. Gilpin. Nashville: Abingdon Press, 1992. Pp. 39-49.

Moore, D. Rick. "The Integrity of Job." *CBQ* 45 (1983) 17-31.

Moran, L. William. "Notes on the Hymn to Marduk in *Ludlul bēl nēmeqi*." *JAOS* 103 (1983) 255-60.

_____, "Rib Haddad: Job at Byblos?" In *Biblical and Related Studies Presented to Samuel Iwry*. Eds Ann Kort and Scott Morshauser. Winona Lake, IN: Eisenbrauns, 1985. Pp. 173-81.

Nicholson, E. W. "The Limits of Theodicy as a Theme of the Book of Job." In *Wisdom in Ancient Israel. Essays in Honour of J. A.*

Emerton. Eds. John Day, Robert P. Gordon, H. G. M. Williamson. Cambridge: Cambridge University Press, 1995. Pp. 71-82.

Patrick, E. James. "The Fourfold Structure of Job: Variations on a Theme." *VT* 55 (2005) 185-206.

Penar, T. "Job 19, 19 in the Light of Ben Sira 6, 11." *Bib* 48 (1967) 293-95.

Plevnik, Joseph. "Honor and Shame." In *Biblical Social Values and Their Meaning: A Handbook.* Eds. J. J. Pilch and B. J. Malina. Peabody, MA: Hendrickson, 1993. Pp. 95-104.

Ringgren, Helmer. "gōʾēl" *TDOT* 2. 350-55.

Silbermann, A. "*Soziologische* Anmerkungen zum Buch Hiob." *ZRG* 41 (1989) 1-11.

Skehan, W. Patrick. "Strophic Patterns in the Book of Job." *CBQ* 23 (1961) 125-42.

Snijders, L. A. "The Meaning of זָר in the Old Testament." *OTS* 10 (1954) 1-154.

Sutcliffe, E. F. "Further Notes on Job, Textual and Exegetical." *Bib* 31 (1950) 365-78.

Vermeylen, Jacques. "Le Méchant dans les Discours des Amis de Job." In *The Book of Job.* Ed. W. A. M. Beuken. Leuven: Leuven University Press, 1994. Pp. 101-27.

Viviers, H. "Body and Nature in Job." *OTE* 14 (2001) 510-24.

_____ "The 'Body' and Lady Wisdom." *OTE* 18 (2005) 879-90.

Wernberg-Møller, P. "A Note on זוּר 'to Stink.'" *VT* 4 (1954) 322-25.

Wharton, A. James. "The Unanswerable Answer." In *Texts and Testaments: Critical Essays on the Bible and Early Church Fathers.* Ed. W. E. March. San Antonio: Trinity University Press, 1980. Pp. 37-69.

Whybray, R. Norman. "Wisdom, Suffering and Freedom of God in the Book of Job." In *In Search of True Wisdom. Essays in the Old Testament Interpretation in Honour of Roland E. Clements.* Ed. E. Ball. JSOTSup 300. Sheffield: Sheffield Academic Press, 1999. Pp. 231-45.

Wildberger, Hans. "Das Hiobproblem und seine neueste Deutung." In *Jahwe und sein Volk: zu seinem 70. Geburstag am 2.*

Januar 1980 H. Wildberger. Ed. H. H. Schmid and O. H. Steck. Munich: Kaiser, 1979. Pp. 9-27.

Zink, J. K. "Impatient Job: An Interpretation of Job 19:25-27." *JBL* 84 (1965) 147-52.

B. Sociological Studies

Books

Andreski, Stanislav, ed. *Max Weber on Capitalism, Bureaucracy and Religion. A Selection of Texts.* London: George Allen & Unwin, 1983.

Ariès, Philippe. *Centuries of Childhood: A Social History of Family Life.* Trans. R. Baldick. New York: Vintage Books, 1962.

Berger, L. Peter. *The Sacred Canopy: The Elements of a Sociological Theory of Religion.* New York: Doubleday, 1969.

_____ and T. Luckman. *The Social Construction of Reality. A Treatise in the Sociology of Knowledge.* New York: Doubleday, 1989.

Cooley, Charles Horton. *Human Nature and the Social Order.* New York: Charles Scribner's Sons, 1902.

_____ *Social Organization. A Study of the Larger* Mind. New York: Charles Scribner's Sons, 1962.

Durkheim, Emile. *The Elementary Forms of the Religious Life.* Trans. Joseph Ward Swain. New York: Collier Books, 1961.

_____ *The Rules of Sociological Method and Selected Texts on Sociology and Its Method.* Ed. Steven Lukes. Trans. W. D. Halls. New York: The Free Press, 1982.

_____ *Durkheim on Religion.* Ed. W. S. F. Pickering. Atlanta: Scholars Press, 1994.

Halbwachs, Maurice. *Les Cadres Sociaux de la Mémoire.* Paris: Presses Universitaires de France, 1952.

Hegel, Wilhelm Friedrich Georg. *The Philosophy of History.* Trans. J. Sibree. New York: Dover, 1956.

Larson, J. Calvin. *Major Themes in Sociological Theory.* New York: David McKay, 1973.

Mead, H. George. *Mind, Self and Society.* Ed. Charles W. Morris. Chicago: University of Chicago Press, 1934.

Ritzer, George. *Sociological Theory.* 2nd ed. New York: Alfred A. Knopf, 1988.

Wach, Joachim. *Sociology of Religion.* Chicago: University of Chicago Press, 1962.

Weber, Max. *Basic Concepts in Sociology.* Trans. H. P. Secher. New York: Philosophical Library, 1962.

_____, *The Sociology of Religion.* Trans. Ephraim Fischoff. Boston: Beacon Press, 1964.

_____ *Max Weber on Capitalism, Bureaucracy and Religion.* Ed. Stanislav Andreski. London: George Allen & Unwin, 1983.

Articles

Curci, Carmen. "The War in Sudan is a Tragic Farce." *New People: The African Church Open to the World* 71 (2001) 1.

_____ "Strangled By Debt." *New People: The African Church Open to the World* 74 (2001) 19.